KEN HAMBLIN

Pick a Better Country

An Unassuming Colored Guy

Speaks His Mind About America

A TOUCHSTONE BOOK
Published by Simon & Schuster

TOUCHSTONE
Rockefeller Center
1230 Avenue of the Americas
New York, NY 10020

First Touchstone Edition 1997

TOUCHSTONE and colophon are registered trademarks
of Simon & Schuster Inc.

Designed by Karolina Harris

Manufactured in the United States of America

10   9   8   7   6   5   4   3   2   1

Library of Congress Cataloging-in-Publication Data
Hamblin, Ken.
Pick a better country : an unassuming colored guy speaks his mind about
America / Ken Hamblin.
p.   cm.
1. United States—Race relations   2. Afro-Americans—Social
conditions—1975–   3. Liberalism—United States.   I. Title.
E185.615.H275   1996
973'.0496073—dc20   96-34163
CIP

ISBN 0-684-80755-6
0-684-84318-8 (Pbk)

Acknowledgments

The ability for me to grow strong in America and to tell the story of my pursuit of the American Dream has been made possible by countless people, including family, friends, and colleagues. These are just a few of them:

My son, Kenneth, and my daughter, Linda, two young adults who I am proud to say are more living proof that black Americans are fully capable of standing as fully vested citizens in pursuit of the American Dream.

Jim Hawthorne (formerly of KOA radio in Denver), without whose confidence I might never have gotten into talk radio or survived my early days there.

Alan Berg (KOA talk host murdered by white supremacists in 1984), a friend and dynamic force in talk radio who greatly influenced my own on-air style.

Chuck Green (of the *Denver Post*), whose invitation to me to pen my views resulted in the birth of my newspaper column and whose support was there when it counted.

Debbie Leider (my publicist), always a calming voice in the storm.

Jan Miller (my literary agent), who understood and believed in my message from the day we met and whose talent and support made this task easier.

Bob Asahina (formerly of Simon & Schuster), who commissioned this book with a smile, a handshake, and a "Let's do it."

John Brewer (New York Times Syndicate), who has been a stalwart supporter in my battles to broaden the dissemination of my message.

Ken Browning (Browning, Jacobson & Klein), one of my favorite legal beagles.

Cecily Baker, Roger Alan, and Jake Arnette (radio staff of *The Ken Hamblin Show*), who help me hone my competitive edge every day.

All of my fans across America—average citizens who are ever present to help me squelch the voice of political correctness that would deny that America is a great nation, with even greater people.

To my wife, Sue, the light of my life,
without whom this book would never have been possible

Contents

Part 3:
The War of Ideologies in America

Part 4:
America Works!

Prologue

Pick a better country.

I throw that challenge out to people almost every day on my radio show.

A while back I talked to a twenty-nine-year-old black trucker who was whining about how bad it was for a black guy out on the American highway. I stopped him cold when, in the midst of our dialogue, I said, "Pick a better country."

"No way," he responded without the slightest hesitation. "I'm not going anywhere. You'd have to carry me out of here kicking and screaming."

"Then why don't you get on board and become part of the very thing that you refuse to give up?" I challenged him.

He had no answer, because he is caught in limbo. He's afraid to get on board as a fully vested American driven by the promise embodied in the American Dream because boisterous African-American community activists are telling him America doesn't work for guys like him.

Introduction: How You?

• • • •

Woman called to say your white listeners are confused because you call yourself "The Unassuming Colored Guy." Been trying to think up a replacement title. How about "The Patriotic Colored Guy" or "The Responsible Colored Guy"? If you weren't so "Unassuming" you could call yourself "The Dignified Colored Guy" or "The Articulate Colored Guy" or "The Respectful Colored Guy" or even "The High Class Colored Guy". . . . No sorry, I like "The Unassuming Colored Guy". Don't change a thing!

VIA E-MAIL 2/1/96
LAWYERETTE

• • • •

We are about to celebrate our birthday! It will be my 72nd one. You are much younger, <u>much</u> better educated, and <u>you are</u> an educator. I have learned so much from you, as you make sense—just plain common sense. You are one of my many loves. There have been times when my spirit has been bruised (not broken) and your words have healed it. You have made me see many things from a different point of view. I guess I might say "I've picked your brain." We share many of the same opinions and I think we are "Right On!"

VIA MAIL 10/95
M.T., AURORA, CO

How you?
Two of the most powerful words in the English language.
H-O-W Y-O-U.
You look a man, you look a woman in the eye, paint a broad smile on your face, extend your hand and say, "How you?" And you know what happens? They become neighborly. They don't have time to notice whether you're short or tall, fat or skinny, black or white, whether you're wearing a straw hat or a yarmulke.

All they have time to do is extend their hand. About then the ice begins to break, and you hear, "Why, fine. How you?"

That's the kind of people Americans are. That's the kind of nation America is.

I joke on the radio that I know these things because I'm a grandfather. But in reality I know them because the "how you" attitude has taken me a long way.

For the last couple of summers I've been getting on my motorcycle, "Wild Thing," firing up its 90 cubic inches of American iron, and like an old hound dog I've gone sniffing across America.

I've met people in general stores in small mountain mining towns who were baking fresh sourdough bread from one-hundred-year-old starter. I've met the RUBS—the Rich Urban Bikers—who get on yearlong waiting lists, buy their new Harleys, and then don't venture far from their cul-de-sacs. I've joined a loose pack made up in part of Denver Police Department homicide detectives who do venture out. They ride hard, as far as they can go and back, every Sunday. I've met two women riders—one Hispanic and one Indian—who are poetry in motion riding in formation with their husbands. I've met my United States senator, Ben Nighthorse Campbell and even buried a couple of political hatchets based on the common ground of our Harleys.

I've joined thousands of other Americans from virtually all walks of life who converge, two-wheeled, on Sturgis, South Dakota, each August.

One year on the way there from Colorado, I stopped at a windswept gas station on a stretch of highway in Wyoming so desolate there weren't even any overpasses for literally hundreds of miles. (I know, because I got caught in a driving rainstorm on that same road coming home.)

As I stood there filling up in my black fringed leather biker attire covered with road grit, a white man in button-down salesman attire approached me. He came straight at me, no smile, and I took a chance.

"How you?"

"I just want you to know how much I envy you," he blurted out.

Sometimes you have to take that chance. And I'll admit there have been times when it hasn't paid off. But my commitment is that I'm the positive end. I know I like people. I know that I'm having a good day. I know that I feel good about myself. So I'm willing to give almost anyone the benefit of the doubt.

If it turns out that I've grabbed the negative end, in the philosophical sense, if the person on the other end is having a problem with black people or with Jews or with Mexicans to the point that every black person is a nigger, every Jew is a thief, every Mexican is a wetback, that's not my problem. I refuse to become an emotional punching bag for those people.

There are too many good, healthy people in the world for me to spend time devaluing myself because I've come into contact with one of the exceptions. The healthy people are the reward, and my experience is that they are on the other end of a "how you" at least nine times out of ten.

I believe the majority of people all over the world are good folks. But I believe Americans are special because our culture is built on saying hi to the guy next to you.

Our culture is one where if the home team is winning, or losing, you interact with the stranger in the seat next to you at the baseball park.

Ours is a culture—at least it was in my native New York City—where if you see the absurd, it's okay to turn to the person standing next to you at the bus stop and say, "Well, I'll be. Did you see that guy hitching on the back of the bus with a pig under his arm?"

And the other person is just as likely to respond, "That was no pig; that was a nanny goat."

Americans are for the most part jovial. We're the kind of people who, if your ship comes in or if you win the lottery, it's expected that you will belly up to the bar and set 'em up for the house.

We're the kind of people who want to share our good fortune because that's what America is supposed to be about—good fortune. What you are doing when you set 'em up is ringing the bell. *Cling. Ding-ding.* You're proclaiming, "I've made it. I'm an American in the fullest sense. I've made it economically. I've had a string of good luck. I'm one of you. I have joined the club."

Success and winning are part of our culture.

That doesn't mean we are Pollyannas. It doesn't mean that we don't have a grip on reality. It means that if you're a farmer and your cornfield is flooded because of extended rain, the other farmers at the general store in town understand your problem and feel sad for you. They understand that in America if you work hard and do everything the way you're supposed to, you ought to win. You ought to have a good crop, and you ought to be able to break out the cider and celebrate under the harvest moon. That's the way it's supposed to be.

But when it doesn't happen that way, they expect you to suck in your gut, go back to the bank, put your John Hancock on another loan, and forge onward, knowing that your failure was just a fluke.

Success is what America is supposed to be about. Opportunity and success. You know that. The bank knows that. And you work together to make a go of it.

My life, like the lives of millions of other Americans, has been full of adventure and laden with success.

Since I'm a radio talk show host today, I guess it's fitting that my curiosity about America began when I was a young boy of eleven or twelve in Brooklyn listening to the radio. New York radio personalities like Jean Shepherd, Barry Farber, and Long John Nebel were my ticket to exploring the possibilities of the American Dream.

This was in the very early 1950s, before television came to my house. In fact, because we were very poor, even the radio frequently was carted off to the pawnshop near the end of the month. Once a radio was gone, that particular set never came back. But at some point it was replaced by a new radio, and I would listen again.

Jean Shepherd in particular captured my attention. He did a show on Sundays on WOR which, in retrospect, I realize was the forerunner of talk radio, though this was long before telephone callers were made part of the show. Every Sunday, Jean Shepherd monologized for five hours about America.

He talked about places far away from my New York and about the hardworking Americans who lived there who had come from even more distant places, like the Eastern Europeans from the Balkan countries whom he affectionately called "bohunks."

He gave me a glimpse of America at a time when the economic status of my family and the color of my skin made it impossible for me to actually go to some parts of America. So through Shepherd, I visited the Midwest, heard stories of steel towns, listened to yarns about people suffering the freezing cold winds blowing off the Great Lakes into towns like Gary, Indiana. I heard him talk about corn and wheat fields in Iowa and Nebraska and about the farmers who worked all day and then what it took for them to muster enough courage to ask for a date with the hometown girl of their dreams.

He talked about cowboys and American heroes like the Wright brothers.

With his eloquent words, Shepherd offered a magic carpet via the radio that instilled in me a curiosity about America that has remained with me to this day. By the end of his five-hour broadcast every Sunday, he had infected me with a desire that made it a matter not of whether but of when I would discover this true American's America. He inspired in me a "can do" attitude to go see America for myself. Despite my circumstances at that point in time, this voice on the radio made all of the trappings of the American Dream seem well within my reach.

The seed was planted very, very, very deep inside me that this was something I had to do. And somehow at that impressionable age, I understood that reform school or twenty years behind bars would prohibit me from fulfilling my dream. I also understood that wasting myself on the momentary euphoria of heroin would stop me.

Radio and the magic carpet it provided were the important things to me back then.

Just as we watch our favorite television shows with regularity today, I was hooked on a host of other radio programs and serials that became my ticket to experiencing adventure and to dreaming about Americana.

I was addicted to *The Lone Ranger*. I listened to *Straight Arrow* and sent to Battle Creek, Michigan, for my secret decoder ring. I listened to *The Shadow* and to *The FBI in Peace and War*.

Today I enjoy a much different legacy from *Amos and Andy* than a lot of supersensitive African-Americans do. Amos and Andy left me with the perspective that, unlike the angry Louis Farrakhan and his stoic Fruit of Islam, the great majority of black people have a keen sense of humor. I think the show may even have helped to develop my own sense of humor.

To my way of looking at it, *Amos and Andy* didn't demean or make fun of black people. It showed that black people could be bright and that black people could be stupid.

You had Amos, who was a hardworking American driving a taxicab. He worked for his money.

And you had Kingfish, who was a hustler, a gamer, a scammer, a daydreamer.

Back then and yet today, there are white counterparts to these two characters all across America.

Listening as a little boy, I think I got the important message of *Amos and Andy*.

You'd get Kingfish saying something like "Ah ya know, ya know, Amos, if you'd just lend me your cab here and let me take it down to Quick Eddy's Pawnshop and it'd be there for just a day. I, ah, want to get Sapphire this coat on a loan, and I'll arrange for somebody to steal it and then I'll take the insurance money down and get you your cab back."

And then Amos would respond with something like "Ah, Kingfish, I don't think that's a good idea. Why's I gonna give you my taxi? That's how I makes my livin'."

This was about good old-fashioned American common sense. It was about basic right and wrong. Here was a guy talking about taking his buddy's cab to get money to buy a coat to impress his wife, and the way he was going to get his buddy's cab back from the pawnshop was to have one of his other buddies come in and pretend to steal the coat. All so that he could come away a hero to his wife without having to get a steady job.

Then there's this hardworking, ethical black man saying, "Ah, pal, buddy, friend, let me give you some good advice. . . ."

That's great stuff. It was a sitcom with a moral.

Yeah, I know. Times back then were such that white people, not black people, got paid for doing the radio show. But I'm just not going to have a bad day about that now. I've gotten over it. Because you know what? It won't ever happen that way again.

. . . .

Not long ago I reaped one of the true bonuses from my own radio show when I had the chance to meet Barry Farber in person in New York—and discover that now he's a fan of *The Ken Hamblin Show.*

Twenty years ago I had another radio flashback as I was piloting my own airplane and realized after checking my chart that the next landmark on that long, slow flight across Kansas was Dodge City. It took me back to *Gunsmoke* and Doc and Miss Kitty. This was the epitome of Americana, and I could hardly believe I was actually out there seeing it for myself.

I saw a lot of America by air long before I went exploring by motorcycle. I learned how to fly at Detroit City Airport, got a loan for about $3,000 to buy a twenty-year-old pea-green ceconite-covered Piper Tri-Pacer airplane, and flew all over this great country in the early 1970s.

My first instructor was a crusty old World War II pilot who, believe it or not, was named Johnny Ruff. Johnny was lost in a time warp. He lived in a rented room within walking distance of the airport. He hadn't seen downtown Detroit on the ground since the 1950s.

But he gave me very basic, commonsense knowledge about piloting. Like the fact that airplanes always warn you—usually in time to fix the problem—before they fail mechanically. And like the fact that when you're flying VFR—visual flight rules—you should always match the landmarks you actually see on the ground to a point on your chart, not the other way around. Johnny Ruff called that the true reality check.

I became a pretty good pilot.

But in a short time, I learned my equipment wasn't adequate and my flying skills weren't good enough to take me everywhere I wanted to go.

I graduated from my beloved Tri-Pacer on a cold trip home from New York to Detroit one winter weekend. Wrapped in blankets—the heater was pretty much a joke in the subzero temperatures 7,000 feet above the ground—my wife looked out her right seat window and announced that the eighteen-wheeler trucks were moving faster along the highway below us than we were making progress crabbing into the wind.

When we finally landed at our home field late Sunday night, I put the Tri-Pacer up for sale and eventually traded it in for a Cherokee 180.

After sleeping a few nights in the pilots' lounge—stuck in airports across the country because I wasn't rated to fly in foul weather—I also went to work to get my instrument rating.

That's when I met Gordon Rose, one of a handful of one-eyed airline-transport-rated pilots in the country. Gordon took me out one Saturday morning in actual instrument-flying weather and purposely tried to rattle me to make a point. The truth is, he humiliated me by eventually leaning over the cockpit in my own airplane, picking up the mike, and in his best pilot's voice, smooth and sarcastic, telling the guys in air traffic control at my home base that his "student" was flustered and wanted to go home. After we landed, I didn't see Gordon for almost a month.

But eventually he taught me that I needed more than guts and the ability to handle an airplane if I was going to fly far beyond touch-and-go's around the patch. If I was going to survive, I would need knowledge of the vast system of navigational airways, precise landing approaches for every runway across America, and complex air-to-ground communications protocol.

I needed to know the rules.

It made sense. The whole concept of instrument flying was that lots of planes could fly through the clouds at the same time without bumping into each other. There had to be rules.

Learning the life-and-death significance of rules in the world of flying translated into an important lesson in life for me. I was unlike a lot of poor black kids today in that there had always been rules in my household. But the realization of the major role that the rules, as opposed to sheer piloting skill, played in instrument flying—along with the magnitude of the consequences if you didn't abide by these rules—made me aware that there are critical rules governing just about everything we do and everywhere we go in life.

It was as if I had been hit by a bolt of lightning. I realized that the concept of rules and regulations went beyond doing what your mother told you to do in order to avoid the consequences. I realized that there were fundamental rules based on universal truths. What goes up must come down. It takes a certain minimum lift—that is, airspeed—to get off the ground.

I also figured out that once you know the rules, it's sometimes possible to break them—as long as you know you are doing so and as long as you are prepared for the consequences.

You have to know that you are breaking the rules when you fly through a thunderstorm, when you push off a ski slope in the back country that's just a little bit too steep, or when you scuba-dive alone. That awareness that you are pushing the envelope, crossing a line, keeps you in touch with yourself and your surroundings, and, for the most part, keeps you out of trouble.

For instance, when I dive alone I know that my survival is less dependent on the chance that a shark might come out of the mist than on my own heightened discipline to keep an eye on my depth, my oxygen supply, my time under water. I know I have to keep particularly close tabs on every part of my body because there is no one else there to save me. I, along with my emergency secondary tank, am my own backup system, my own dive buddy.

Once you learn society's rules of courtesy, of appropriate dress and behavior, you understand that if you're painting on a Saturday and you run out in your paint clothes to buy something, you're less likely to arouse attention at K mart than you are if you run into Saks Fifth Avenue.

At Saks you might well encounter Security. But if you know the rules, your primary instinct should be to assume that Security is trying to be helpful, thinking you're a workman, rather than immediately jumping to the conclusion that Security thinks you're a thief. You'll know that you are the one who has broken the rules, so you are less likely to presume that the store is trying to admonish you or discriminate against you.

Learning the rules of instrument flying presented a huge challenge to me. I was forced to learn disciplines like mathematics, which I had glossed over in school. I failed the written instrument test twice. Eventually I got my rating because I really wanted it. I knew I needed it to see Jean Shepherd's America.

When I was learning to fly, I met a group of pilots who had started up a black-owned flying club at Detroit City Airport. I shared a special camaraderie with these men in the adventure of flight.

Flying was about competition in many ways. There were guys who were licensed pilots, and then there were guys who commanded their airplanes. But the competition wasn't about one-upmanship. It wasn't about "See how bad I am, nigger? Don't you dis me."

Winning in this competition came from the silent strength you derived from opening your wallet and showing your pilot's license—private pilot, multiengine, commercial and instrument ratings. It came from opening your logbook and displaying entries to Port-au-Prince, Haiti, Boston Logan, or Toronto Island Airport.

Those accomplishments set the standard of pride. Everybody understood it was a fair game of competitiveness. You couldn't say you flew somewhere if you hadn't gone there. You couldn't lie about passing the FAA test. You had to show the paper. And there were no excuses, no shortcuts. If you didn't pass, there was no talk about the tests being culturally biased. Everyone knew the test was passable because eventually we all passed it.

These guys knew I was a student of a white guy, Gordon Rose, but they never chastised me for flying with "the man." They knew Gordon Rose was a son of a bitch when it came to being a tough teacher, and I think they felt, as I did, that it gave a man a sense of pride to graduate under his tutelage.

Just as the radio had been my armchair ticket as a young boy to see America and experience its adventure, as a young man I saw the airplane and my pilot's license as the ticket to see and partake of the real thing.

Over the next three or four years, I landed at America's biggest and smallest airfields, from Chicago's Midway and "Teter Tower" in Teterboro, New Jersey, to a single strip on Beaver Island in Lake Ontario. I flew single engine from Detroit to the island of Saint Thomas in the U.S. Virgin Islands.

On one of my first flights out west, I landed at South Pass "International," a dirt strip not more than a mile from the wagon ruts that are still visible along the Oregon Trail in Wyoming. As a boy from Brooklyn, I was flabbergasted. Seven miles down a dirt road was Atlantic City, population 44. There was no casino gambling in this Atlantic City, but I did find the Buffalo Chips, a musical ensemble led by a grizzly-bear tracker who, rumor had it, felt that his real claim to fame was that he had once played the accordion on *The Ed Sullivan Show.*

Last I heard, the Buffalo Chips were still playing at the Atlantic City Mercantile every Saturday night.

My connection to Atlantic City was fellow photographer and good friend Mike McClure, whom I had met when I was working at the *Detroit Free Press.* One day he just up and quit his city job and went home. Most of us were surprised to learn that Mike's home was on the high plains of Wyoming.

When I touched down there, I had planned only to visit him overnight on my way to San Francisco. But because of Mike and the other good American westerners I met, I left eight days later.

This was the firsthand look at the Wild West I had been dreaming about. The town was frozen in time and could have been a set for an episode of the TV version of *The Lone Ranger* or *Gunsmoke.* I met practical and resourceful westerners, the kind who kept toilet paper, Tampax, and bullets in the glove compartment and rifles on a rack in the back window of their pickup trucks.

I am very comfortable with guns. I have owned them since I was in the army, and I ardently support the Second Amendment right to bear arms. But I've never been much of a hunter.

That was never proven more true than on one of my first nights in Atlantic City, when I talked Mike into taking me jackrabbit hunting. We left the Mercantile Bar about nine o'clock, got into Mike's International Scout and took off for the Red Desert on an unmarked system of four-wheel trails that seemed to go on forever. We bounced over sagebrush as high as my thighs. We forded creeks. We went through a succession of barbed-wire gates. We rumbled over cattle guards. We spotted a dozen jackers, but I couldn't hit a thing.

About that time, the unfathomable happened for this city boy.

As we were barreling along in hot pursuit of a rabbit, off even the beaten four-wheel trail, the Scout came suddenly to rest atop a rock that bottomed us out and shut the engine down. It must have been well past midnight, and we were stuck somewhere high in the desert God only knew how far from Atlantic City. We got out of the Scout and quickly realized that we couldn't fix it.

And then, for the first time in my life, I looked up and I saw the heavens just as the pioneers must have seen them.

It was a perfectly clear night, and I know I saw at least a million stars in that velvet black Wyoming night sky. It was an overwhelming spectacle, beyond anything I had ever anticipated when I ventured out of Brooklyn to see America.

I remember the thrill of that moment with such clarity that to this day, when city friends come to visit me in my Colorado mountain home, I drag them away from the cozy evening fire to the top of a nearby mountain pass, 11,990 feet above sea level, to experience this exhilaration for themselves.

That night in Wyoming I learned that the wondrous sky also would provide the way home to Atlantic City for us. We had taken so many turns out there on the open desert that by then, celestial navigation was our only guiding light.

Being a true tenderfoot, that night I also learned the effects that high altitude has on your body. We figure we trekked about seven miles back to Atlantic City—seven miles at 7,000-plus feet. Coming from sea level in Detroit, I did my share of huffing and puffing and wondering why my boots felt so heavy.

As we came over the last ridge, Atlantic City below us, we saw a string of lights from a caravan of pickup trucks leaving the Mercantile and heading our way. Figuring we should have been back by then, the townsfolk were coming out to find us.

Once again I had tangible evidence of what's right about America and its neighborly American ways.

On that trip and in the course of many more back to Atlantic City and Wyoming's Red Desert, I saw glimpses of the heritage that this country was founded upon. The Oregon Trail became a symbol to me of people giving their all—for the adventure, for each other, for a better life for their babies. People from different cultures and backgrounds who were bonded together with a "can do" American spirit.

The risks out there were real and raw. Along the Oregon Trail, I saw the Fourth of July Rock, the mile marker to reach by that date in order to be sure you could cross the California Sierras before the early winter snows made them impassable. I heard stories of the Donner party, who failed to keep the schedule. Nearly half of the group died, cannibalism becoming the stopgap solution for the last survivors.

I closed my eyes and envisioned the trail strewn with hope chests and family albums, all of the priceless personal articles that had to be discarded along the way as the pioneers stripped down to their true essentials.

I sensed that the westerners driving out into the cold desert that night to rescue Mike, their friend, and me, a stranger, were just doing what had been done as a matter of course for decades in the American West.

You can never have American experiences like the ones I remember from Atlantic City, Wyoming, or learn about the greatness of America if you live in fear of people unlike yourself or of places outside your familiar environs. Thank goodness, my attitude about the unknown has always been "What's that? Show me."

. . . .

I'm a West Indian boy, first-generation American, and I'm sure there are foods that I grew up with that are probably not known to all Americans.

Like pigeon peas and rice, coconut bread, sorrel, and couscous. We grew up making ginger beer from the gingerroot. We coveted pieces of sugarcane, which we chewed like candy and which we bought at neighborhood markets that catered to the thriving West Indian community. Fish was a staple of our diet but we didn't eat exotic seafood like lobster and crab.

As I grew up, I came across foods that were strange to me at first, but I learned that people from other backgrounds relished them just as we enjoyed our West Indian culinary delights. In New York I especially enjoyed some of the Jewish delicacies like knishes and bagels. I liked Italian cannoli. When I ventured out to Chicago and the Midwest, I tried Polish kielbasa.

In the early 1980s I was in Baltimore on a job interview at a TV station (a job I didn't get) and I drove down to the Chesapeake Bay in Maryland to visit some friends before flying back to Colorado. When I got to their house in Easton, they weren't there, so I decided to get something to eat while I was waiting for them.

By this time in my life, I had tried crab and I liked it. I had never had the local specialty, soft-shell crab, although I had heard of it.

So I went into this little restaurant in this quaint little town and I ordered one. There were quite a few people in the restaurant—a state trooper was eating by himself, there were several tables of customers in twos and threes and a couple of people behind the counter. As I waited for my order, somehow I could tell they knew that I had never had one of their local delicacies.

I was the only black person in there. No one was giving me a double look. No one had refused to serve me. I wasn't kept waiting an inordinate amount of time. That wasn't it.

But at that time in my life I was living in Ski Country U.S.A., and I had experience myself in spotting tourists—turkeys, as we affectionately called them. They were the flatlanders who stomped wooden-legged around Summit County from November to April in their ski boots and their brightly colored one-piece ski outfits, looking for all the world like Big Bird.

At that moment I could sense that I was Big Bird in Maryland.

My order came up. The guy handed it to me—a plate with the soft shell crab on a hamburger bun. I held it up to eye level to examine it. Here was this crab about the circumference of the bun, shell intact with all of its legs hanging out! I had no idea how to eat it. Were you supposed to pull those legs off?

So I turned to the people in the restaurant who were looking at me, just for the sport of watching a greenhorn, and I said to them, in general, "How do you eat this thing?"

The state trooper said, "You just bite it."

"Legs and all?"

"Yeah," came a chorus from everyone in the restaurant, as if cheering me on.

I bit into it, it crunched through the bun, and I found it to be one of the tastiest things I'd ever eaten.

My question was kind of like the icebreaker "How you?" I got into a conversation with everyone in the restaurant about soft-shell crab, about where I was from, who I was visiting.

I had ridden up and down Main Street killing time before I went into the restaurant. No local police car had followed me. No one had put me up against the wall and asked for ID.

The myth of the stranger in town—the stranger who happened to be black—was shattered by some American-style curiosity answered by friendly help at this local lunch stop.

Sadly, I know a lot of black people today who miss the greater part of America because they are afraid to venture far from other black people and from their urban homelands. They are afraid of ghosts of the past.

My message to them is this: Get over it. Seeing and experiencing America is worth the gamble that you might run into an isolated bad experience.

I'd be the first to admit that my path en route to the American Dream has included obstacles, sometimes because I was black and other times because obstacles are part of every man's road to success in America.

Like a lot of New Yorkers, for instance, I couldn't figure out how to take that first big step out of town. To begin my expedition to see America, I had to get a bus ticket from Uncle Sam.

I was seventeen years old, at the age when a lot of poor black boys like me run away from home, never to look back. But I couldn't bring myself to do that.

I also couldn't get a job. I don't know whether it was because I was black or whether, like every young person starting out, I simply had no job skills.

The army provided a means of escape, and it also gave me an allotment I could send home, the financial support that I thought I should provide.

I went down to the Army, Navy, Air Force, Marine Recruitment Center in Times Square intending to join the air force. But as I was sitting there waiting my turn, I couldn't keep my eyes off a large poster showing a man hanging under a parachute. A very astute army sergeant noticed my curiosity and struck up a conversation.

"That's Airborne," he said. "The enlistment is three years instead of four. *It pays fifty dollars more a month.*"

Today I am an alumnus of the 101st Airborne Division of the U.S. Army.

I was sworn in on Whitehall Street in downtown Manhattan, then put on a bus at dawn to travel the New Jersey Turnpike until we arrived close to dark at Fort Dix's Reception Depot Center—Repo Depo, for short. There I was hustled, shuttled, cajoled, sorted, directed, and shouted at until like most new recruits, I wondered, "Oh, my God, what have I done?"

I did my basic and advanced infantry training at Fort Dix.

Then I was shipped out from McGuire Air Force Base to Fort Campbell, Kentucky, for jump school. It was the first time I had ever sat in an airplane. I think it was a DC-3, the old gooney bird of World War II fame. Here I was all signed up to go Airborne, and I'd never even flown in an airplane before. The plane rumbled down the runway, rotated, got to flying altitude, and leveled off. I remember that I looked down, assessed the size of the cars, and I said to myself, "Yes, I can do this."

When we went off post at Fort Campbell for some fun, we headed for Clarksville, Tennessee, or Hopkinsville, Kentucky. Now, this was about 1958.

I was a first-generation American, born and reared in New York City. I had never been exposed to the South. I didn't have a guide to the South. I didn't have any cousins in Georgia or Mississippi or Tennessee.

Very early in my tour of duty this group of us—including one other black soldier besides me—went to Clarksville, and we stopped at this restaurant to get something to eat. At least I had the presence of mind to be in uniform.

The restaurant looked to me like any eating establishment up north. We sat down, and customers came and went. The waitress seemed to know most of them.

"How are you, Charlie?"

"Fine."

"Want some coffee?"

"Uh-huh."

Occasionally she glanced at us and then went on about her business serving the others.

Finally I said to her: "Excuse me. I'd like a cheeseburger, please."

She looked at me, wiped her hands with a towel as she moved toward the other end of the counter, and said, "We don't serve no niggers."

And I said, "Well, ma'am, I don't eat niggers. I just want a cheeseburger."

My buddies got me out of there with rapid speed, enabling me to live to see more of America.

I started spending a lot more time on the base.

I had heard some of the boys in my squad talking about things that were completely foreign to me, and it caused me to think that I might have missed a few things in school. For no particular reason one of the things I had heard them talk about that piqued my curiosity was Greek mythology. I went to the post library and found some books to fill my free time.

So here I was, a poor little colored boy from Brooklyn, out in America for the first time. I was jumping out of airplanes during the day and hanging around the army barracks in Fort Campbell, Kentucky, at night reading the *Iliad* and the *Odyssey*.

One of the benefits of my media forum becoming national in scope over the last few years is that I have heard from countless old friends, most, though not all, of whom have been happy for my success. Likewise, most of my black friends from the old days agree wholeheartedly with my message, because they have experienced the same America I have.

My radio show was broadcast live on C-Span in January 1993. One of the callers was Reggie Joseph, whom I hadn't heard from since we were paratroopers together at Fort Campbell. Reggie nearly brought tears to my eyes when he recounted, in almost the identical words I had used numerous times with my wife, the pride we felt when our post commander, General William C. Westmoreland, pinned our wings on us at our graduation ceremony from 101st jump school.

By the time I got out of the army, my initial outrage over the cheeseburger incident had passed, but I still was simmering a slow burn in my gut, which caused me to sign up as a yeoman in the early 1960s fight for black civil rights.

Interestingly, though, my tour in the South didn't kill my desire to see America. Clarksville didn't look like the America Jean Shepherd had been talking about, and I was certain I hadn't heard some subliminal message from him, like "Negroes need not apply for this adventure." I still took his yarns about the America he loved as an open invitation. I just figured the South wasn't for me.

By the mid-1960s, I had had quite a few bad experiences with white people in the South, including more encounters while I was in the army and still more when I went South with Brooklyn CORE to register Negro voters in Greensboro, North Carolina.

But on one trip home to Brooklyn from Greensboro, I experienced the flip side of the coin.

By this time some buddies and I back home in New York had become entrepreneurs.

Ed Booker, Bob Taylor, Tommy Gaffney, and I had opened a foreign-car repair shop in an old miserable cold garage in Brooklyn. We were all sports car enthusiasts and competed in Sports Car Club of America events. I drove an F production TR-3, not especially successfully, in competitions at Bridgehampton, Long Island, and at Lime Rock, Connecticut.

We all had full-time jobs, we also had wives and families, and sports cars were expensive to operate. So we decided the best way to maintain our cars was to run our own repair shop, which we called Triumph Service Unlimited. Before long, word got around, people started to bring their cars by, and we made enough money to keep our own cars running.

But more important, we garnered a certain degree of respect from the community, not just as young working men, husbands, and fathers, but as men who could do things. We serviced our own cars. We could fix other people's cars. We drove in the SCCA races. None of us ever went to jail. We had arguments, but no one ever stabbed or shot the other guy. I don't remember any one of us sitting around talking about how unfair life was to us.

Around 1964 or 1965 I was driving an MGTD home from Greensboro, where I had been visiting Cecil Butler, another good friend of mine from New York who had become a full-time civil rights activist in North Carolina.

It was wintertime, and as car buffs know, that model of the MG has a little tiny heater box way forward, so at full power it blows out little more than a warm tropical draft. It was a cold, cold, cold winter on the seacoast that year. And somewhere on the back roads of Virginia or West Virginia—I don't remember which—I ran out of gas.

I knew I was running out of gas, but I didn't know exactly where I was or where the next gas station would be. The engine went *ugh-ah-ugh* just as I crested a hill. At the bottom, as luck would have it, was a gas station. I coasted pretty much right up to the pump.

A woman came out—a white woman. I was close to frozen in the driver's position. As I struggled to unfold my stiff limbs and get out of the car, she looked me over and said, "My God, boy, you look like you 'bout froze to death."

We got the MG gassed up, and she said, "Well, come on in here. Let's get you warmed up."

I walked into the forerunner of today's convenience store. I remember there was this cherry-red potbelly stove in there that stood about four and a half feet tall. It was huge. I don't think you could have gotten your arms around it. And it was putting out heat like I couldn't believe.

Two white men in coveralls were sitting by the stove. Today I would describe them as looking like characters out of *The Beverly Hillbillies*. By now I was apprehensive.

But they moved over, and I took that as an invitation to join them around the stove. They asked me where I was from. Told me I better take my shoes off to warm up my feet.

I carried that experience away in my soul. Up until that time, I didn't have a good feeling about me and white southerners. And I had been fighting hard in the South for civil rights for black people. But I knew in my heart that these folks hadn't extended hospitality to me because a civil rights law had been passed declaring that they had to be nice to Negroes. These people were representative of what's always been right with America and with most of the American people.

Like any young person who leaves his or her birthplace, my real American adventure began when I decided to depart New York for good. I was lured west by the Mamas and the Papas' "California Dreamin'," by warm weather and sandy beaches. California also promised to be a land of opportunity where I might find the kind of work I wanted to do.

Notice that I did not say I was looking for work. Since the army, I had always worked. But I was at a point in my life where I was considering my options.

The realization that I had options hit me when I was a packer at IPCO Hospital Supply in Manhattan. As a kid, I had suffered from asthma, and the dust in IPCO's warehouse caused me to spend most of my eight-hour workday sneezing and wheezing.

Al was a clerk-typist at IPCO. He was black like me, and I didn't feel inferior to Al in the least. I was just as articulate as Al. I was just as alert as Al. But I was punching in and out in my work clothes while Al, in his white shirt, seemed to me to be the master of his own workday fate. He set his own work pace, which included taking an extra half hour for lunch on some days. For weeks I calculated what Al was doing that I wasn't and tried to figure out how I could get from where I was in the back packing boxes to a desk up front. Typing seemed to be the key.

I went to my father and told him I needed a typewriter. He scrounged up an old Underwood. Then I took one of my wife's sewing patterns—I guess because the type was large—and decided it would be my typing workbook.

I put my butt down for thirty days and repetitiously typed and typed and typed and typed. Eventually I became a good typist—55 words a minute— and decided I was ready to apply for a new job. On my first interview, I was told, "You passed the typing test, but you don't have any experience."

When I went to the next interview the following week, I had two years' experience, and I got a job as a shipping clerk at Botany Bow Ties.

I lasted maybe ninety days. It was apparent early on that I was going to lose the job because I couldn't *do* the job. But I gained experience, not the least of which was succeeding in figuring out how to get from here to there in the world of work.

With that first typing job, I knew I had broken through the membrane. I was very aware of myself every morning sitting on the subway in a suit and a tie, my shoes shined, going to work. I was conscious that now I was making a living as a clerical white-collar worker. From that point on, even though I soon realized I had a lot more to learn, I was committed to not sliding backward. I would maintain my new ground and only grow to higher levels.

I was convinced that America would allow me as a black man to be a full participant in the world of work, and California seemed like the land of opportunity where I could find the kind of work I wanted.

I have seen America by land, by air, and by water.

I have climbed 14,000-foot mountains for the fun of it and bivouacked in swampland on rainy nights under military orders. I've piloted my own airplane from one coast to the other.

I've sailed the Miami Flats and weathered the two o'clock afternoon squalls on Lake Dillon, Colorado. I've floated in my motorboat in secluded coves on Lake Powell, mesmerized by the moonlight illuminating ancient petroglyphs on towering canyon walls around me.

Thanks to the 101st Airborne, I've jumped out of airplanes. Thanks to pushy friends from Detroit, I've skied bottomless powder. Thanks to my own curiosity, I've sniffed out scuba diving, horseback riding, and fly fishing.

I have been honored to recite the words of Martin Luther King during a live performance by a symphony orchestra comprising the finest young musicians in America. I once beheld a herd of wild horses in their natural habitat.

I cradled my son's daughter in my arms when she was just forty-five minutes old. I stood up with unmatched pride to give my daughter, an accomplished television anchor, away on her wedding day.

I have been so broke that my mouth and my throat broke out in ulcers from fear that I would lose everything I had fought to achieve. I have had the joy of undreamed-of riches in America.

But I am not the exception. It is seeing America, living its adventures, and reveling in our success in this great country that makes us Americans. I am just one of the 70 percent of black Americans who, like the Irish, the Mexicans, and the Poles, went after and ultimately got a piece of the American Dream. Along the way, my black friends were right beside me.

Together we were soldiers.

We were entrepreneurs.

We were adventurers.

We were soul mates.

I can only describe my Detroit friends—Larry Ephriam, Nate Parker, and Frank Manning—as a black rat pack. They were the compatriots I found in Detroit to match the guys I had run with in Brooklyn, all of us with the attitude that whatever you did, you "had to be pretty." No matter what you did in life, you had to do it well. We were looking for success, and we were willing to work for it.

We partied hard, but all of us got to work the next morning.

My experiences and the experiences of my black friends over the last four or five decades have been like those of millions of other black people who fought for the chance to participate in America.

I refuse to be considered exceptional for my accomplishments in America or to believe that the obstacles I have met along the way were particularly exceptional.

As I say on the radio, I'm just an "unassuming colored guy."

Like a lot of Americans, though, I've come a long way.

Part 1

The American Dream and the Myth of the Hobbled Black

Chapter One

Bedford-Stuyvesant

. . . .

Ken, I am 1/2 Korean. I was born in South Carolina in a Fort Jackson hos-
pital in 1956. I am 100% American thanks to my mom. She understood
the importance of melding with the American society—becoming part of
the American Experience. . . . She never once said "You must celebrate this
or that Korean custom" or "You are different. You are a Korean-American."
No! It was "You are an American." For that I am forever grateful to her.

VIA E-MAIL 1/21/96
G.F.,
HOUSTON, TEXAS

. . . .

. . . . [You and I] are close in age and grew up in the same area of the coun-
try, namely Brooklyn, and share family values. . . . There is one incident I
would like to share with you. Growing up on Eastern Parkway near Utica
Avenue, as a young (white) boy, I wanted to join PAL. The nearest precinct
was several blocks down in the heart of the "colored" neighborhood. I
thought nothing of walking down by myself to get an application. When I
was returning, a group of 10–12 young (Black) boys surrounded me in a
threatening fashion—although other than words there was no exchange (I
am not a physical fighter). Out of nowhere came my (colored?) Guardian
Angel—an older probably teenager, who observed the goings on, and inter-
vened. He asked if these guys were bothering me, shooed them off with a

reprimand, and told me to look for him if they ever bothered me again,
when I came around. Although somewhat insignificant, it is the type of ex-
perience that can set one's perspective and/or biases forever.
I consider myself a discriminating person (I have the right to choose who I
want to associate with) but not prejudiced.

VIA MAIL 7/10/94
A.S.,
EAST BRUNSWICK, NY

A trip through New York's predominantly black ghettos in the spring of 1991 chiseled a deep and profound resentment into my soul about the underclass today and its seemingly passive acceptance of an impoverished quarantine in that city. I had been invited to serve as the guest host of a weekend talk show on CNBC and I used the occasion to visit Brooklyn. I hadn't been home in nearly a decade.

When I arrived, I rented a car, eager to return to the streets of my youth. But as I rumbled off the Triborough Bridge into Harlem, I was unprepared for the vivid urban filth and poverty. The stench of rotting garbage and human refuse took my breath away.

On Central Park West, once a much-sought-after address, I gawked in disbelief at the entrances to buildings and the rims of fire escapes adorned with barbed and razor wire. In Brooklyn, the groceries and other shops had been converted to citadels of commerce—entrances encased in steel and iron, windows literally bricked over.

As I motored through these murky districts of New York, I marveled at the decay on Harlem's 125th Street, in Bedford-Stuyvesant, in Brownsville—all neighborhoods that had fallen far from the way they were during the period in American history when their black residents were proud to be greeted as Negroes. I've since considered that despite the obvious inequities of those days, in a way it was a glorious time for the people of my race, a time when we were determined to command dignity and respect, determined to fight with our every fiber to make the best lives for ourselves and for our children. We were seeking a simple but powerful status in America. We wanted to be given an equal opportunity and then to be judged according to our honest efforts.

I studied the teeming sea of dark-skinned faces in those streets while I sat in the car waiting for the traffic light to change at the intersection of Flatbush Avenue and Fulton Street in Brooklyn, and I wondered who those people had become. What were the dreams of this motley assembly of street-corner vendors who looked like a multitude of excited ants busy peddling every conceivable black market knockoff from Rolex wristwatches to Chanel No. 5 cologne?

It was clearly a Third World scene. The trash-laden avenues looked more like roads in the heart of Port-au-Prince, Haiti, or a desolate barrio in Nicaragua than the streets I remembered in Brooklyn, New York. I wondered how my old neighborhood, symbolic to me and to my family as the promised land beyond a Third World Caribbean island, could possibly have regressed to this.

I reflected long and hard on what causes a man to foul his own nest, about what stimulates him to drop his trousers and urinate in the same elevator that he needs to carry him and his children to the floors above.

How had my people allowed a struggle for the finer qualities of our civilization to be replaced by this culture of depravity that cuts far deeper than the scars of poverty I had known?

When did the American Dream dry up in my old Brooklyn stomping grounds?

I am certain that there are thousands and thousands of Americans like me, both black and white, who have experienced the degradation of poverty but who somehow held on to the belief that we could reach for a life better than a mere existence dependent on a handout from the government.

I imagine they are as mortified as I am to observe the blatant immorality and lack of hope displayed by the most visible majority of today's black underclass. Perhaps, like me, they are convinced that at the core of the problem is a warped metamorphosis of the American welfare system—a multifaceted welfare culture so pervasive that it has created a completely new paradigm for the poor, one that denies all of the tenets and the hopes of the American Dream.

As I grow older, I have come to appreciate my own American upbringing, however poor, because I was lucky enough to grow up believing in this great country and the opportunities it offered me. At the same time, I worry a great deal about the future—not just of poor black people, but of all Americans.

Life for me began the way it has for millions of little black boys in this world. I was born into terrible poverty in the Brooklyn neighborhood of Bedford-Stuyvesant on October 22, 1940. I was the eldest of five children, all of us raised for the most part by women. My father—like my mother, an immigrant from the Caribbean island of Barbados—was a New York City cop. He left home after my brother and I were born, and my mother became dependent on welfare.

As the firstborn, I was aware early in my life of the seemingly endless shortages that my mother suffered trying to care for me and my brothers and sisters. Today, decades later and long after her death, I still can remember the knot tightening in my belly when I saw the worry in her eyes as she faced another day not knowing where she'd get basic resources like milk and bread to feed her babies.

While I can't recall ever going to bed hungry, I can remember that more than once she took the food from her own plate to provide seconds for my brothers and my sisters when they complained that they were still hungry. As I watched them devour the food from our mother's dish, I made a subconscious promise to myself never to be held captive by food. I would think of eating only as an inconvenience necessary to staying alive, not the pleasant social occasion most people of the developed world enjoy. Today I realize that promise cheated me of a connoisseur's palate, and even of an appreciation of good food, for decades to come.

Like any child, I got my first signals from my mother that something was wrong. A sadness—a sadness that was ever present in her eyes—always seemed to dog her as she went about her never-ending quest for food, shelter, and a couple of extra dollars to play the numbers—her one crippling vice. It didn't take long for me to identify with her melancholy.

Observing her suffering and her disappointments, I gathered that when you were poor, life was unstable and unpredictable, and I learned to be a bit distrustful of any occasional moments of bliss, always wondering what tragedy might be lurking right around the next corner.

I also sensed from her that poverty made us different from other people. And so I hated welfare. I thought welfare was dirty, that it cheapened the soul.

From my perspective, being on welfare meant we couldn't raise our voices or make any other noise when we played in the furnished rooms where we lived. It meant perpetually moving from one public school district to another. It meant regularly having to cower in silence behind a torrent of thunderous blows against the door from landlords and landladies demanding the rent.

I learned that when you are poor you must learn to be invisible. When I left home, I met people who seemed to be the masters of their domain. They stomped and made noise. Their very presence seemed to say "I'm here." Not only could they make themselves known, but they assumed the right to demand exactly what they wanted. They could tell hotel clerks, "The room's not right," or tell waiters, "Please take this back; I asked for it rare."

I realized that poverty would require me to sneak through life, saying little. And I didn't like that prospect.

I suffered the shame and the indignity of welfare firsthand because, as the oldest, I often traveled with my mother. She made me her companion and her confidant.

We got groceries almost daily at the neighborhood store owned by a Jewish man named Jack on the corner of Atlantic and Brooklyn Avenues. Jack had the build of an athlete, a head of fiery red hair, and a freckled face. I remember him as always pleasant to his customers and respectful of my mother even when she begged for additional credit on our account despite the bills she hadn't paid.

Nonetheless, our poverty was embarrassing to her. She never wanted anyone else to hear her pleading for credit, so we would go into the store and wait until the other customers had left. Jack would see her and let out a little sigh that I suspect only we observed. I remember loitering in Jack's grocery, standing on that hardwood floor and feeling very insignificant. I would try to escape mentally by meticulously assessing my surroundings.

Jack's was typical of many Old World–style grocery stores in Brooklyn. There were bins crammed full of loose rice, beans, sweet potatoes, onions, peas—all contributing to the store's cozy aroma and all for sale by the pound. Jack stocked all kinds of items guaranteed to tantalize a kid. There was everything from big barrels of giant juicy pickles to chocolate and hard rock penny candy displayed neatly in a case behind sparkling glass.

But I learned that being poor meant you couldn't have the peppermint candy you salivated for. We didn't buy Wheaties and Cheerios at Jack's. We bought the basics, like margarine that you mixed in a bag with coloring to make it appear yellow like butter, and flour, which my mother would blend with the margarine to make island peasant food like the little flat cakes she called "bakes." There were times when we couldn't even afford enough of the staples—the rice, the flour, the split peas, and the beans—to feed the family.

And, of course, besides what we could and couldn't buy, there was the difference in how we bought things. We couldn't just walk up to the counter and say "How much is this?" or "Tell me about that."

I learned that being poor meant you had to wait and wait and wait. And just when you thought you could step up to the counter, the bell would jingle as the door opened, signaling the approach of another paying customer, and you would lose your chance for a private audience with Jack once again. I vowed back then to be able one day to walk up to any counter and lay down my money for what I wanted, just like everybody else.

I'm not sure whether or not my mother's obvious embarrassment reached the level of painful humiliation. She did what she knew she needed to do to feed us. I know I was humiliated, though, when finally, alone in the store, she would beg Jack: "Please, I don't have anything to feed the kids. The check is due. The check is late."

Interestingly, we never hated Jack, the Jewish merchant, the way some black New Yorkers have come to hate the Korean merchants and the new Jewish merchants who have taken Jack's place today. We saw Jack as a lifeline. Most of the time he extended credit, and we got fed. My mother didn't hate Jack because he was a white man doing business in our neighborhood.

She didn't blame him for our poverty. She saw him as a way to feed her children.

Our welfare check for Aid to Dependent Children came twice a month. In emergencies we would ride the bus to the Fort Green Welfare Center in downtown Brooklyn to request additional assistance. On the way I would see bums lying in the doorways along Fulton Street. Sometimes I would wonder how long it would be before I became one of them.

Even if we got there by nine in the morning, we'd sometimes sit literally all day waiting to see a welfare caseworker. We had to take a number, and if the office closed before our number was called, we were supposed to come back the next day and start the sequence all over again. I remember once when time ran out, my mother ran over to the window and pleaded: "We don't have anyplace to go. We don't have any food. We're not leaving. We're staying right here."

Occasionally I went with my mother on the subway to One Centre Street in Manhattan, often only to find that my father had not deposited the check for our child support that month.

Lest I give the impression that every moment of my youth in Bedford-Stuyvesant was spent living in utter destitution, I assure you that I managed to have many of the same experiences as did the thousands of other city boys who did not have a trust fund.

Roller-skating was my passion for several summers. It was about the time that the Roller Derby was being broadcast on television, and my friends and I spent every waking moment playing our own rough-and-tumble games of Roller Derby around the manhole covers in the street.

I still carry a scar on the palm of my right hand because I disobeyed my mother one afternoon when she pulled me from a game to run to the store for a bottle of Clorox bleach. Her parting words to me were "Kenneth, leave your skates in the house. You can go skating again when you come back."

But of course I could not ignore the fact that skating was faster than walking. And my haste to get back to the game resulted in a nasty cut from the broken bleach bottle and a trip to the emergency room at Saint John's Hospital for stitches.

Midwesterners may believe the fiction of a single tree growing in Brooklyn, but my buddies and I could attest to the fact that there were many trees, most notably crab apple and pear trees that tempted us to commit minor thievery over backyard fences every summer.

There is one boyhood memory that I know Iowa boys couldn't have shared, though, because it was strictly an urban adventure—a sprint through a stretch of dark subway tunnel carefully timed between trains.

There's probably not a boy in Brooklyn who hasn't clutched his mother's hand on the subway platform and wondered what monsters lurked in the darkness between stations. My young friends and I were no different.

When we finally reached an age at which we had proved ourselves responsible enough to travel on the subway alone, we planned our adventure to explore the half mile or so of tunnel on the Eighth Avenue subway line along Fulton Street between Franklin and Nostrand Avenues. We waited for the subway cars to pass and checked to be sure no one else was left on the platform who would see us. Then we jumped down into the tunnel, each of us cautioning the others to beware of the third rail.

It wasn't as dark as I'd imagined it would be. There was a sort of eerie semidarkness, and the air was heavy with soot and the smell of electricity. But it was wet and dirty down there. The walls were lined with murky portals that none of us was interested in exploring.

I remember that toward the end of our sprint, I was on the verge of panic. What if a train came early? What if I tripped? What would my mom do to me if I killed myself?

I think we all saw the Franklin Avenue platform at the same instant. We dashed straight for the iron steps and averted our eyes from the people waiting for the train, who were momentarily dumbfounded at seeing three little colored boys crawling out of the tunnel. Not to mention that we were as filthy as a swing shift of West Virginia coal miners.

By the time I approached my teenage years, I was embarrassed to have my friends over to my house. We would rendezvous at the local candy store or on a street corner, sometimes using the Police Athletic League as our meeting place.

At that age I began trying to control the image of who I was through personal grooming. I didn't have a lot of clothes; certainly none of us had the sports jackets or pricey Reeboks and Nikes that even supposedly poor, disenfranchised black teenagers wear today. But I was compulsive about neatness, always pressing my shirts and pants.

Today, ironing has become a hobby. I have a professional presser set up in a room in my basement, and I use it for therapy when I feel the need to produce something tangible.

There is no question that the poverty and welfare that I experienced growing up left me with lifelong scars. I saw the negativity of poverty—I saw what it took to get the room rent, what it took to get food. There was a constant struggle just to survive. There was grief and depression—when we had to beg at Jack's, when my mother sent me to ask my aunt Merle, her eldest sister and the family matriarch, for a dollar or two to tide us over to check day.

At times these emotions seemed to cancel out any possibility of happiness, even from what should have been the simple joys of life. During those times we didn't enjoy the sunshine or the summer. We didn't stop to window-shop. We never did the things that even I, at my young age, thought we could and should be doing for fun, like going to the zoo. It was not a healthy way to live.

Sometimes my mother would take my brother and me to a park in Brooklyn. Actually, it was a vacant lot where a military armory had been torn down. High grass and broken glass were all that remained. But there was one green area where we would sit and try to regroup—to figure out how we would get food for dinner that night or how we would sneak back into the house without the landlord catching us, knowing time was waning and it was only a matter of days before the eviction notice would catch up with us. The "park" was like a way station, a depot, where, among other things, we waited for someone to come by who knew the latest winning number.

Clearly, I know firsthand about welfare and the plight of the conventional welfare family.

When my mother collected welfare in the 1940s and the 1950s, she received a stipend from the Aid to Dependent Children fund based on the fact that she had no means—namely, no husband—to support her children. In those days few specialized welfare programs existed, like food stamps. You received a check and you were expected to budget to cover your living expenses.

Interestingly, food stamps were introduced, in part, to help people like my mother learn to budget better. Now, decades later, some liberal social scientists are arguing that we should go back to welfare cash to teach poor people money management skills. I'd say some poor people are pretty skilled already. They know how to turn food stamps into cash and buy whatever they want— forget what they and their families supposedly need.

Today at least seventy-five different assistance programs make up our United States welfare system. Tens of thousands of social workers and clerks are employed to supply all manner of aid, from hard cash to medical care to rent supplements to short-term emergency stipends to those black-marketable food stamps.

Many of these programs came into being after President Lyndon B. Johnson declared the War on Poverty in 1964 and opened the floodgates, loosing this ravenous bureaucratic monster and allowing it to grow. Through 1992 more than $5 trillion—that's *trillion*—had been spent on this war.

But along the way, welfare strayed dramatically from its early charter.

The origin of ADC during the Depression was in the concept of widows' pensions, stipends designed to help provide for children whose fathers had died, or whose fathers had abandoned them. Today the concept has evolved to one of aiding parents or guardians of children who have lost support because of the "prolonged absence" of a parent, including mothers who have never married. In essence we are subsidizing out-of-wedlock births with little thought of the fathers—be they alive or dead—as any factor at all. And that concept, Mr. and Mrs. America, makes modern welfare a thriving enterprise.

In 1960 there were 800,000 American families living on Aid to Families with Dependent Children, the successor program to ADC. By 1987 the number had risen to 3.7 million families. By 1995 more than 4.7 million American households were receiving AFDC benefits.

Most Americans agree that more than three decades after we made conquering poverty a national crusade, it remains a significant social illness in our country. The statistics show a growing, not a diminishing, poverty problem.

At the root of the growth and at the center of most debates over poverty and the welfare system are the single mothers—more and more of them black—who continue to have babies out of wedlock and then to collect public charity from AFDC.

Nationally, illegitimate births now account for more than 30 percent, or one out of every three babies born, while the rate of illegitimate births among blacks has risen, incredibly, to more than 65 percent.

Let me pause here and respond to a question I often field when I talk about welfare and focus on blacks on welfare. Yes, I am aware that there are lots of white single mothers on welfare, not to mention white men and entire white families, as well as Hispanics, Asians, American Indians, and "others."

According to the Department of Health and Human Services, in 1994 there were, in fact, a larger number of whites than blacks receiving AFDC benefits—38.9 percent of the total recipients were white compared to 37.2 percent who were black. However, consider those percentages in light of the overall racial makeup of America, which is less than 13 percent black. From that perspective, the actual count of blacks on welfare signals, to me at least, a crisis that should be of concern to all Americans, particularly black Americans.

For that reason I have made a conscious decision in this book to focus primarily on blacks who are on welfare. As a black man, I am writing from personal experience and with great compassion about an issue that is facing my people in disproportionate numbers.

But an even greater threat than the sheer numbers is the far-reaching anti-American welfare culture that has developed around these growing hordes of blacks on the dole.

Because of my family's attitude, the stigma of being poor far outweighed any distinction I ever felt because I was black or West Indian. Furthermore, I never assumed poverty was a logical extension of the color of my skin or that it was necessarily a lifelong condition. I just recall being somewhere I didn't want to be, and the message I got was that you can always change your fortunes in America.

I can remember as a young boy standing outside the New York Public Library on Forty-second Street and Fifth Avenue and looking at the majestic stone lions that sat as sentinels in front of the building. I remember looking at the grandiose structure and wondering what was inside and how I could become a part of all that magnificence. I remember looking up and studying the skyscrapers in Manhattan.

From an early age I had a firm grip on where I was and where I wanted to be—on the Manhattan side of the East River. I wanted in. It never occurred to me for one moment that I couldn't get in.

I don't know precisely where that determination came from. Perhaps my inspiration and my resolve to achieve came from walking through Manhattan, being exposed to the wealth there. But I am certain that being an American, particularly having a mother who was proud be an American, had a lot to do with my "can do" attitude.

The welfare generations today have been bred to know only the perverted lifestyle embodied in a welfare culture based on racism, victimization, and defeatism. It is a lifestyle completely devoid of the promise of the American Dream. Without the belief that you can be all that you can be, this culture leaves people with no drive to fight their way off welfare.

Today the Bedford-Stuyvesant section of Brooklyn is known for its ramshackle condition. But the physical dilapidation is only one aspect of Brooklyn's demise. Far worse to me is the isolation brought about by everyone living at the same level of misery.

Today's welfare recipients seem to have no real dreams or aspirations at all. In that sense they remind me of the lowest form of biological life, a condition not far removed from the single-cell state of an amoeba taking in food and giving off waste. They see only other welfare families and thus have accepted their sad life as the norm.

Unfortunately, what aspirations they claim to have are hallucinations boiled from a pot of ignorance.

That's not the Bedford-Stuyvesant I remember from almost four decades ago when I walked down the steps to the subway train that would carry me away from my childhood home to join the army.

Bedford-Stuyvesant back then was like many other American communities made up of haves and have-nots. With a single mother and no father to support us, we were a brood from the wrong side of the social and economic tracks.

But there were other Brooklyn families—including middle-class black and West Indian families—who occupied the brownstone dwellings that my mother dreamed about.

As a child, I had friends who lived in those houses. I was probably eight or nine when I began to notice the difference between them and me, and I would be lying if I didn't admit I envied them.

My mother and I, like many others in the 1950s, viewed our dependence on welfare as blatant evidence of shameful poverty. Our view of welfare was derived from the philosophical roots of our American welfare system, which lie in the Poor Laws of nineteenth-century England. These laws offered public charity but only to the truly deserving and at a cost of disgrace to the recipients.

Compare that attitude to the contemporary concept of "welfare rights," a reparation-like philosophy akin to owing all freed slaves forty acres and a mule, which is embraced by many of today's black welfare recipients.

Unlike my mother, many young black single mothers today have acquired a victim's mentality, believing that their poverty for the most part is the white man's fault, that it is rooted in a racist agenda sanctioned by our government and by the majority of Americans. Therefore, struggling against poverty is futile. Besides, they reason, welfare represents merely the justified redress to which they are entitled.

A couple of years ago I naively accepted an invitation to appear on the Ricki Lake television show to discuss bigotry—specifically how white racism works to retard the advancement of African Americans. I found myself face-to-face with the mentality of the new black welfare generation.

The panel of guests included a black comedian certain that racism had stopped his career short; a black welfare mother complaining that white police weren't doing enough to solve the murder of her husband on Fourteenth Street in Washington, D.C.; a black Harvard Law School graduate who, instead of using his trade to further black Americans' entry into the mainstream, had posed as a common laborer in order to write a book exposing lingering white racism in America; a young white woman, the consummate liberal, who added her eternal compassion for poor black people who, like her, are dominated by white men; and me, filling the slot of the Uncle Tom conservative who had succeeded only after betraying his people and abandoning the black ghetto.

As the debate heated up, I pulled my gold American Express card out of my suit coat pocket and held it up to try to make my point that most of us earn our way in America. We pay our bills in order to keep our credit cards. My point was that any black person, even if they'd once been poor like me, could earn the spoils of the American Dream.

A young woman from the audience, mustering her insolent "colored girl" attitude, clearly missing my entire point about self-reliance, jumped in: "Ken, you gonna buy me an apartment with your Amex?"

I didn't miss a beat. "No, I'm not the welfare office."

I am certain I wasn't well versed in the heritage of the Poor Laws when I first encountered Dorothy King, but I knew from my own experience that something was very wrong with her crusade.

Dorothy King was a welfare recipient who rose to national prominence through her activity with California welfare unions. She began her incredible lobby in Denver in the late 1980s when she organized a protest against the Denver Housing and Urban Development office, demanding that they turn over houses they had repossessed to her and to her legion of homeless followers.

Why?

Simply because the government had these houses, and her followers had none. She called her organization the Yellow Brick Road, a name befitting her fantasy of receiving something for nothing.

One of her tactics was simply to occupy the repossessed houses and then to challenge the police to lock her up. She brought strength and daring to the welfare rights cause, and local groups like the Colorado Coalition for the Homeless provided the numbers to turn her audacity into a movement that is still evident today as marchers with placards in Washington demand welfare rights—in stark contrast, I might add, to the civil rights we demanded in the 1960s.

Dorothy King represented a moment of utter absurdity to me. It may have been the moment when I realized that the welfare system had run completely amok. Here was a woman actually getting sympathetic consideration for her demand that the government give away the houses that some sad folks probably had invested their life savings in and lost. If the government was just going to *give* these homes away, I couldn't help wondering why it didn't give them back to the people who had worked hard to try to keep them in the first place. Why would we seriously consider giving them to people who likely had never made an effort to get anything beyond what they believed they were entitled to be *given* by the government?

My interview with Dorothy King on my Denver radio talk show gave me a close encounter with a growing welfare rights perspective. Actually, I think my very first encounter with this concept occurred when I was a photojournalist at the *Detroit Free Press*, covering the many protests that followed the Detroit riot in 1967. I took a picture of a black woman wearing a huge button, like a political campaign button, pinned to her dress that said simply "Welfare Rights."

I have a print of that photo in my archives today. I don't recall exactly where I took it or in what circumstances, but obviously it made an impression on me even back then. The concept of welfare rights seemed just as absurd to me when Dorothy King presented it on my radio show some twenty years later.

King struck me as a fairly bright woman who probably could have been successful in the traditional world of work. But I concluded that she saw her job as "getting over"—hustling, intimidating, manipulating, using any means possible to achieve her goal of getting something for nothing from whitey's system.

"Getting over" is a term dating back to slave days. It was used to describe the practice of black field hands working as little as possible, shirking the hardest physical labor, without the white overseer becoming any the wiser.

Many black welfare recipients today appear to spend all of their initiative trying to "get over," trying to exploit the welfare system for its monthly spoils, rather than expending whatever energy is necessary to break free from the shackles of welfare dependency. This attitude is the absolute antithesis of my perspective on welfare when I was growing up.

Chapter Two

Black Trash

. . . .

Ken, the liberals always say that trash (color doesn't matter) that commit crimes don't know any better. They claim they are just trying to get by. If they don't know any better, why do they always hide their faces when a TV camera shines upon them? Because they don't want anyone to see how stupid they are? A passing thought. Keep up the good work, Ken.

VIA E-MAIL 1/11/96
DUDE, SACRAMENTO

. . . .

Hey Ken!
I love your show, keep up the great work!
I ran across a quote today I thought you might enjoy:

"There can be no fifty-fifty Americanism in this country. There is only room for one hundred percent Americanism."

—THEODORE ROOSEVELT

Never quit, Ken, never quit.

VIA E-MAIL 2/1/96
SPITFIRE, ROANOKE

I am the product of a mixed marriage. My parents were married at a time when such things were frowned upon. While my father was in Vietnam, my mother was constantly receiving crank calls dealing with her race and her marriage to my father.

The town I grew up in was mostly white, and I was THE minority kid in school. Well, that was true up to about the 8th grade. The consequences of that fact often proved, to my physiognomy and constitution, dire in the extreme.

I often hear minorities crying about injustice. I wonder how many have really experienced it as I have. What these experiences taught me was to be stronger, faster, and smarter than the others. Perhaps they would do well to follow my lead rather than expect the opposition to come down to their level.

Ken, the first black kids I met were in Junior High School. They were the African Americans everyone seems to dread. That is to say, they were the equivalent of white trash. My first experience at their hands coloured (no pun intended) my view of all blacks, even though my parents' black friends pointedly served as an example that not all were this way. Needless to say I never had any black heroes, even though many of my friends idolized OJ Simpson and Rosie Greer.

Ken, you are my first black hero. I just wanted you to know that. You are right up there with John Wayne, and Charlton Heston, right behind my Dad and Jesus Christ.

VIA E-MAIL 12/26/95
J.H.,
MORGAN, CALIFORNIA

* * * *

Ken, there would not be raceisum in this country if the people that insisted they did'nt get what thay want, tryed to be americans. I believe JFK said "ask not what your country can do for you, but what you can do for your country" I feel today that the statement is "do on to your country before they do onto you"

Meny people tell the mynorty to go out an get what you want; however they forgot to tell them "get it by working for it, not steeling it."

VIA E-MAIL 11/10/95
M.F.,
JACKSONVILLE, FLORIDA

* * * *

While reading (your column African American, Pick One), I couldn't help but think of an experience I had last Spring as a student teacher of World History at a San Diego high school. We were studying imperialism in

Africa during the 19th Century and I had the students write an essay about the topic. At least three of the students referred to the native Africans as "African Americans" in their essays and I was dismayed. The rhetoric and labeling has grown to such a degree in this country that people have blurred the line between true Africans and "African Americans." I had to explain to the class that it would have been virtually impossible for any "African Americans" to be living in Africa in the late 19th century unless there were some very old repatriated ex-slaves still around in Liberia or elsewhere. But, this labeling process has grown to such sickening extremes that people have started to blur the lines when referring to "blacks," no matter where they may be located geographically. . . . Sign me, an English-Irish-Scottish-Dutch-Cherokee-American, or the way I prefer for all US citizens to be labeled, simply an AMERICAN (no hyphens or extraneous labels).

VIA E-MAIL 11/30/95
R.M.,
SAN DIEGO, CALIFORNIA

• • • •

Ken, God bless you for bringing your message to the airwaves every day. You are right on target in saying the problem in America today is not "race" but "class." I use "class" here in a broader sense, to mean "character" rather than strictly social class. Material wealth is not a prerequisite for, and may not even be a good predictor of, the kind of "class" in people that made America great. . . . As a black man who rose from humble origins, you are uniquely situated to challenge the "conventional wisdom" that a large segment of society should be exempt from standards of human decency because they believe life wasn't fair to them or their ancestors. As a white man who grew up in an urban neighborhood among what is now called the "white underclass," I can assure you, "trash is trash." It's high time we quit "giving out a pass" to those who behave in ways that are destructive to themselves, their families, and our society.

The dominant media not only rationalizes this behavior, it "glorifies" it. How else do you explain the "wannabe" phenomenon, where "mainstream" teens seek to dress like, talk like and act like . . . well, thugs? I think this is why illegitimacy and drug abuse are spreading not only among the "underclass," but throughout our society.

It burns me when I see how those who overcame their supposedly insurmountable limitations . . . are dismissed or held in contempt. Stay the course, fight the good fight, and keep the faith. America needs you.

VIA E-MAIL 11/1/95
S.F.,
MARYLAND HEIGHTS, MO

• • • •

True story to relay to you—my daughter (in Germany) did financial coun-
seling for the Army and had a Black couple come in for help. In gathering
information, she asked for the name of their child. She was told (phonetic
spelling) Shi-tea-add. Assuming it was an African ethnic name, she asked
for the spelling, and this you may not believe: but it is S-h-i-t-h-e-a-d! I find
it incomprehensible that anyone would do that to their child, what an aw-
ful thing to live with! I swear the story is true!

VIA E-MAIL 6/5/96
G.B.,
WAUNAKEE, WI

When I was growing up in Brooklyn, one of the rituals, particularly in the summertime, was that my brother and I were sent down the street
to the neighborhood candy store, called Dissick's, around eleven at night to
pick up the early edition of the next day's *Daily News* for my mother and my
aunt Merle.

I remember several occasions as vividly as if they happened last night,
when my aunt Merle opened the paper to the center picture spread, which
always featured a crime story, and called me over to impart one of her wise
lessons in her West Indian accent.

"Ya see. Ya see how dem boys, how dem young black boys, get in trouble because dey don't behave demselves? Lord knows, you got to behave yourself."

Dutifully I would go over to her, and sure enough, there would be a picture of some black scumbag with his hands cuffed behind him and his head
hung low and turned away from the photographer's flashbulb. Leading him
away would be two or three officers dressed like my father, in blue jackets
with brass buttons down the front and their New York City Police caps.

My aunt Merle would go on and on.

"Ya see, ya see how when de police got dem they hang deir heads down in
shame, how dey can't look you in da eye. Ya see how dey ain't got no pride."

Then she would turn on me, wagging her finger.

"Boy, don't you never bring dat kind of shame on your family."

Her words have stayed with me to this day.

I interpreted them loud and clear as "Nigger, Nigger, We don't want no
niggers in the family. Don't roll over. Don't let your back bend. Don't be
swayed by others."

The fact is that I was far more strongly influenced by Aunt Merle's un-
nerving admonishments and her dread that I might do things that would reflect on who I was and, more dreadful yet, on the people whose name I
carried than I ever could have been by the bad boys on the street.

Even though I was poor and black and on welfare, this was a time when there were clear boundaries between right and wrong. These boundaries governed the standards of civilized behavior. Right conduct was rewarded. Wrong conduct was punished. There was a sense of strong community among those who chose to do the right thing. Those who chose to break the code of good conduct were ostracized and punished.

Not only were the values of right and wrong, good and bad, made explicit, but it also was made clear that you would be held accountable for wrongdoing.

In most families, this moral training started very early with decisive disciplining of their children.

The few times the police had to come into our house or my mother had to walk down to the school because of me or because of one of my brothers or sisters, she was devastated. I still remember the tears and the stress that it caused her.

A good part of her misery was for moral reasons. She obviously felt the despair parents feel when their children fail to live up to the standards that they thought they had set for them. But I'm sure she also was devastated by the added burden that our misdeeds had inflicted upon her. Life was difficult enough. She didn't need new and unexpected problems, like having to take one of her children to juvenile court.

I had a genuine compassion for my mother, and I truly felt bad when I disappointed her. Besides, neither my siblings nor I wanted to bring any more grief into our house than we already suffered because of our poverty.

Being a normal kid, however, I did have a couple of very memorable encounters with New York's Finest. The first one took place during one of the times when we were living with Aunt Merle at 1406 Pacific Street.

Because we didn't grow up with any excess material possessions, the belongings we did own were easy to inventory. We never received allowances that might account for things we bought on our own. As a result, we couldn't bring things into 1406 Pacific Street that didn't belong there. No stereos or TV sets or Rolex watches or toys or money could just appear without my mother or my aunt noticing them.

I must have been about seven years old. Edgar, who lived upstairs, was about nine. We both went to P.S. 41, about four blocks from our apartment building, and Edgar had this swell idea. He suggested that we go back to school some night and remove some items—clear-cut theft by any definition.

I had very little interest in taking anything from that school save one thing. There were these marshmallow cookies—some were white and some were pink, and all of them had coconut sprinkles on top. I was addicted to those cookies. Our teacher allowed us to buy only five cookies a day, no matter how many pennies we had.

As a result, I was positive that I suffered from a constant state of cookie deprivation. So when Edgar suggested a surreptitious return to P.S. 41, I had a fairly modest, seemingly innocuous goal: grabbing all of the marshmallow cookies I could eat.

We devised a plan.

As we left school on the day that I would become a thief, we stuck some paper in the door to block the lock. Sure enough, when we returned after supper, the door opened easily. We went directly to my homeroom. I opened the cabinet where the cookies were kept and commandeered a box of two hundred Marshmallow Delights. As I headed for the door, I did a double take: Edgar was carting away a typewriter and an adding machine. At that moment it occurred to me that this caper could be getting out of hand.

We sneaked into the apartment building on Pacific Street and stowed our goods under the stairs in the entryway. It appeared we had committed the perfect crime.

In spite of my advanced state of cookie deprivation, however, I could not consume all two hundred cookies before a green mold began to form on the uneaten ones. So after a day or two, my attention turned to the typewriter.

I took it upstairs to my aunt's apartment, and I was pecking away when she came home and immediately identified something new in the house. She spoke to me directly, without a moment's hesitation, in her singsong West Indian voice.

"Where you get dat?"

"I found it."

"Where you find someting like dat?"

Having no idea how to respond, I just kept pecking away on the typewriter keys.

Before long, two of New York's uniformed officers were standing in the doorway of the bedroom peering down at me.

My aunt Merle, arms flailing, screamed in her thick accent, "Take him away. He know better than to steal. I don't want no tief in my house. Take him away. Take him outta here, Officer. You hear me? Lock him up!"

Faced with my aunt Merle's wrath, I did not hesitate. I ratted out Edgar and threw myself on the mercy of the cops. My mother and my aunt returned the equipment to the school and made restitution for the cookies.

I realized at that young age that if I was going to be a thief, a lowlife, a brigand, I would have to leave home.

Sadly, a growing number of poor little black boys today never benefit from morality lessons like the ones I learned. They are simply not being taught right from wrong.

. . . .

At the heart of the black welfare culture today is a black underclass, which I say should be called out for what it is—black trash.

"Black trash" is one of several terms I use that send my critics into a frenzy, claiming that I hate black people. But indulge me, and consider my logic.

There is a universal comprehension of what "white trash" means. The label is a disparaging term for a category of poor people considered to be from the wrong side of the socioeconomic tracks. It refers to an unskilled and unemployed class of white America—the illiterate, the poorly housed, the welfare dependent. Poverty is only one facet of white trash. Their distinctive lifestyle and culture are the earmarks that prompt criticism from most people.

So it's obvious, at least to me, that if human trash exists among whites, it also can exist among blacks. And the members of this culture, like their white counterparts, would tend to be socially inept, possess limited education and few salable job skills, demonstrate a minimal regard for civilized society and the generally accepted rules of humanity, and have a firmly entrenched attitude that welfare is a God-given right.

This definition is also transferrable from white to black, because like white trash, black trash are a minority among the populace as a whole. Of the 32 million Americans who are black, the great majority, more than two-thirds of us, have stepped very comfortably into the American mainstream in terms of academic achievement, in terms of employment status, in terms of income, and in terms of the aspirations we espouse for our children.

Just like the majority of white Americans, we have progressed along the path toward the American Dream by accomplishing many of our personal goals and by moving further and further away from poverty and the need for welfare.

But while the great majority of black people embrace mainstream American values, there remains a clearly identifiable underclass that does not. In the 1960s we referred to members of this class as the hard-core unemployed. Back then America gave them the benefit of the doubt, granting that racial inequities had kept them from achieving economic and social independence. We made them the poster children in our fight for civil rights and later in the War on Poverty. The goal then was to enable them, along with all black people, to be free and self-sufficient Americans.

But despite a successful civil rights revolution and the millions and millions and millions of dollars spent over the decades to fight poverty, today there is a group of poor blacks who still have not even set a course to achieve the American Dream. They have not even accepted mainstream values as their own. They have not recognized a work ethic; they have not put a value on education for themselves or for their children. They still believe they are the victims of crippling racism, and thus they refuse to accept any personal responsibility for their own shiftless attitude and sorry predicament.

Their ever-growing dependence on welfare and their isolation from traditional American values and rewards have worked together to make this underclass society within the black urban ghetto not just poor folks but socially and morally deviant black trash.

Once you admit it exists, it's pretty easy to identify black trash. Like the black boys who went "wilding" and brutally attacked a white woman jogger in Central Park. Or the fellas who attacked Reginald Denny during the 1992 L.A. riot. Or the twin teenage girls who pursued, taunted, and beat up a white suburban woman at the Detroit riverfront Freedom Festival.

Or the grandmothers and mothers who routinely use their preadolescent offspring as mules in the drug trade. Or the countless sons who follow in their fathers' footsteps to the joint.

One of the more graphic descriptions of black trash was in an Associated Press story out of Chicago in 1994. Police broke into a four-room apartment where they found nineteen children living in conditions worse than we have ever heard about slave quarters.

The story speaks for itself:

> The four-room apartment was littered with filth and crawling with cockroaches, its windows broken and covered with blankets that flapped in the wind. It was home to nineteen children—the oldest fourteen years old, the youngest just one.
>
> When police barged in on a drug raid, they found five of the children sleeping in their underwear on a bare floor. Others fought with a German shepherd dog for scraps of meat on bones scattered on the floor.
>
> Six adult relatives of the children—four mothers, a father and an uncle—were charged with contributing to child neglect, a misdemeanor. A fifth mother of some of the children was in custody but had not been charged, and a sixth mother was in the hospital giving birth, police said. . . .
>
> "The apartment was cold, the apartment was filthy," police officer Linda Burns said. "I'm talking feces, garbage, food on the floor. I don't even know how to describe it—it was just filth."
>
> "They were eating food off the floor out the bowls the dogs were eating out of," said police Lieutenant Fred Bosse. "The remaining food that was on the floor was being fought over by the dogs and the children."
>
> Some of the children begged officers to be "my mommy," said police officer Patricia Warner. . . .
>
> A child-abuse expert said poverty, ignorance, alcohol, and illegal drugs all play some part in most such cases.
>
> "There are chronic problems among people who grow up in violent, poor, disintegrating communities," said Anne Cohn Donnelly, executive director of the Chicago-based National Committee for the Prevention of Child Abuse. "Young parents who grew up in these situations never really learned that there is an alternative way to behave."

Is it any wonder that by 1996 the experts were talking about the children of these generations of children-having-children turning into superpredators?

In fact, in the spring of 1996, a six-year-old was suspected of brutally attacking a one-month-old baby in California, and a ten-year-old was being held in Colorado for bludgeoning an eighteen-month-old baby to death.

In most cases, these are not just bad eggs or black sheep in a family. They are members of entire predatory tribes who appear to be completely devoid of morality.

I believe much of their moral decay is rooted in the changing attitude about poverty and welfare, the attitude that is broadcast openly and loudly by black-trash welfare recipients today.

My mother certainly never would have let us use the fact that we were poor—or black—as an excuse for not knowing right from wrong, as so many black-trash offenders and their families do today.

It has become fashionable and acceptable to blame even the most blatant wrongdoing on anything and anyone but the perpetrator.

"Why, I cannot be held accountable for my behavior because my mother was a crack addict, my father was a child molester, or my mother was molested, or I'm short. I'm ugly. My mother was short. My mother was ugly. Why, if you could only live in this tortured state that I exist in. . . . If you could only know for a few moments what it's like to be black, to be gay, to be Jewish, to be the underdog. To be a victim!"

It's out-and-out rubbish! And in most cases these whiners get away with it.

Once upon a time in America all of us were fully clear about what constituted right and wrong, about what good values and bad values were.

If you were a child, you learned very early that you would be held fully accountable for stealing the change from your mother's purse. This was a nondebatable, nonnegotiable fact of life.

Furthermore, if a child was caught stealing, not only would the child be judged guilty of wrongdoing, but the child would be considered evidence of bad values in his household. The community would want to know why the family elders had failed to pass along the most basic knowledge of right and wrong to this child.

Likewise, children were fully aware that even after they left the nest, their actions would continue to reflect on their families. They knew they were a direct extension of their surname.

What has happened today to that crystal-clear standard of right and wrong, that standard that even little black boys growing up on welfare with single moms knew with absolute certainty forty years ago?

I suspect again that thousands of Americans like me are asking that question.

. . . .

I am convinced that America's lack of resolve to treat black trash with the same disdain as they do white trash is firmly rooted in the prevailing liberal mandate of political correctness. The fear is that the plight of the underclass might just be—as black trash claim it is—attributable to racism. Most Americans do not want to be thought of as racists or to appear insensitive to the victims of racism. I argue that because of this abundance of irrational liberal commiseration about the sorrowful quality of life of black trash, we dismiss the real facts—real facts that we never ignore when we consider white trash.

Like the fact that black trash seem to be programmed to precipitate their own self-destruction. Children are having children. Disregard for education has resulted in a lack of job skills and thus an inability to achieve economic independence. And without even the desire to be self-reliant, there is no self-esteem among black trash. Well beyond the breakdown of the traditional nuclear family and an absence of fathers, the black-trash value system has disintegrated to the point where essential human principles are no longer being passed down from generation to generation.

The startling statistics created by this minority within a minority have been cited by many different factions to support a range of positions regarding both the causes and the effects of this human crisis. But today few debate the stats themselves or argue against the fact that growing numbers of people are being raised without sound human values.

Not only have we permitted excuses for the black-trash culture to exist, but certain attributes of this culture—like its street argot and its high rate of teen pregnancies—are actually extolled by some white liberals and black community leaders as perhaps worthy of consideration as multicultural counterparts to the values of the white American middle class.

Think about that. When have we ever glorified the poor grammar or the shabby dress of white trash? Or even remotely considered them or their cultural attributes as candidates for alternative mainstream values?

Nonetheless, debate over the merits of certain aspects of the black-trash culture has escalated to the point where they are put forth by some African Americans as the core of the only authentic black culture in America.

I was speechless after I encountered this logic when I visited my old middle school, P.S. 258, on my 1991 trip home to Brooklyn. In the hallway, tacked to the door of a janitor's closet, was a handwritten narrative. It was an explanation of why some black women, especially poor black women, are overweight. It reasoned that this was a carryover from slave days when pretty young Negro girls purposely put on poundage to avoid being desirable to and ultimately raped by the white slave master. The conclusion was that being fat today should be considered a trait of beauty for black women, a trait firmly rooted in African-American history. This was a new standard invented out of clearly ignorant black-trash logic and passed on as a cultural quality to be preserved.

The overriding rationale was that mainstream American values, which these African Americans deem to be only white values—even such commonsense values as not being overweight and unhealthy—simply were not relevant to black people.

A couple of years ago I went to the wedding of one of my daughter's friends. At the reception, the groom's brother stood up and thanked everyone for coming to share in his brother's happy day. He was chided later by a family member from the inner city of Detroit who accused him of trying to "act white"—just because he was courteous and gracious.

Sadly the welfare recipients are not the only losers in today's corrupted culture of entitlements. The expanding black welfare culture has the potential to harm all Americans, most certainly to affect all black Americans, in ways that go far beyond the tax dollars levied against them to pay for it.

The rejection by today's black welfare culture of the American Dream, the single thing that I credit with giving me the strength to claw my way out of the world of poverty, is epitomized in the back-to-Africa movement and the pressure to call Negroes African Americans.

These anti-American crusades emanate from the fact that black trash generally still harbor a hatred of America based on the ancient history that their ancestors were brought to our shores as cargo in slave ships generations ago. They refuse to embrace America today. Instead, they remain emotionally tethered to their community's rhetoric, which insists that only white people can claim the heritage of having wanted to come to America. Only white people can say, "Hey, I came to this country so my kid could be an American." Therefore only white people and those who came to our shores by choice can want to be here today.

They ignore the fact that compared to the opportunities they have in America today, much of their African homeland offers a lifestyle equivalent to an unclean public outhouse in terms of sanitary conditions and human rights.

Nonetheless, rather than reveling in the accident of their own birth as Americans and taking advantage of the unique opportunities they have as American citizens today, this subculture of trash is consumed by useless wonder about what might have been if their ancestral parents had not been captured and forced from their African homeland.

It's conceivable that the 1990s back-to-Africa frenzy is just a twisted evolution of the black pride movement of the 1960s. Most of us took strength from that movement, strength and inspiration that we used to compete in American society. But clearly some of my people cannot move beyond their blackness to the greater state of full citizenship in the melting pot of America. Unlike the Irish, the Italians, the Germans, the Japanese, the Koreans, black trash can't seem to get beyond their sub-Saharan African ancestry.

And so they revert to foreign costumes of kufis and dashikis and they endow their babies with African-sounding monikers like Moesha or Katisha, names that few can pronounce and that sometimes even they don't spell consistently.

They celebrate new holidays like Kwanzaa because they can't bring themselves to enjoy a white Christmas. Kwanzaa was created in 1966, one year after the Watts riots in Los Angeles, by Maulana Karenga, whose authority to invent such a holiday apparently derived only from the fact that he was chairman of the black studies department at California State University at Long Beach.

They even try to reinvent history with the help of pseudo-intellectuals like Leonard Jeffries, a professor at City College of New York, who has been dubbed a "black prince" by some of his many followers.

Jeffries, an African-American neo-historian, has created a tale of black African superiority to counteract the reality of miserable economic and social failures represented by black-controlled American cities and sub-Saharan black African countries.

Jeffries further plays to his unsophisticated audience by labeling white people in general as "pathological . . . dirty . . . dastardly . . . devilish folks."

It's bad enough that African Americans and white liberals have given people like Jeffries a free hand to rewrite history in order to ease their emotional distress over black failures. What's worse is that many are demanding that these delusions be taught as fact in American public schools, and in some cases the demands are being met.

For years the spokespersons for black trash have claimed that education in America isn't relevant to minorities. This serves to cover up the fact that the students are not encouraged to study or disciplined to learn. At first, they said there weren't enough black teachers who could relate to their black children. So we rushed a horde of black students through teachers colleges on special scholarships, often with lowered standards of excellence.

And what did we get? Obviously we didn't get a crop of smart, proud black students. What we got was too many classrooms with black trash teaching black trash.

I remember going to an inner-city elementary school in Detroit in the early 1970s to talk with my son's teacher. I was astounded when this young black teacher opened her mouth and I realized she had a limited command of English. Today it's obvious to me that, just by her presence, this teacher played an early role in the movement to validate black argot as the legitimate voice of blacks.

No wonder the test scores of blacks consistently run below those of whites, Hispanics, and Asians.

In the effort to be blacker than black, we have abandoned the standards of education that have made it possible for generation after generation of American children to succeed beyond the boundaries of their parents. We have allowed these standards to be thrown out with everything else deemed to be white people's business—and thus not relevant to the authentic black culture.

Their excuses and their lack of logic are the real downfall of black trash. I contend that they can't blame anyone but themselves for not attending school and getting an education in this country where schooling is free. The low level of occupational skills that prevails among these poor blacks is directly related to their own disregard for education. It is not, as black-trash propaganda puts forth, because great masses of white racists in the suburbs are plotting to keep them down.

The whole philosophy of black trash, the whole philosophy of the black welfare culture, however, is based on a defeatist outlook when it comes to mainstream America and the American Dream.

"What you going ta school for? You black. You ain't gonna write no column for the *Denver Post*. What makes you think you're gonna be syndicated by the *New York Times*? You go ahead and act white all you want, nigger, but I'll tell you this, them white folks ain't never gonna let you get nothin'."

Sound preposterous? Think I'm exaggerating?

Consider these actual words from the Reverend Reginald C. Holmes, a black minister in Denver, who wrote a letter to me in 1991 saying that I struck him as "a young brother who's trying to 'pass' and 'escape' the reality of being black."

He went on: "No matter how far you move from the 'ghetto,' no matter how little you associate with the 'ghetto leaders' and the ghetto inhabitants; no matter how proficient you become with a knife and a fork, to those whom you seek to mimic, you are still, in your 'whitest state,' a 'nigger.' Never forget that, Ken!"

This fatal undertow of defeatism that flows through black-trash tribes in the ghettos of America has produced generations of black people who are afraid—afraid of the challenges awaiting them outside the borders of their urban reservations.

The propaganda and the misinformation, particularly about white people and America, that are fed into those reservations breed a barrier of xenophobia that is more effective than the Nazi troops who guarded the Warsaw ghetto during World War II. It is more effective because black trash won't even approach the boundaries of their ghettos, much less try to sneak out—except, that is, to forage for what they can take by force from America's rich mainstream society.

Chapter Three

Black Thugs

I was about thirteen when I was permitted to hang on the perimeter of a gang that used to gather regularly on the corner of Fulton Street and Franklin Avenue in Brooklyn. It was the territory of a sixteen-year-old gang leader whom everyone called Dice. I never knew his Christian name.

Dice was a tall, lanky black kid. He took great pride in wearing a green felt fedora with a Tyrolean brush in the hatband. With his alpine hat cocked to one side in a very rakish manner, Dice would hold court with his homeys—whom my uncle Roy referred to in a demeaning way as "jitterbugs"—near the hot dog stand on that corner.

I was at an impressionable age, and I had a certain fascination with Dice. But from the moment I was allowed to observe him up close, I had the strong and definite feeling that I didn't like him. I didn't like the way he grabbed his genitals to punctuate his street-level boasts or threats. I didn't like the way he pimp-rolled—walking as though one leg were shorter than the other in an attempt to put bravado in his stride. I didn't like the way he kept a constant scowl on his face when he talked.

I experienced an overwhelming instinctive rejection of Dice and his culture, the same reaction some people have to walking up on a snake. Dice hit me like a bad odor.

Maybe there is something to genetic memory, because if there's any truth to reincarnation, Dice hit me like a man who had murdered me or my mother in a previous life. I felt a strong and total rejection.

Fulton and Franklin was the interchange where you got off the Eighth Avenue subway and went up some stairs to catch the elevated train to Coney Island. It was a transfer point for the girls who attended Girls High School. I didn't like the way Dice and his boys talked to those girls. They didn't use the brazen expletives that the black gangs do today. They didn't reach the degree of disrespect for women that is portrayed in today's gangsta rap videos. But it was understood that the more blasphemous Dice's boys were toward these girls, the higher the status they gained among their fellow gang members.

About the same time I encountered Dice, I was listening to the radio and hearing Jean Shepherd talk about America. While I don't think I consciously related the two events in my life, obviously the power of the adventure Shepherd offered outweighed anything Dice could have offered me, and it didn't take long for my fascination with Dice to turn into deep dislike.

Dice was despicable. He was not a nice person. Back then and still today, I don't want anything to do with people who hold their genitals, who scowl, who are always boasting—or, in the African-American vernacular, "fronting."

Dice and his boys came to represent the bad boys my aunt Merle was always admonishing me about.

To this day I see some of Dice in every low-life gang member I run across in the newspaper or see on the TV news.

The existence of gangs is not new, or limited to blacks only. But today's black gangs, like the black-trash welfare rights proponents, have grown incredibly bold and brazen.

The Bishops and the Chaplains were the two main gangs in Brooklyn in the 1950s. One reason I wasn't one of them had to do with my mother and my aunt Merle. The other reason had to do with my father.

While he didn't live with us, my father definitely loomed as a no-nonsense authority figure nearby in the local police precinct house. It was unfeasible, even for me as a carefree adolescent, to believe that I could run with a gang and go unnoticed by him and the other men in his law enforcement brotherhood. It was especially unfeasible in light of the fact that I was named after him—Kenneth Lorenzo Hamblin II.

Even if I hadn't reasoned all of this as clearly as I recall it today, I had one other even more memorable encounter with the police, after Edgar and I broke into the school, which undoubtedly convinced me to go straight. It occurred because once again I followed some boys who had a swell idea. This time it was to pop open parking meters on Jay Street in downtown Brooklyn.

We were taking in quite a haul of dimes when two uniformed patrolmen showed up. They collared us and carted us off to the nearest precinct house. There an officer sat us down in the squad room and started filling out juvenile delinquency cards. But my interview was short. As soon as I gave him my name, Kenneth L. Hamblin, the policeman realized that I was, in fact, NYPD officer Kenny Hamblin's kid.

"You Wahoo's kid?" the officer asked as he abruptly stopped typing. Wahoo was my dad's nickname for a reason. He was a tough guy when it came to crime.

"Yes," I squeaked.

"Sit right there."

The officer disappeared, and the next thing I knew, my dad was towering over me.

My punishment was meted out first as a father-son matter and later as a mother-son matter. To this day, I believe it was far worse than anything that could have happened to me in the juvenile court system, even in the juvenile court system of some forty years ago.

Back then there were no liberal-minded social workers to cloud the message to me. There was no one to counsel that my wrongdoing was predictable and thus excusable because we were poor or because I was black or because my father had abandoned me or because my mother played the numbers.

Nope. There was no question in my mind—even when I was in the very act of popping those parking meters—that I was doing something wrong. I knew there was no viable excuse I could give that would be accepted by my mother or by my father or by the arresting police officer. I knew I was wrong. And I knew that I had punishment coming.

Aside from the fact that joining a gang was considered unacceptable behavior in my West Indian household, the fact that my dad was NYPD also presented the possibility that I might be marked as a snitch. I deduced that I would be in harm's way no matter which gang I might join. So as I grew into my teens and the peer pressure escalated to affiliate, I decided to sidestep the entire issue by becoming a neutral arms dealer, supplying my own handmade zip guns to both the Bishops and the Chaplains.

Zip guns probably are as old as the horse-drawn buggy. I don't remember how I learned about them or how I learned to make them, but for a summer or two I had a reputation for producing some of the best.

I started with a block of wood, which I cut into the shape of a pistol grip. Then I got—i.e., stole—a motorcar antenna, which happened to be roughly the diameter of a rimfire .22-caliber bullet. I cut the lower half of it to the length of the barrel and taped it to the block of wood.

Then I got a nail and filed the tip into an angle like a spearhead, and it became the firing pin. I used another piece of the antenna to create a shaft so the nail would run true to hit the rim of the bullet. I placed it so the rimfire bullet would slip in between the shaft and the barrel. And then I loaded it for spring pressure with rubber bands.

Firing the zip gun was a two-handed process. If you were right-handed, you would point the gun with your left hand and pull the nail—the hammer—back with your right hand and release it. The nail would hit the rim of the cartridge and fire the shell.

Just like molded steel guns, zip guns fired .22-caliber bullets. You could use them to kill somebody.

I didn't peddle my zip guns on the corner. Guys would hear that I made them and would come to me to buy them. I sold them for just a couple of bucks; sometimes I even traded them for records.

My cottage arms dealership was not a big moneymaking enterprise like drug dealing is today. It simply served the greater purpose of relieving the peer pressure on me to join a gang. Thanks to a good sense of right and wrong instilled in me by my mother and by my aunt Merle, I had already made the right choice about Dice, the neighborhood gang leader. I had withstood my share of taunting, being called a sissy—as in "Na, na, na, na, na, you're afraid to join. You're a sissy." While I may have been wrong to participate in this enterprise at all, even by supplying zip guns, it nonetheless gave me a good excuse to ride the fence a little longer.

Back in the days of the Bishops and the Chaplains, gang activity seemed almost harmless compared to today's. You might hear that there had been a rumble the night before and somebody was in jail because he got busted with a zip gun or somebody was in the hospital because he got stabbed. Very seldom did you hear that somebody got killed.

Only occasionally, you would read in the *Daily News* that there had been a gang revenge killing. Sometimes the vendetta was carried to the point that the rival gang would go to the funeral parlor and turn over the coffin, dumping the body out in front of family.

Disrespect was a tactic then as now.

Likewise, adolescent testosterone and bravado drove the Bishops and the Chaplains just as they drive the Bloods and the Crips today. Two of the most powerful positions in the old Brooklyn gangs were the gang leader and the war counselor. It was the job of the war counselor to incite encounters between opposing gangs. It was the war counselor who walked up front and faced off with the other war counselor—both backed up by their respective gang members. The ritual was akin to Indians counting coup.

After the war counselors struck the first blows, the rumble would start. They fought with bottles, garbage cans, garbage can lids, and sometimes zip guns. But seldom did the zip guns come out.

If a gang member packed his piece, often just showing it was enough to make the other side back down.

Today's gangs have replaced zip guns with high-powered sophisticated automatic firearms: Berettas, Glocks, "nines," and large-caliber Smith & Wesson revolvers. Rumbles, or street fights, have escalated to drive-by assassinations of rival gang members, which frequently result in stray bullets hitting innocents as well as the intended enemies. In Omaha in the spring of 1996, local street thugs even went so far during drive-bys as to boldly shoot at uniformed police officers standing out in front of their own headquarters.

A gang-related killing—sometimes more than one—is an everyday occurrence in a growing number of big cities in America today.

Two of the most infamous contemporary rival gangs, the Crips and the Bloods, started in the South Central section of Los Angeles. Today these young thugs, who mark their turf with bullets and cryptic graffiti from $1.98 cans of spray paint, have contaminated more than a hundred inner-city ghettos in more than thirty states. What's more, they have fanned out into mainstream America, spreading their mayhem and terror.

Like a lot of mainstream Americans, I am angry that these modern-day black thugs have been allowed not just to escalate their adolescent bravado but also to reach out to threaten the peaceful lives of law-abiding citizens.

Their sagging pants, bandanna colors, and backward baseball caps—and unfortunately their black skin—make up the stereotype that instills fear among us. Even Jesse Jackson, a career defender of the community, admitted a while back that he was relieved to turn around and see a white instead of a black face when he heard footsteps following him in certain neighborhoods.

The self-professed life philosophy of Shahid S., an eighteen-year-old black thug, was profiled in a 1994 *New York Times* report on juvenile crime.

Shahid told the *Times* he had snatched more than two hundred automobiles, robbed between fifty and sixty people, and shot at least four more. The article described the following outlook on life as recited by Shahid as "a blunt Darwinian philosophy": "Deers eat grass. Lions eat deers, and men kill lions. I'm the lion. The working people are the deer, the grass is the money and the men shooting the lions is [sic] the cops. You take one thing out and everything will get screwed up."

By sanctioning some of the anomalies of today's black trash and their perverted welfare culture as possibly being on par with mainstream American values, we have opened the door for black gangs and gangsta wannabes to elevate their common street violence to the status of guerrilla warfare for social justice. These black thugs, these street punks and predators, have been allowed—in some cases, encouraged—to believe that their acts of violence against innocent people and property are merely blows for justice, blows for black liberation and black sovereignty. They envision themselves as the point men leading the fight against the unfair system of the white man.

The fact is these boys are a far cry from social crusaders. These boys are empty vessels.

By that, I don't mean they are stupid. They are dumb when it comes to the skills they need to survive in mainstream America. They don't, or maybe they can't, speak beyond a mumbled "Whatsup" or "Yeaaaahh." Most cannot read or write beyond a minimal grade school level. They have few, if any, job skills beyond petty street sales in the drug trade.

Gang members have not prepared themselves to be the proud bearers of attaché cases; they have not prepared themselves to be mathematicians or scientists. They dress for success in their own world, not in mainstream America, which holds the promise of true rewards for them. In place of the pressed shirts and creased trousers that would grant them access to the mainstream, they have substituted sagging pants, dark hooded jackets, and $300 athletic shoes.

But the accepted excuse for their failure is that they have been disenfranchised from traditional American path to success because they are black.

And so organizing a gang is validated as an alternative for their unfulfilled entrepreneurial energy. They are granted every right to be angry about their plight, and they also are validated to strike out at the system that supposedly made them resort to this lifestyle.

Some people reason that these thugs join gangs because they are seeking the families and the love that they don't have at home. I say that is more liberal hogwash to condone clear-cut wrongdoing. There can never be a moral justification for consorting with this kind of family, which is completely without values.

What is never easily explained away is why they strike out at their own. Why they shrug off the poor black babies who are killed and maimed when they are caught in the line of fire of the gangland drive-by shootings. Why they look for excuses to shoot each other on the flimsy grounds that they have been shown disrespect, or "dissed," in their argot. And why they use their African-American sisters as objects of rape and abuse for gang initiations. Today in almost every American urban community, at least one out of every three young black males is either in jail, on parole, on probation, or awaiting trial on a criminal charge.

The irony of the gang members' phony social-justice crusade on behalf of their race is that these black thugs probably have snuffed out more of their own—more black teens, more black women, more innocent black babies—than any white racist gang, including the Ku Klux Klan, ever dreamed of exterminating. Their behavior boils down to cold, unremitting fratricide.

I call them empty vessels because they are devoid of morals.

But as I said, they are not stupid.

They are street-smart and institutionalized enough to know exactly what to say to the police, to their mothers—and to the media, when given an opportunity.

To the police: "I didn't do it."

To their mothers: "I didn't do it."

To the media: "I'm disadvantaged and restless because there aren't any jobs or recreational centers in my neighborhood."

Gangs have become the most immediate and tangible threat to American society emanating from the black-trash welfare culture.

In many American cities the threat of an unprovoked gang attack has made it unsafe to use public parks, particularly to take a stroll there in the evening. We husbands and fathers legitimately become uneasy when our wives and our daughters are late coming home. I know at least one young white businessman who lives in the city and, in this age of equal rights for women, asked his wife, a professional like him, not to go to their urban neighborhood grocery store unescorted.

Many of our once-grand downtown centers of commerce have been all but abandoned because people—not just white people—are afraid to do business there.

In Detroit, people joke about not letting their cars break down on the John Lodge Freeway, a major artery that passes through the black ghetto en route from the suburbs into downtown Detroit. They make jokes about it, but more and more people stay put in the suburbs.

The gangs long ago marked the streets as their turf—streets in ghettos like Brooklyn's Bedford-Stuyvesant, where my friends and I used to escape from hot apartments to play children's games like ring-a-levio or to roller-skate around manhole covers in a fantasized game of Roller Derby in the street.

In 1995 in Little Rock, Arkansas, two young black thugs took their terror and mayhem beyond the streets when they broke through security locks on a mother's door and executed her four young children with bullets to their heads in front of her. The gang members reportedly were angry at the mother's oldest daughter, who wasn't home, so they took revenge on her siblings.

Many of the gang killings are senseless. In 1993 in Denver, stealing a Jeep Cherokee was the initiation rite required of new members in one of the gangs. Purportedly the challenge was that stealing this vehicle, which was driven only by wealthy white people, required a daring venture beyond the familiar territory of the black ghetto. A fifteen-year-old black thug shot and killed a woman in the vestibule of her town house because she didn't turn over her Jeep keys on demand. The woman was found lying in a pool of blood with her groceries strewn about her several days later, after police arrested the boy still joyriding, celebrating his initiation, in her Jeep.

I had my first close encounter with these black-trash hoodlums when I asked to ride with the Aurora, Colorado, police gang unit a few years ago. Aurora is a large Denver suburb that has made national headlines for its nononsense crackdown on gangs.

The gang unit was formed to create a presence among known gang members by making frequent contact with young people on the streets who either are in gangs or are being tempted to join one. Some liberals think this kind of policing violates civil rights. Some black community leaders back up the gang members who claim they are being harassed. I call it holding the thin blue line between them and us.

That first night in Aurora, I rode with two gang officers in an unmarked vehicle. We weren't out long before we spotted and followed some young black boys in a car who appeared to be passing a marijuana cigarette one to another.

We put the bubble light on the car roof so that anyone could tell we were cops, signaling for them to pull over. But the boys must have driven another six or eight blocks. Finally one of the officers said, "There it goes; there's the drop out the window."

I never saw a thing.

But when the boys finally pulled over, one of the officers ran back down the street and picked up a small bag of marijuana.

There were four kids in the car. The driver had a license, and the car wasn't stolen. So the cops decided just to contact their parents and get them out there to deal with the dope on the spot.

The expression on these boys' faces was of total disdain. Their attitude was abrasive, indifferent to the seriousness of their situation, as if they were being scolded by the school librarian, not detained by city police officers. Their behavior wasn't anything at all like mine had been when I was sitting terrified in the precinct house after my daring parking meter escapade. These boys were used to this. They had done this before and had learned the ropes.

It took almost an hour before another car pulled up with the mother of one of the boys inside. As she approached, I could smell alcohol on her breath.

She totally ignored her son's alleged misdeed, but marched right up on the officer: "God damn it, what have you got him handcuffed for? What are you people doing to him?"

She was completely oblivious to the responses from the officers, nor did she show any concern when confronted about her boy having drugs. She never once scolded her child for breaking the law or for getting into this predicament.

Her boy did not see her show the least bit of respect for the authority those officers represented.

Frequently a boy like him does see his mother in complete denial, however. She lies to the cops and to the media, telling them that her son isn't even remotely connected to a gang, telling them he's a "good boy."

Later that night we stopped another carload of homeys. One of the cops found a .25-caliber automatic gun in the car, and the boys were arrested. As we started back to the station house, one officer said to me that the kids would be out before the police finished their paperwork. And he was right.

Furthermore, not only were these kids unruffled—like the other group, they obviously had been through this drill before—but when one of the mothers came to bail her kid out, it was clear that this was a routine ride on a summer night for her.

She and her boyfriend and the boy's kid sister came into the precinct bantering back and forth. There was nothing solemn about going to the cop shop to pick up their son, their brother. They had done this before.

Mom asked, "How are you?" The kid said, "I'm fine." And after a few words from the desk officer, they all left, as jovial as when they had come in.

The kids themselves had been down in the holding cell joking and high-fiving the entire time.

It hit me that these petty teenage thugs—many of whom ultimately become muggers and killers—had been institutionalized already.

They had picked up the jargon of the liberal social workers and public defenders who talk about extenuating circumstances, starting with the fact that these boys are juveniles and thus all but immune from punishment. Then the boys hear the politically absurd argument that too many blacks are arrested and put in jail in proportion to the population of blacks in America.

Therefore, even though these kids know very well that they have committed a crime, that fact is presented simply as evidence of what good kids do when they are "socioeconomic prisoners of racism in America."

When the neophyte thug queries, "What's that?," the response from the black thugs who are more savvy about the system is "That's what will get you out of here, nigger."

By the time the neophytes take the next fall, they know exactly what kind of rhetoric to feed back to the social workers and the judge. They also feed it back to the liberal reporter from the TV station, and he or she makes it the truth by broadcasting it to America.

Since taking my first ride in Aurora, I've tried to hook up with the local police whenever I'm traveling and ride the night shift in a patrol car. I've seen these thugs in action in cities across America. There is little difference from one gang to another or from one city to the next.

These black thugs are a menace to society. They need to know that they represent something totally wrong and fundamentally immoral and that mainstream society has every intention of putting them out of commission. But unfortunately that message has yet to be even formulated, let alone explicitly communicated.

The embodiment of these black thugs surfaced in a Denver courtroom in the summer of 1994. Steve Harrington, age twenty-three, and Shane Davis, twenty-one, were found guilty of the murder of young Denver businessman Tom Hollar and the beastly beating of his wife, Christina.

Perhaps this crime was more graphic for me because I knew the Hollars. They were good friends of my son's, and I had met them at his wedding just a couple of years before the attack.

And perhaps it was especially vivid for me because it occurred in my neighborhood in Denver, in the parking lot adjacent both to the Hollars' apartment building and to a grocery store where my wife and I, along with thousands of other urban dwellers, shopped almost daily.

I compiled the following account of the grisly crime from reports in the local newspapers, on TV newscasts, and by talking with the homicide detectives on this case:

The Hollars were attacked in the Denver Capitol Hill neighborhood about 1:00 A.M. on a balmy July night when two men, later identified as Davis and Harrington, approached them and demanded money and their car keys.

Some police officers later surmised that these black thugs were hanging around that night specifically looking for trouble, what cops call "an opportunity" to commit a crime.

They executed Hollar in front of his terrified wife after he told her to ignore the thugs in an attempt to avoid a confrontation. The killers then ordered Christina to get back in the car.

They drove her into an alley, where they stripped, sexually abused and beat her so severely that the two Denver police officers who found her in the car thought she was dead.

According to Denver newspaper accounts of the murder trial, one officer testified that as he approached Christina's car, he noticed that all the windows were splattered with blood and when he pointed his flashlight through the car window, he saw a woman with "extreme facial injuries—a lot of trauma to her head and face."

Officer Vince Lombardi told his partner, Scott Hartvigson, to call for an ambulance, Code 10—an emergency run with overhead lights turned on. While Hartvigson was summoning the ambulance, Lombardi said he received the scare of his life when Christina moved her head. He had been certain she was dead. During the trial Lombardi testified that "The face didn't look human at all, it was so mangled. It was about twice the size of my head. It was the worst beating I've ever seen on a live person."

But in spite of the unmerciful attack against her, Christina Hollar lived to identify the men who beat her and to testify against her husband's killers.

While in custody for the Hollar murder, Shane Davis was charged with another first-degree assault and aggravated robbery for shooting another man in the head during a robbery attempt a month before the Hollar killing. Davis and Harrington showed virtually no remorse for killing Hollar.

Throughout the trial Denver gang members, identified as friends of Davis and Harrington, were present in the courtroom, threatening prosecution witnesses and friends of the Hollars with icy glares and gang signs. Harrington glared at Christina and mumbled expletive-studded remarks in what appeared to be an effort to intimidate her and discourage her from identifying him and Davis. But he failed to shake her, and although Harrington claimed to have been miles away at his mother's home in Montbello, a predominantly black Denver neighborhood, making love to a woman at the time of the crime, eyewitnesses testified that they saw him pull the trigger.

Davis told authorities he couldn't remember where he was that night but guessed he was drunk, adding that he drank almost every night. A coin purse found in the hijacked Hollar car was tied to Davis.

In the end, despite the defendants' denials, a Denver District Court jury found Davis and Harrington guilty on eight counts each: felony first-degree murder, premeditated first-degree murder, attempted first-degree murder, first-degree assault, second-degree kidnapping, aggravated robbery, first-degree aggravated motor vehicle theft, and attempted first-degree sexual assault.

More than ten sheriff's deputies were present in the courtroom to ensure that order prevailed when a jurist read the verdict—guilty—on each of the counts.

As the verdict was being read, Christina Hollar finally wept. Harrington flashed gang signs and mouthed obscenities.

Outside the courthouse, liberal Denver District Attorney Bill Ritter was busy patting himself on the back and insisting he stood "100 percent" behind his decision not to seek the death penalty in the Hollar murder case.

According to Ritter, "These guys don't come out of prison except in a pine box. People talk about swift and certain justice. In a murder case, this is as good as it gets. Guilty on all counts."

While the jury was deliberating, Denver homicide detectives got a tip that resulted in their discovering the actual gun used to kill Hollar. It matched shell casings they recovered from Davis's house. He apparently was keeping them as souvenirs.

The Hollar murder trial was a big event in Denver, and it was watched by Americans across the nation on Court TV. When the trial ended, local newspapers wrote about the aftermath for weeks. The *Denver Post* assigned a liberal reporter named Alan Katz to get a street perspective on the verdict from friends of the defendants.

Here is his story:

> *In the harsh afternoon sun, four neighbors of Shane Davis—all men under twenty-five—gathered on a front porch to commiserate over yesterday's guilty verdicts.*
>
> *All seemed saddened by the news that Davis and Steve Harrington were [found] guilty of eight felony counts each, including first-degree murder.*

A familiar figure in the neighborhood, Davis lived in a tidy-looking red brick home at 2304 Williams Street. He won't be returning home, ever, since in Colorado the mandatory sentence for first-degree murder is life in prison without parole.

"Life in prison?" One of the men said bitterly. "They'd-a got parole if they'd-a shot a black dude. A fat parole."

The men laughed.

"The judge would've let them do charity work."

They laughed again.

"Yeah, I knew Shane," said one of the men. "I was locked up with him once when we were juveniles. He was cool to me. He was laid back. What did he talk about?

"Bitches."

The men chuckled again, then launched into a complicated discussion of the defendants. They talked about rage, and the feeling of being unwanted in America, and of feeling shut off from mainstream society. They talked of the boredom of life without prospects, and the frustration over not having money.

Each man had read newspaper accounts of the Tom Hollar murder; several had watched the trial on Court TV.

"Crying widow this. Crying widow that," said one, speaking of Christina Hollar, who survived a brutal beating to testify at the trial. "Court TV was hyping her the whole time. What I can't figure out is why the dudes raped her. Why didn't they kill her? They must've wanted to get caught. They didn't use their brains."

"Aw, now wait," [said another man] who identified himself as a rap singer. "I feel sorry for her. The whole thing had to be very traumatic for her."

"I agree," [a third man chimed in]. "'I honestly think the two dudes got what they deserved. I mean, why do you got to kill somebody you don't even know?"

"I feel bad for the two brothers, though," [said a fourth man]. "I can understand how they feel, too. Look how everything has been taken away from us. There's no recreation. There's no jobs. We can't even go to a club to hear music. They stop you at the door and card you. They claim you ain't got the right identification or they find some other reason to hassle you. At least this Hollar dude, he had it good up until he got smoked."

"For me, it's hard to watch brothers go up [to prison]," [said the third man]. "Everybody is born with something, some talent. You have to find your place where you fit into society. You have to find a direction and make it work for you. But I do feel more sorry for the lady that had the loss."

On the Montbello block where Steve Harrington lived, the mood was anything but convivial.

"Get the f—— out of here," said a man identified as Harrington's relative. "I ain't talking. It was the media that got him sent away."

These boys epitomized my portrayal of black thugs as empty vessels. They displayed the sickening twisted values characteristic of much of modern-day black trash.

While I'm convinced the reporter, Katz, missed this point, I think he was a witness to the only lesson that Davis and Harrington's homeys learned from the trial of their two friends: "What I can't figure out is why the dudes raped her. Why didn't they kill her? They must've wanted to get caught. They didn't use their brains."

With those words, I believe those African-American brothers in that Denver ghetto were reasoning that killing was the only way to deal with witnesses. Witnesses who, by their deduction, shouldn't be left alive the next time this particular band of black thugs conspired to hijack a car or snatch a purse. The only lesson these dusky predators learned from their convicted gangsta brothers was that in the long run it pays to be sure that anyone who might be able to convict them is dead.

Another fitting epilogue to the Hollar murder trial was written in the *Rocky Mountain News* by Lynn Bartels. Bartels interviewed Shane Davis at the Denver County Jail and asked him what he thought about being convicted for murder.

"The evidence against me is great," Davis admitted, although he, like Harrington, still maintained his innocence.

Asked to describe the kind of person who would have hurt the Hollars, Davis fed back the standard institutionalized rhetoric: "Somebody who didn't value themselves, who didn't feel good about themselves."

The *News* printed part of a protest rap written by Davis and Harrington from jail:

> *We as a minority race*
> *must always see the problems we face.*
> *The justice system hates us. They want to lock us all away.*
> *They're the strongest-growing gang called the KKK.*
> *If you think about it for awhile, you'll see what I say is true.*
> *They've been convicting us of crimes we didn't do.*

Davis insisted to Bartels that race played a big part in the trial because he and Harrington are black and the Hollars are white: "To come in here for a drive-by shooting in your own community, a person will get up to eight years, something like that.

"That's black-on-black crime.

"But when it's black-on-white crime you face the death penalty, life in prison, all of this stuff."

According to Davis, Christina Hollar's testimony bothered him the most when she calmly pointed to him and Harrington as the two men who killed her husband and almost beat her to death.

"I just hate it when they say she's such a good person and her husband's such a good person and her husband's this and her husband's that and something bad was done on her.

"I understand that.

"But for her to get up there and say, 'Yeah, that's him who beat me up.' Damn, well, I didn't beat that woman up, and she knows I didn't beat her up.

"She knows what happened as well as Tom, but Tom's not here to say. I can't get mad at her no more, but she knows."

In the end, Davis sounded like the many other misguided African-American men and women who get wound up talking the talk.

"I was raised good," he said. "To tell you the truth, I was raised with values."

Other wars on civilized American society that emanate from fringe elements are perceived as a threat to the foundation of life as we know it. At a minimum, they are scorned. In some cases, such groups are literally snuffed out. Consider the reaction by the Bureau of Alcohol, Tobacco and Firearms to an armed and isolated religious sect in Waco, Texas.

Now compare that to the black gangs' threat to the well-being of peaceful American city dwellers which is not only tolerated but excused by many.

In a twisted way the gang organization is what puts black trash on the map. But for the prominence of gangs, mainstream America probably never would have heard of ghetto communities like South Central and Compton in Los Angeles.

But by making these murderers and crack dealers poster boys for the "misguided youth" line of propaganda, these woeful communities remain on the front pages of newspapers and on network television news programs to advertise the terrible monsters that racism has created. That spin on black trash helps to keep the entitlements, purportedly to finance social solutions, rolling into their communities.

Average Americans are drawn further into feeling sorrow and guilt for the "poor downtrodden people." They fail to label the gangs and their criminal activities as the vicious scourge on society that they are. Mainstream America fails to turn against black trash as it logically should turn on any community that would tolerate such behavior from its young men.

Instead, black community leaders like Jesse Jackson go unchallenged when they appear on national television and tell talking heads like Dan Rather that a boy from South Central L.A. isn't deterred from killing and pilfering by the threat of arrest because the amenities offered in jail are a move up from his own home and run-down community.

The Jesse Jacksons don't use their voices to mobilize the community to take responsibility for its offspring in the manner that my mother and my father took ultimate responsibility for my actions. They don't challenge the community to put a stop to the gangs and their unspeakable behavior. Instead they call for more taxpayer-supported liberal social solutions to "save" these boys.

In my decade and a half on the radio, I have staunchly refused to invite these black thugs to come on my show as guests so they can exploit me and my audience with their carefully honed rhetoric of oppression. I have talked a lot about them on the radio and written a lot about them in my newspaper column, however. And I've talked about some of the politicians and the cops whom I believe they have bamboozled.

That's gotten me into a couple of tight spots, including one that was captured on video by the CBS magazine program *Eye to Eye* in 1994. Correspondent Bernard Goldberg and I were being taped walking and talking in Five Points, Denver's black hood, when we were confronted by some pimp-rolling thugs with a mission to get in my face on national television.

Leading the pack was a local thug and small-time hustler named Michael Asberry. Some people credited him with starting the local Denver chapter of the Crips when he moved here from Los Angeles a few years before. He soon came to the attention of the Denver police gang unit as one of the ringleaders in petty crimes and was eventually involved with more serious offenses, including being charged with assault and arrested for attempted murder.

I took special notice of Asberry when he was mentioned as a point person in a new program called Reconstruction, Inc., which liberals had pressured corporations and government to put into place, supposedly to curb gangs. The idea of this program in essence was to let the gangs police themselves in the community.

I saw this, plain and simple, as a move to turn over the community to urban terrorists. By taking authority away from the men and women who were commissioned to protect our cities and by handing that authority over to the bad guys, the Reconstruction program, in my opinion, was demeaning to the police.

But proponents of Reconstruction saw it as giving these disadvantaged kids an opportunity to hold a position of authority. Of course they missed the point entirely that these kids already held positions of authority on the street, positions which, when disputed, often resulted in cold-blooded killings.

Former gang members designated as "My Hood Communicators" were to patrol the streets and were issued pagers, cellular phones, and Denver Police Department radio scanners.

Well, the police balked at the scanners, expressing concern that My Hood Communicators soon would be monitoring police frequencies in order to warn their homeys that the cops were on the way. That became the topic of a column I wrote for the *Denver Post*, which resulted in my taking a long, hard look at Michael Asberry, including his rap sheet, which was several pages long.

Needless to say, I concluded in my column that Reconstruction was another foolish liberal enterprise, and I nailed Asberry for what he was—a street thug. I also talked about the folly of Reconstruction and the absurdity of making Asberry a leader of this folly by putting him on my radio show.

Michael Asberry soon developed a hatred for me. He called my radio show and whined that I was picking on him. I laughed him off and said he had me confused with some white liberal he thought he could bully.

"Excuse me, kid," I said. "I'm from the streets too. And I know what you're up to. It's a big scam."

Then a guest column by him appeared in the *Post*. But if you had ever spoken to Michael and heard his ghetto argot, you would have had to deduce that someone else had written the column for him. It was quite an eloquent attack on me for being unfair to him, not giving him a chance, and coming down too hard on black people. It said I had ascended to some high perch and had forgotten where I came from.

While doing an interview for *Eye to Eye*, Bernie Goldberg asked me to go down to Five Points, the center of Denver's black ghetto, to get some footage of me walking on the streets. The "drum" quickly dispersed the word that Ken Hamblin was in the hood, and soon after our arrival, Asberry walked up on us, backed up by three of his little thugs, and tried to intimidate me with the cameras running.

"Hey, man, you know who I am?" he opened.

"No, brother, how you?" I countered.

He launched into a tirade to Goldberg and the cameras about how I had said bad things about him and I didn't even know him.

"He comes down so hard before he gives a person a second chance," he ranted.

"He's selling the community out. He downgrades this community, when he's got it so lavish. Look at how he's dressed. The man's got it made."

I was wearing a suit and tie, a topcoat, and my trademark fedora. These thugs were dressed in typical gangland attire. I was the one who stood out in their community. That's one of the reasons I usually don't go there. I tried to talk to them, but my words fell on deaf ears.

"I'm angry," I began. "I'm angry that when somebody who looks like you walks up on people today, they're afraid. You perceive it as power but . . . you try to relate to me on a level that is going to keep you on your back. I fought to change that, brother."

It was clear that Asberry had no desire to communicate with me, as he claimed he did. He wanted only one thing—to punk me out, to "dis" me on national television.

After meeting him, I was certain that, despite his ability to pull the wool over the eyes of the liberal social workers, I had been right on the money when I pegged him early on for exactly what he was—just another empty vessel.

Chapter Four

Brood Mares

. . . .

You are "right on" with your ideas. Mandating control of births within
the welfare sector is a must to reduce the "welfare state" that this
nation is in!
There is a way to use the Norplant to accomplish this end. . . . This system
will reduce the number of children born into the "welfare state." . . . How
can we get a program started like this? We have politicians who love this
"welfare state." Why? Because these people vote for their re-election! Without these votes, the other political party would win the elections. What I'm
saying is the number of welfare votes is sufficient to change a majority vote
for one party to a minority vote. The liberals have "developed" the "welfare
state." Without this vote they would become the minority party. Do you believe the Democrats will institute a Norplant system?

VIA E-MAIL 12/15/92
L.P.,
GRAND JUNCTION, CO

. . . .

Congratulations on your Nov. 8 column on teenage mothers in the Denver
Post. . . . It's a sad reflection of the times that such a subject has to come up
at all. But it's here—all around us. Something must be done or we'll be

overwhelmed by a tidal wave of illiterate, illegitimate, unwanted children
irretrievably lost in society.

VIA E-MAIL 12/2/90
C.S.,
HOUSTON, TEXAS

The birth of a baby was somewhat less than a happy, blessed event in poor households like the one I grew up in, and for good reason. While most poor babies were loved, the overriding emotion associated with their birth was concern about having another mouth to feed. Poverty kept families from experiencing the exuberant joy of birth that I later came to know.

I admit that embracing that joy did not come naturally for me. When my own two children were born in the early 1960s, the wonder of their birth was overshadowed by my panic that they would grow up experiencing the same shame and insecurity brought about by poverty that I had known as a child.

Like so many American parents, I was driven to make certain that they didn't suffer the desperation of my youth. I was committed to changing things for them, and I believe, for the most part, I succeeded.

It took the birth of my first granddaughter, Olivia Christine, in 1991, however, for me to experience the complete happiness that can and should be associated with birth in America. Her other grandfather and I were able to hold her when she was barely forty-five minutes old, still enveloped in a delicate film and carrying a slight scent of the placenta.

We were captivated by her and her every new development. In the first year of her life, the family assembled regularly—at first weekly and later monthly—for birthday parties complete with presents and doting. We shot hundreds of rolls of film in an attempt to document our euphoria. We looked at her long, slender fingers and wondered whether she would play a musical instrument like her other grandfather. I proudly mused with other family members that indeed her facial features had a strong resemblance to my own. We tried to project into the future just far enough to wonder what her voice would sound like when she began to talk. We planned trips and experiences to expose her to the wonderful world of choices that this great country offered her.

Perhaps that level of joy was what Pulitzer Prize–winning black author Toni Morrison innocently wished for her young sisters when she declared in 1990 that having babies out of wedlock was a laudable aspiration for black girls. But I, for one, was astounded at her words of encouragement to them.

From a feminist perspective, it might be debated as laudable for a woman of means, like Ms. Morrison, to choose to have a baby as a single mother. But unfortunately, I believe the girls who accepted her statement as a sanction were the sad, vacant young black girls living on welfare in housing projects like Chicago's Cabrini Green and Robert Taylor Homes—girls fighting an uphill battle for their own survival and utterly unprepared emotionally and practically to take on the responsibility of a child. They, after all, were still children themselves.

Today these are the black teenage girls who are breeding in unspeakable numbers. Some sources indicate that more than 90 percent of their babies are born out of wedlock.

If the gang members are the foot soldiers of the black-trash welfare culture, then these young girls are the brood mares whose sole function is to keep replenishing the rank and file, collecting another welfare entitlement for each newborn.

Not only are these ghetto births absent of unmitigated joy, but according to Jane Deacon, a nurse at Denver General Hospital, in many cases the mothers lack even the most basic maternal instincts.

I interviewed Deacon on my Denver radio show in 1994, after she had kept a journal the previous year while on duty in the newborn nursery at Denver's city hospital.

She made the startling observation that, although she began making entries on June 6, it was not until July 22 that she attended a birth by a married mother. She said almost all of the mothers she cared for were in their teens, and the great majority of them were not having their first child. The oldest mother mentioned in Deacon's journal was twenty-three years old and giving birth to her seventh child.

Nurse Deacon recounted brood mare horrors that even I had not envisioned:

- When one sixteen-year-old new mother was asked to fill out a form with her baby's name the day after she gave birth, she had forgotten what she named him. She knew the precise number of the form she needed to fill out to request welfare payments, however.
- A fifteen-year-old was rushed in to deliver a premature baby by cesarean section after she was shot in a gang squabble over drugs. Her thirty-six-year-old mother, who had a prison record and drug-abuse problems, reportedly was to care for the baby when it left the hospital.
- A thirteen-year-old came in by ambulance, ready to deliver full term, but claimed she never knew she was pregnant. Her mother came to the hospital just once—with the new mother's fifteen-year-old pregnant sister. But she never returned to pick up her daughter and new grandchild, both of whom tested positive for cocaine. The thirteen-year-old ultimately was discharged to a waiting cab in a hospital gown and slippers with her baby in hospital blankets.

Needless to say, all of these mothers were either already collecting welfare or signing up in the hospital.

Only rarely did the fathers appear. If any male was there at all, he was usually a new boyfriend.

I didn't have the firsthand input of Nurse Jane Deacon in 1990 when I read Toni Morrison's statement, which in essence supported the birth of more black babies to young mothers. Even so, back then I judged it not only idiotic but cruel to the babies who, if they survived the gunfire in their urban neighborhoods, probably would grow up neglected, abused, and delinquent. And it was cruel to the girls, these young mothers whom Ms. Morrison was, in fact, inspiring to become little more than brood mares.

It is impossible to experience the kind of joy or hold the aspirations for your child that I finally experienced with my granddaughter when you become a mother at fourteen, fifteen, or sixteen years of age, when you yourself have no future, little education, no dreams, and no life experience beyond your own isolated upbringing on welfare. It's impossible when there is no father for your baby and no partner in your life. It's impossible when your own mother, your only role model, cut her life short with your birth a scant decade and a half ago, when she was no more than a teenager herself.

I know that level of joy and the luxury of those dreams are not possible because even though my mother was not a teen mother and even though there were strong role models in my extended family, still the arrival of each of my brothers and sisters added a burden to my family that greatly diminished our joy. Our poverty and our dependence on welfare stopped us short of the unconditional happiness I eventually experienced when Olivia was born.

I was raised by women, on welfare. But the similarity to many of today's single teen welfare mothers stops there. My mother and her sisters were far different from today's evolutionary disgrace, the brood mares.

While we weren't wealthy in material things, my mother and my aunts provided me with the priceless strength of my heritage—a heritage that began in the West Indies and continued with my family's fateful move to America. They endowed me with the hope of the American Dream and the will to achieve it.

Sadly today, these girls, who become mothers before their time—these brood mares—can offer no legacy of strength and dreams to their children, because with each succeeding welfare generation, they have less substance to draw upon. Each generation is left more isolated in a world of illiteracy, violence, and contempt for America and American values. Each generation is more deeply embedded in the black-trash welfare culture.

My mother was an unsophisticated Third World woman. She never even learned how to drive a car, an irony that came to my mind as I was piloting my own airplane over the craggy peaks of the Rocky Mountains one day many years after I had left home.

Her vice was betting on the numbers, always in anticipation of overnight riches. And more than once we were forced into more pressing financial predicaments because of it.

My childhood was spent moving from one sparsely furnished room or shabby apartment to another in Brooklyn. I remember one particular time when, as had happened frequently, my mother misappropriated too much of our monthly welfare stipend to the community numbers man, and we were evicted in the middle of the month. At other times like this, my aunt Merle had taken us in. But this time, when the eviction notice came, Aunt Merle must have hoped she would teach her sister a lesson.

And so, at barely ten years old, I recall helping my mother herd my younger brother and my little sister onto a New York City subway car, where we rode the line through the night.

Sometimes on hot summer nights, well after my siblings were asleep, I would sit with my mother in the dark and listen to her fanciful notions about hitting the number big, about getting off welfare and buying a three-story Brooklyn brownstone where we would live forever after, never to be evicted again.

I would listen to her talk about "home," a word that carried a meaning of strength and warmth, a word denoting to all immigrants the comfort that they had roots. She would reminisce about being a little girl in Barbados, about the folklore of duppies, the imaginary ghosts that every superstitious adult and every little child knew rustled in the sugarcane fields when the wind blew. I didn't really understand why she was remembering these things back then, but today I realize she would recall anything pleasant to talk away the pain of her situation.

But despite all of our struggles, my mother maintained an unwavering belief in her ability to do better than welfare for herself and for her children. Besides her pipe dreams of hitting the number, she had dreams for personal accomplishment and success that would enable her to break away from government dependency. In her youth she had wanted to be a professional singer and even competed—unfortunately somewhat unnoticeably—in talent shows at the Apollo Theatre in New York. In spite of her naïveté and our difficulties, the constant in our lives was that she held on to hope, albeit frequently impractical.

Neither my mother nor her sisters would ever allow themselves to become resigned to a lifetime of poverty on account of being victims. They had been sent to America, after all, to find a better life than they could have hoped for back home on an isolated island. They loved this country and always told us we could and should become proud *Americans*.

My mother told me in no uncertain terms that I could succeed in America. She and my aunts told me education was the key. "Stay in school and get yourself an education" was their mantra. I never heard anyone in my family speak ill of education.

As poor as we were and as bleak as our future looked sometimes, my family was convinced that mainstream education—consisting of the basics of reading, writing, and arithmetic—was the way to get ahead, the way to ensure a better life for the children.

I don't know exactly how old my brother and I were when my mother found out, quite by accident, that neither of us could read, even though we had been going to public school for some time. It was summer, and my memory is that after her shocking discovery we were kept inside all day, every day, away from our friends and play, while she patiently taught us.

I also remember the moment some months later when we were walking down the street and I glanced down and *read* a matchbook cover as though it were speaking directly to me. Even as a young boy, I had a sense that an entire part of the world that had been foreign to me had opened up. The next fall my mother enrolled us in Catholic school.

I admit I hated school, be it parochial or public. One reason probably was that, while I don't recall being the subject of a lot of prejudice for being black, I do know that school was one place where my poverty showed. I have a vivid, sickening recollection of being taunted by other kids because I wore my mother's laced shoes to school at the end of the winter one year after my own had worn out. And my defiant attitude today may be due in part to a teacher who told my mother, in my presence, that I would be in prison by the time I was seventeen.

But my mother didn't hold a protest rally in front of the school or complain about the teacher to the local NAACP.

Instead, she continued to encourage us to get an education and to make better lives for ourselves. She never made excuses for us because we were poor, and she sincerely believed that anything was possible in America . . . even for a poor black single mother in the 1940s and the 1950s.

In retrospect, I realize that the American Dream may have been all that kept my mother from slipping into the traps that undoubtedly contribute to the defeatist welfare mentality so prevalent today. She had few skills suitable for the job market, and she did little or nothing to acquire new ones. I remember her working only for short periods of time doing piecework as a seamstress in the Garment District in Manhattan. Yet she continued to have children with no means of her own to care for them and almost never with a father in our home.

The difference between my mother and many welfare mothers today, however, is that my mother knew welfare was wrong. I think she was conscious every day of the fact that she was being judged poorly by black society and white society alike, by the American mainstream society of which she desperately wanted to be a part and by which she wanted her children to be favorably judged.

Children are resilient so I am certain that despite my poignantly painful memories of childhood poverty, it was my mother who bore the brunt of suffering for the family.

Whenever Mrs. So-and-So across the street came outside to sweep her steps, I know it was painful for my mother to watch. She wanted nothing more than to have her own brownstone where she could proudly sweep her steps and prune her flowers. She felt trapped in a welfare culture that she instinctively knew was wrong based on every value system she had inherited.

Her sisters often chastised her, even though some of them were guilty of similar lifestyles. I remember being humiliated—being the invisible kid in the corner, just as I was at Jack's grocery—as I would listen to them tell her how she had ruined her life, how she didn't adequately provide for her children, how we were not their responsibility, when she solicited help from them on our behalf.

My mother lived in a bit of a fantasy world in terms of how to get the better life that America promised. She even used her children just as welfare mothers do today, to plead for unconditional help. But I'm thankful that at least she envisioned the American Dream and somehow passed it on to me.

The sad phenomenon of brood mares also represents a prime example of how a substandard value cultivated in the black-trash welfare culture has spread to mainstream America.

Having a baby out of wedlock, particularly in your teen years, used to be shameful and stigmatizing, just as poverty and welfare once were. Pregnant girls were banished in a hush from school, sometimes to a home for unwed mothers, sometimes out of town to live with a relative. They were outcasts because they had failed to meet the standards of the community.

But today, inch by inch, step by step, with the aid of prominent voices like Toni Morrison's, we have allowed these community standards to be dismantled.

And thus sanctioned, illegitimate pregnancy has spread beyond the black ghetto to mainstream America. By 1994 the percentage of all babies born out of wedlock had reached more than 30 percent.

The acceptance of unwed teen pregnancies reached the ridiculous a few years ago when a controversy erupted over a Texas high school's decision to bar pregnant girls from the cheerleading squad. Think about that. Cheerleaders traditionally have been role models in high school—the most athletic, the most wholesome, the smartest, the prettiest, the most popular girls.

A pregnant cheerleader in an American school even a decade ago would have been considered not just scandalous but a true oxymoron.

But as the debate over the Texas case raged on television talk shows and in newspaper editorials, the argument came down to whether the pregnant girl might be hurt while leading a cheer, not whether she presented a suitable example of leadership for her classmates.

We began tearing down the stigma of illegitimate births on TV talk shows hosted by supposedly compassionate liberals like Phil Donahue. They provided a credible platform for the psychobabble of so-called experts who bemoaned the trauma we inflict on innocent bastard babies when we stigmatize their immoral and primitive mothers.

Gradually, instead of banishing pregnant girls from school, it was advocated that not only they but their newborn babies as well stay. School nurseries were built to provide day care for student mothers. The theory was that this girl, now more than ever, needed an education.

In the end, we have altered our community values and disrupted our once orderly educational system to make it convenient for teenage unwed mothers to have the same access to school that "good" girls have.

The unmarried teen mother, with virtually no means of support of her own, gets extraordinary attention and perks as a result of her irresponsible behavior. Not to mention that we have removed the stigma and the discomfort that always has followed improper actions.

As a by-product, we have set the stage for these pregnant teens to pollute their peers. With nurseries in the high schools, these young mothers can show off their cute and cuddly doll babies to their friends. Teenage pregnancy and unmarried motherhood are losing any sign of disgrace at all. On the contrary, they now are viewed as being normal.

Unwed pregnant girls existed in my neighborhood when I was growing up. But back then they were summarily ostracized.

Today, like their counterparts, the black-thug gang-bangers, they are held up as poor downtrodden victims of racism and poverty. And so, as with other kinds of decay brought about by the runaway black-trash welfare culture, America has validated their behavior and is standing aside while they increase their tribe.

Whenever I address the problem of black-trash teen mothers on my radio show or in my syndicated newspaper column, inevitably I get calls and letters reminding me that there are fathers somewhere who need to be held just as accountable for these babies as their young mothers.

To them I say: What a joke.

I am well versed in biology. I know that there is a father somewhere for each and every one of these babies. I also know that most of them are the black thugs, empty vessels, who procreate as nonchalantly as they shoot rival gang members.

Biology also dictates that it's the mother who ends up experiencing the painful birth process—frequently alone. It's the mother who ends up with the kid slung over her hip for several years after that.

And it's the mother, according to the standards of the black-trash welfare culture, who has been led to expect that the government will take care of her babies, just as the government took care of her and probably her mother as well when they were babies.

These generations of brood mares are the valve of the welfare crisis. They are the machine that perpetuates the black welfare rolls with more and more new dependents, multiplying welfare generations with amazing speed. They produce innocent babies and use them as pawns for their own lazy existence.

Today girls as young as twelve and thirteen are having children. If you sit and talk to them, they justify the fact that they continue to have children at the state's expense because they have a right to breed at will. They honestly feel no obligation of their own to take care of the offspring they produce. Once again they feel society owes them because white people cheated and oppressed their ancestors sometime in the past.

They stand in the way of any real resolution to the welfare crisis because whenever cuts or reforms are offered for consideration, these mothers ask with brazen bluntness and mock poignancy, "Who's going to take care of my babies?" It simply never occurs to them that they should have asked themselves that question before they had babies.

But the liberal Democrats recognize the true impact of such a query, especially when it is delivered by this poor black girl, this symbol of downtrodden Americans.

The Democrats quickly perceived that the threat of "starving babies" was the hot button they could hit when all of their other flawed logic failed to persuade the American public that the welfare budget had to be kept intact.

They wasted no time or resource in using this destructive ploy, and in the end it precipitated the single most important impediment to the Republicans being able to fulfill their Contract with America in the area of welfare reform in 1995.

As the welfare debate in Congress heated up, full-page advertisements with editorial-style headlines ran in the New York Times: "IF CONGRESSIONAL EXTREMISTS WIN ON WELFARE: California Kids Will Be Begging on the Streets by the Year 2000."

That ad, run in July of 1995 and paid for by the Fair Share Network in Los Angeles, claimed that if welfare reform was passed as the Republicans proposed, California streets would resemble the streets of Calcutta.

Another ad, run in May of 1995 by the San Francisco–based National Committee on Child Nutrition, carried a similarly ominous headline: "A STARK AND URGENT WARNING ABOUT HUNGER AND MALNUTRITION: Will Congress Let Our Children Go Hungry?"

This one showed an unflattering close-up of a grim-faced Newt Gingrich along with the symbolic hollow-eyed face of a little boy.

A controversial study published in 1995 by the Food Research and Action Center in Washington, D.C, claimed to determine levels of hungry children by asking eight questions of welfare families.

Answering yes to five of the questions classified the respondents as "hungry," and a yes answer to between one and four questions put them "at risk of being hungry." In my monthly newsletter I called the study "The Science of Liberal Propaganda."

Here are the eight questions. Judge for yourself whether the answers would provide an accurate reading of hunger in America:

1. Does your household ever run out of money to buy food to make a meal?
2. Do you ever rely on a limited number of foods to feed members of your household because you are running out of money to buy food for a meal?
3. Do you or adult members of your household ever eat less than you feel you should because there is not enough money for food?
4. Do you or adult members of your household ever cut the size of meals or skip meals because there is not enough money for food?
5. Do your children ever eat less than you feel they should because there is not enough money for food?
6. Do you ever cut the size of your children's meals or do they ever skip meals because there is not enough money for food?
7. Do your children ever say they are hungry because there is not enough food in the house?
8. Do any of your children ever go to bed hungry because there is not enough money to buy food?

Of course, the liberal media accepted the study results at face value. *CBS Evening News* broadcast the following as part of its report about the study: "A startling number of American children are in danger of starving . . . one out of eight American children is going hungry tonight." And more headlines began running on front pages of local newspapers around America, like the following:

In Madison, the *Wisconsin State Journal* ran this headline: "69,000 state children go hungry. That's nearly 8 percent, three-year study says."

In Columbia, South Carolina, the *State* ran this one: "Hunger gnaws at one-third of S.C. poor."

Without question, brood mares, like their counterparts the social-crusading black thugs, play a pivotal role in perpetuating the black-trash welfare culture. Together, as they build generation upon generation, they are reinforcing and intensifying an anti-American, antisocial culture that threatens the proven American way.

Chapter Five

Dark Town

• • • •

A ghetto is a government designated place where an identifiable people are forced to live under penalty of the law. There are slums in America but no ghettos. A slum differs from a ghetto in that one can escape by changing one's life style and you are one among millions of Negro Americans who have escaped. This is an American tradition.

VIA MAIL 7/5/94
H.J. & F.J.
FREEPORT, NEW YORK

The first time I rode with the police gang unit through the inner city of Aurora, Colorado, it struck me that the people I saw there were not part of the twentieth century. Instead, they appeared to be living by standards of the Dark Ages.

There was a lack of regard for the rights of other people—their right to peace and quiet, their right to property, their right to a secure environment—and a seeming lack of regard for the value of life itself.

The black trash there—the black thugs and the brood mares—were isolated in a community that was shut off from the advancements and the potential of the greater American community around it.

As a result of their isolation, they were reverting to a primitive social order. The gangs reminded me of the British schoolboys in *Lord of the Flies* who, when marooned on an island, reverted to the savagery of the jungle.

After a number of trips into these communities, communities emotionally and physically locked inside urban centers across the country, I began calling these ghettos Dark Town.

Dark Town is Anyplace, U.S.A., where your child might come home in a body bag because he or she wore the wrong color headband or jacket on the street. It is any place where your baby might be shot down by random violence, any place where mothers put their children to bed at night in pig iron bathtubs to protect them from flying bullets as they sleep, any place where you're taught that breeding for welfare dollars is acceptable because your mama did it, any place where the pimps and the drug dealers hold sway on the street corners, any place where you have to install bars on your windows.

I call these ghettos Dark Town because of the ignorance and the ugliness that predominate there. The name Dark Town is not intended to imply a racial designation of its residents. I have seen predominantly white, black, Hispanic, and Asian Dark Towns in cities across America, but you don't need to know the racial demographics to find a Dark Town. You can easily identify Dark Town in any given city by going to the local police station or to the coroner's office and looking for the areas with high concentrations of crime and homicide statistics.

The fact is, however, that a great many Dark Town communities are inhabited predominantly by black trash.

Why won't black trash leave Dark Town? Why won't they venture across the East River, as I did, if only to take a peek at the other side?

Because they are held captive by what I call the Myth of the Hobbled Black. Black trash play a starring role in this growing mythology. They have been brainwashed by a line of propaganda from groups like the black political caucuses, the Nation of Islam, and the NAACP to believe the myth.

Simply put, the myth is that they cannot make it in America because they are black.

They can't get a "good" job. They can't go where there are too many white people—where they are in a minority—for fear of being stopped by the police. They believe they are not welcome to live in good neighborhoods or to visit America's vacationlands.

They believe they remain hobbled by their skin color today just as the slaves were hobbled in shackles more than a century ago.

Well, I contend that the slave generation is dead. Many of the people who have firsthand memories of slavery—the first and second generation of people who remember the legacy of that of bondage—are dead, too. I believe that every black American, every black American whose ancestors survived slavery should kneel before an elder and be knighted an American hero. We are survivors, not victims.

Not only have we survived, but today we are living in a country where we are sampling the nectar of our success. Black people are governors and police chiefs, mayors, lawyers, doctors, and dentists. The slave ship is no longer relevant.

But between the days of slavery and today a liberal movement has grown out of an environment where America was trying to say I'm sorry, mea culpa. This liberal political movement grew to extremes, and out of it has grown the black-trash welfare culture, which today breeds people who are culturally blank. They have no knowledge of and no conscious tie to their immediate past.

They can't tell you who Harriet Tubman was or about the debate between Marcus Garvey and George Washington Carver. They can't tell you any more about Detroit Red than they can about the X in the name Malcolm X. Armed only with a perception of the wrongs perpetrated against them, and with no knowledge of the history of the successful struggle to right those wrongs, they cannot grasp the promise of the American Dream.

That forward-thinking message is not being sent to the children in Dark Town. It is not being sent to the children of black trash. And as long as they are tethered to Dark Town, a ghetto community that is at odds with itself about America, these people always are going to be in crisis.

People, like water, seek the level of the boundaries around them. If you live your life among people who have no dreams, you can expect that these people will laugh at you if you pursue your dream. They will belittle you for having ridiculous aspirations. You will be like a duck looking up at eagles and wishing you could soar. The other ducks won't encourage you; they will laugh at you.

For instance, if young people are encouraged to believe that pursuing an education is a wasted effort because they are black and the majority culture won't give them a break, they won't go to school and they won't learn.

Likewise, if your only expectation in life is the government dole, then there's little reason to squirm beyond that low point, especially when the elders in your community confirm that the welfare lifestyle is the norm.

You don't leave your neighborhood. You just wait for things to come to you. You wait for the food stamps, the crack, the gin. You live with the garbage, the fights. You don't do anything for yourself. Your sustenance is airlifted to your mailbox in the form of a welfare check—airlifted the way the French dropped off supplies for their troops trapped in Dien Bien Phu, Vietnam.

After the L.A. riot in 1992, I watched the people of Dark Town on television as they got their welfare checks and then stood around in the rubble while Representative Maxine Waters determined what they wanted and what they needed before she conducted a caravan into the rest of California to fill their needs. Her constituents obviously couldn't conceive of getting on a bus and venturing out of Dark Town to get what they needed for themselves.

I've concluded that this happens because the residents of Dark Town are like single-cell animals with nerve systems that don't match those of people working to get ahead—working as waiters at the Village Inn and maybe working a second job while trying to get through school.

It is a matter of common sense—a commonsense American truth—that you must set your sights on some higher goal and then strive to reach that goal, in order to gain dignity and self-esteem. Fighting the good fight affords you a sense of purpose and the resilience to run the gauntlet of life. It outfits you in a strong, weather-resistant coat with which you can ward off the hailstorms and acid rain attacks that come with life. Without this dimension to your character, you are prone to become a purveyor of hate and bitterness as opposed to ambition and dreams. In the case of black trash, this basic truth is evident. They have become little more than brood mares and empty vessels.

As in any Third World country, where the people bustle about from dawn to dusk but collect no official paychecks, there is an underground commerce run by the gangs and thriving in Dark Town. In addition to their enterprise of crime, which they justify in connection with their alleged crusade for social justice, the black gangs view drug sales as their legitimate industry.

As my aunt Merle told me on my trip home to Brooklyn in 1991, "What they talkin' 'bout? No jobs, no money. These people got plenty money—there's drug money all 'round this place."

Liberal indulgence of the Myth of the Hobbled Black, like every other black-trash scam, has dictated that mainstream America actually engage in a debate about the possible merits of this deadly trade.

A few years ago, I saw a black woman participating in a live town meeting on television say that young African-American men had a legitimate right to sell drugs because that was their way of getting into business. She contended that they were excluded by white bosses from the opportunity to become junior executives with General Motors, so they had no choice but to engage in commerce where they could find it.

According to her argument, I guess you could say these corner drug dealers were nothing more than the Ace Hardware store managers of their community.

Liberal-minded journalists tend to reinforce the Myth of the Hobbled Black by going into Dark Town, always with expectations of talking to people who are one-dimensional—just poor victims—and therefore not to be challenged about their adherence to the myth or their absurd logic relating to it.

So even though logic must have told him that the woman had said something absurd, the host, apparently attempting to fathom the dark mysteries of the black psyche while also trying to maintain a level of political correctness, all but allowed her statement to go unchallenged.

I believe he did so because in the eyes of the predominantly liberal media, when you're black and poor and living in a place where the murder rate is high, it's considered immaterial that you might be stupid or dysfunctional. The overriding reality is that you're a victim of white oppression.

Of course, there is some commerce in Dark Town besides drug sales, although most poor uneducated black trash have a dysfunctional attitude toward business in general, even black-owned business, in their "communities."

I think the black merchants who set up shop in Dark Town are very interesting creatures, however. Seldom do they reach out and appeal to any broad base of customers. For the most part, I've observed that they advertise little, even in the black press and on black radio stations. The black merchant tends to depend on word of mouth.

My observation also is that the black-owned stores in the ghetto can be broken down into no more than a handful of businesses: beauty parlors, barbershops, dry cleaners, mom-and-pop groceries, and liquor stores.

Seldom do you see restaurants, other than a few greasy spoons. And black-owned drugstores, hardware stores, and service stations—businesses that offer the basic necessities for a mass audience of consumers—are few and far between.

As a matter of fact, for anyone reading this page, stop a moment and think. Think about your own neighborhood. Think about the businesses you expect to find nearby.

Within walking distance of where I'm sitting right now, in my home, there is a major supermarket as well as a hardware store, a card shop, a barbershop, two gas stations, an espresso shop, several restaurants, including fast-food chains, a flower store, two video rental stores, and a couple of bookstores—businesses you seldom find in Dark Town.

If they were magically to appear there, the periodic community "uprisings" by black trash would be one thing that would make their long-term prognosis poor.

When an urban riot explodes, it matters little who owns the corner business. There is an equal-opportunity grab for the merchandise, followed by an equal-opportunity torching.

Whether it's a grocery, a clothing store, or a liquor mart, the justification offered by the looters always seems to be the same: "They were overcharging us."

Looting is never seen by black trash as an infraction of the law or as an action that will reflect poorly on the community. Nor is it ever perceived to have an effect on the future of commerce, black or otherwise, in their community.

The looters justify their lawlessness on the grounds that it is a legitimate form of economic retribution taken by the community against the inflated prices poor people are forced to pay in inner-city stores, whether the merchants are Korean, Jewish, white, or black.

In a word they, the people, rebelled because "capitalists" were ripping off the community.

According to one black man who showed no remorse after looting stores in his own neighborhood during the 1992 Los Angeles riot, "If you're a few pennies short, they [the Korean merchants] throw the money back at you. They treat us like dogs."

Even without a full-fledged riot, the cost of doing business in Dark Town is so high that most merchants do not stay. Stable businesses, the kind that offer steady jobs with weekly paychecks, are driven out by the attitude that says: "Whitey has got insurance, so we'll rip this off. It's our way of getting even." The result is wholesale theft of the merchant's profits right off the shelves. Mainstream companies like A&P and Wal-Mart have made a prudent business decision not to try to survive in that environment.

Then we come to the often-raised issue of financing—the plight of every entrepreneur in America, black or white, who has to go to the bank and buy money. Money is bought with collateral or with good credit, with your signature.

When you buy money, you buy it at a certain rate for a certain period of time on the promise that you will pay it back according to specific terms. But in a situation where the neighborhood is burned down periodically or where day-to-day shoplifting runs rampant because the residents have a perceived grievance against City Hall or with white people or with the capitalist world in general, it may not be the smartest idea to open an establishment—and risk your life savings—in a location that puts success in jeopardy even before your business can begin making a profit.

But when banks refuse a loan for a prospective Dark Town business based on a reasonable forecast of its success—in this case lack of success—they are accused of racist policies.

So the bottom line is that welfare, drugs, and crime drive Dark Town. And these are not healthy enterprises that can function as paths to the American Dream.

Several years ago I was talking about the depravity of the ghetto on my Denver radio show, and a woman called to challenge me. I told her I refused to pretend that an outhouse is culturally superior to a bathroom with indoor plumbing. I'm not going to choose the well or the creek over fresh running tap water. The argument is absurd; it defies common sense.

Furthermore, I said, the black community is not by definition the ghetto. The minute I buy the Wilson house in the "white community," in mainstream America, I've expanded America's black community.

I don't want to live in a black ghetto, and I won't apologize for that. Ghettos are not places to be revered and nurtured. Ghettos are terrible places where the Dark Town mind-set is perpetuated, where people's dreams are squelched. They are places people should be encouraged to leave.

After wrangling with me for several minutes, this woman concluded her argument with great finality: "The ghetto is beautiful."

I have carried that comment with me since then. I can only conclude that when people isolate themselves, when they begin to fear the unknown world beyond their self-imposed boundaries, when they embrace the Myth of the Hobbled Black, they become blinded to reality. They become attached to their captors just as hostages sometimes do.

Encountering Dorothy King, the welfare activist who wanted free HUD homes, marked the point at which I began forming many of the strong opinions I have today about the evolution of the black-trash welfare culture and the parallel deterioration of black people on the dole.

When I was growing up poor, I was committed to doing anything possible to get off welfare and to get out of the ghetto. I refused to settle for poverty.

The American Dream and the scars of poverty have fueled my lifelong struggle to achieve. I have fought all my life to free myself of the shame of charity. And my success has turned me into an adamant believer in self-reliance and strengthened my disgust with those who lack the ambition to grab a fistful of life, saddle up, and ride it for all it's worth. I don't know when I rid myself of the conscious fear that I might end up as a bum on the Bowery in New York, but I am certain that dread subconsciously drives me yet today.

While my circumstances may have been extreme, I'm convinced that some degree of fear of the shame of poverty has driven and continues to drive many Americans, particularly first-generation Americans, to reach for this country's promise of achieving self-sufficiency and a comfortable life.

But sadly, many of today's black charity cases seem to be missing both the dream and the shame. There is no shame in Dark Town, and I'm not talking just about welfare.

There's no shame in your fourteen-year-old daughter having a baby, no shame in having to go down to the courthouse because your son has been arrested for stealing a car or for mugging someone or for carrying a gun. As a matter of fact, your neighbors commiserate with you because you were hassled, because you had to go downtown, because the system is indifferent to your plight. The accepted party line in Dark Town is that the white people downtown don't give a hoot about you and the middle-class blacks have forgotten what it was like to really be black.

By accepting poverty and condoning violence, by ripping off the system, and by living off the dole, you prove that you are fighting the good fight against the white man's system. The American Dream is jive. It is tantamount to selling out on your blackness. So you cling to welfare and its warped culture as part of your rebellion. You buy into the Myth of the Hobbled Black and that "the American Dream" is just a code phrase for "racism."

Today I see poor black people living in wretched poverty, perhaps worse in some ways than the poverty I once lived in.

The American Dream, the driving force I employed to move beyond poverty and welfare, has been replaced in Dark Town by the hallucination of a back-to-Africa movement. The shame associated with charity has been replaced by a bogus badge of honor worn by the martyred underclass as they play out the Myth of the Hobbled Black.

They cry out that they shouldn't have to suffer the way they do. But I say yes, you do have to suffer; you're poor. Your life is hell. You have to understand that you have chosen a lesser quality of life. You cannot have what we have, those of us who embraced the American Dream with all of its hard work and rewards. You haven't worked for it.

You can go to Macy's, but you can't buy Joy perfume for $150 a bottle because you don't have any money. You don't have any money because you can't read, and you can't read because you chose to pick your nose or dig in your ear when you should have been learning to read in the free public education system that we have set up in the United States of America. You passed up all the checkpoints. So now your life is the equivalent of an unclean outhouse. Sorry.

We have to debunk the Myth of the Hobbled Black.

We have to communicate to Dark Town that if people maintain a victim mentality, they will die. This is America, and Americans can be whatever they want. People are not victims just because they themselves have made bad choices. White people and mainstream blacks like me are not oppressing them.

The kind of struggle I employed to reach for the American Dream has been replaced in Dark Town by a street fight aimed at shoring up welfare as a well-entrenched ghetto-based industry.

Today I see a lot of people in the black-trash welfare generation who would do just about anything to stay on welfare instead of doing anything possible to get off of it.

What wasted energy! And what an injustice to the millions of black American kids who will never extend their lives beyond the boundaries of the poor communities where they happened to be born, because their parents have grown fat, lazy, and pitifully satisfied to settle for a life of isolation and fear. What a sad state that these urban-bound children will never experience the luster of an aspen tree turning from a splendid green to a brilliant gold, or the magnificence of the snow-capped peaks of the Rocky Mountains, or the thrill of an elk walking in a hushed prance in the woods.

For them, welfare programs, federal handouts, teenage pregnancy, the penitentiary, and an early grave will be their inheritance from a culture where poverty and public assistance have risen to a place of honor—in a country where opportunity abounds as in no other.

I certainly am not the only one who has observed the repercussions of the corrupted black-trash welfare culture. I am not the only one who can see the stagnation in Dark Town or the bleak prospects of black trash. If your response to this situation is not compassion, then it is disgust and outrage at what welfare is costing America—a cost that is bad enough in dollars but goes far beyond money in the threat it poses to our way of life.

It is almost impossible to ignore the need for reform.

In state after state, legislators are feeling pressure from constituents who are fed up with subsidizing the stereotypical lowly lifestyle of today's most visible welfare community. President Clinton apparently was motivated by this dissatisfaction among the electorate when he vowed to "end welfare as we know it" as he entered the White House in 1993. Welfare reform was a major part of the Republicans' Contract with America, published when they took over Congress in 1995.*

But the partisan approaches to reform are as different as day is from night. The Democrats, led by the president and his band of liberals, seem to believe that the solution is to put dignity into the welfare system and thus instill dignity in welfare recipients. But to me, their attempts to make welfare a "normal" and "accepted" lifestyle stand in stark opposition to their objective of restoring human dignity.

In Maryland, there is something now called the Independence Card, an ATM-like card that welfare recipients can use to withdraw their monthly stipends. I call it the magic credit card, because unlike my MasterCard and Visa, this one recycles itself every month with new available credit and wipes out what for me and most Americans would have been a balance due.

This magic card was designed by the welfare office in the state of Maryland ostensibly to bring dignity to poor people so they wouldn't be embarrassed by the traditional ways of using welfare, like redeeming food stamps at the local supermarket.

What I want to know is why in the dickens would somebody strive to get off the dole if the dole is modernizing and streamlining itself to meet their every need? Making welfare easier only makes welfare recipients more comfortable and thus less motivated to alter their current state. People do not gain dignity from a free ride.

As I argued with Dorothy King, you cannot give someone a home—only a house. A home comes only from the hard work you put into getting it and keeping it.

---

*As this book goes to press, President Clinton has promised to sign a welfare reform bill passed by the House and Senate. Only time will tell whether it succeeds in bringing about true reform.

The Republican plan for welfare reform, most notably presented by Speaker Newt Gingrich, takes what I categorize as a tough-love approach. Their theory is that taking tough measures—immediately labeled Draconian by some—such as placing certain children of welfare mothers in orphanages, would strip every bit of dignity out of welfare, and thus logically people would want to get off of it.

While I agree with many of their measures, the Republicans, because of their historic role as the political party of the cold, calculating rich, are scrutinized for their motives and thus have failed to mobilize adequate popular support, or political votes in Congress, for their hard-nosed solutions.

The reality is that there are no neat solutions to the welfare predicament. Welfare is out of control. We have millions of Americans literally addicted to the public dole. And as we rapidly add generations to this new corrupted welfare culture, we move farther and farther away from welfare's original function as an apolitical temporary helping hand.

Politics aside, I believe the American people expect welfare reform to be a very straightforward task. Fit welfare recipients should be obliged to go to work after no more than a couple of years of receiving benefits. The government should find a way to stop subsidizing out-of-wedlock births and other socially destructive types of behavior that fuel the engine of the welfare machine. And thus welfare costs, and presumably taxes as well, would be controlled.

The fact is, though, that the welfare system, particularly the black-trash welfare culture, has mutated into something so grotesque that I liken it to a 500-pound canary with atrophied wings.

There is no gentle way to extricate that canary from its nest—even though we know that the canary is killing, not incubating, its eggs. You can't tickle it. You can't prod it. It won't go on a diet. That 500-pound bird cannot fly. And when eventually we push it out of the nest, it's going to make one big nasty mess at the base of the tree. And it's going to die.

The canary personifies every crack addict, every alcoholic, every bad-luck Charlie, every parasite who is sucking on the blood gushing from the welfare artery of the American taxpayer. And those bloodsuckers won't go away quietly.

But America has to make a decision. We have to deal, conclusively and soon, with that continuously growing canary, which I believe is spreading decay throughout this country—which I believe most certainly will wreak havoc on the majority of black Americans, whether they are on or off the welfare dole.

Most probably we will lose the canary, but I believe we have to make a choice in favor of the eggs, which represent the future—a choice in favor of healthy growth and the historic promise of America.

Ken's elementary school picture from P.S. 41 in Brooklyn.

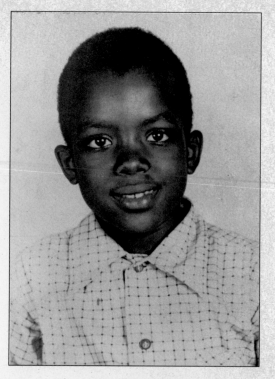

Ken's dad (right) was known as "Wahoo" in the New York City Police Department. He's shown here with his partner after they rescued children from a fire.

In 1969 and 1970, Ken was a staff photojournalist for the Detroit Free Press, best known for his street action photos.

Ken took this photo at the 1969 March on Washington, one of the largest organized protests against the Vietnam War.

This Ken Hamblin photo, taken inside the headquarters of the Detroit chapter of the Black Panthers, ran in the February 6, 1970, edition of Life magazine to accompany an essay on the Panthers by Gordon Parks.

After leaving the Detroit Free Press in 1970, Ken produced 16mm films for WTVS, Channel 56, in Detroit and through his independent film company, KLH Productions.

In 1973, Ken shot and produced a television commercial featuring his daughter, Linda (left), and a friend's daughter to support Coleman Young's campaign to become Detroit's first black mayor. The commercial was shot early on a Sunday morning on Woodward Avenue in front of the J. L. Hudson department store. (Photo by John Collier)

Ken's first airplane, purchased in 1971, was a 1959 pea-green, cloth-covered Tri-Pacer, which he flew from Detroit to Nassau in the Bahamas—17 hours one way. (Photo by Hugh Grannum)

Ken takes pictures for fun on one of his many trips to the Caribbean in the 1970s.

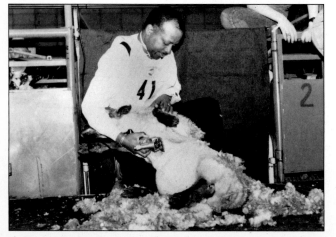

Dressed in a tuxedo and sneakers, Ken won a me... sheep-shearing event a... Denver Stock Show in 1... representing a Denver r... station.

For years, fans in Denver recognized Ken by his license plates.

Ken meets his fans at Dan's Bake Sale, the promotional event for Rush Limbaugh in Fort Collins, Colorado, where Ken's moniker, The Black Avenger, was born.

One of Ken's charter radio affiliates to his syndicated show, WTDY in Madison, Wisconsin, has promoted Ken with local billboards. (Photo courtesy of Adams Outdoor Advertising, Madison, Wisconsin)

Ken and his son, Kenneth Hamblin III, on a Colorado mountain adventure in the 1980s.

Ken and his daughter, Linda, on her wedding day, March 25, 1995, in Kansas City.

Estelle with her four oldest girls in Barbados. She is holding Ken's Aunt Alma; from left, Aunt Winifred, his mother, Evelyn, and Aunt Merle.

EMIGRANT IDENTIFICATION CARD
UNITED STATES
DEPARTMENT OF LABOR

Forde
SURNAME

Estelle
GIVEN NAME

Barbados, B.W.I. July 7, 1883
COUNTRY OF BIRTH   DATE OF BIRTH

British   Brown
NATIONALITY   COLOR OF EYES

Boston, Mass.   Lady Drake
PORT OF ARRIVAL   STEAMSHIP

DATE ADMITTED   STATUS OF ADMISSION

IMMIGRANT'S SIGNATURE

ORIGINAL   IMMIGRANT INSPECTOR

After several trips to the United States, Estelle Forde, Ken's grandmother, emigrated permanently from Barbados in 1934.

President George Bush sent this note after he read Ken's column pledging his vote to Bush.

THE PRESIDENT

a personal letter please
4-23-92

Dear Ken,

Someone sent me the column of 4-18-92.

I will continue to try to merit your trust. Tough and ugly times these; but the

economy is looking up and some of my severest critics in the arena have or are in the process of self destructing.

Sincerely,

G. Bush

Ken with Aunt Merle and Aunt Alma during a visit home to Brooklyn in 1992.

Ken received some 8,000 pieces of mail after his Denver radio show was broadcast on C-Span in January 1994. (Photo by Glenn Asakawa, Rocky Mountain News)

Part 2

The Beneficiaries
and Purveyors
of the Myth

Chapter Six

Poverty Pimps

. . . .

I was thinking about the repercussions from the MM (Million Man)
march today. . . . I am still startled about the growing racism in America—
growing mainly in nonwhite America, I think. I have been trying to find its
roots.

I am convinced that its major roots are in liberal policies; but where?
I think it is because liberal policies begin with the assumption that
there is only so much pie. If one group thinks they are not getting
enough of it, then liberal policies direct society to take a slice away
from one sector to give it to the other—it is up to government to decide
how to split the pie.

In contradiction to liberals, conservatives are suggesting that if one sector
of society is not getting enough pie, THEN MAKE THE PIE LARGER
so that if someone wants some more pie, they can have it. And the conservative ideal is to let the private sector decide how to make the pie larger.
But it doesn't hand a piece of pie to anyone. (And it doesn't punish anyone
for having a piece of the pie now.)

Obviously, this takes all the power away from the liberals, who have long
decided who gets a piece of the pie. (Hence the vitriolic talk in Washington
these days.) But it also lays the burden of gaining a piece of the pie onto
the INDIVIDUAL.

So under conservative policies, the individual gains power while the
group loses power. If the group loses power, then the "leader" of

the group loses power. Bye bye, Jesse. Bye bye, Kwesi. Bye bye,
Louie. Unless . . .
Cry racism. Raise the fears of the group. Tell them that "we" won't let
anyone else have any more of the pie unless "we're" forced. You get your
power back.
(I don't know if it's anthropology or prejudice, but I find I fear the group,
not the individual.)
P.S. I thank you for your work and I want you to know you make a big
difference in people's lives.

VIA E-MAIL 10/31/95
J.D.,
PHOENIX, ARIZONA

In 1973 I met Robert Millender and Coleman Young. Coleman, who had been a longtime state legislator from Detroit's Black Bottoms, was running to become the city's first black mayor. Bob had been the kingmaker behind a number of pioneer black politicians, including John Conyers Jr. when he was elected the state's first black congressman. Millender became Coleman's key strategist and campaign chairman.

At the time, I was producing and hosting programs for WTVS Channel 56, Detroit's public television station, and I was making films through my own independent company. I was hired to produce television commercials for this historic political race.

As a black man, I was very proud to be a part of Coleman's campaign. I considered him a role model who was blazing the path for blacks in big-city politics, just as I felt I was blazing a trail for blacks in the media in Detroit.

One of the television ads that I conceived and produced featured two little girls. One was black, my own daughter Linda; and the other was white, the daughter of my friend John Collier, whom I had met when we were staff photographers together at the *Detroit Free Press.*

The spot began with very tight shots of the girls playing hopscotch—their hands tossing a stone, their feet hopping from square to square. Their little voices could be heard giggling and chatting on the sound track.

When the voice-over narrative began, we did a slow pullout to a wide shot revealing that they were playing in the middle of Woodward Avenue in front of the J. L. Hudson department store in the heart of downtown Detroit. Woodward Avenue was one of the busiest downtown streets, a landmark thoroughfare representing the retail center of the city of Detroit. We shot the commercial very early on a Sunday morning with the street blocked off by Detroit police, who at that time wanted no part of a black mayor and only grudgingly followed the procedures granted to us by an official permit.

The commercial's message—"Save the city for our children"—is sadly ironic today, because the stark drama we depicted to represent the exaggerated threat of a dying city was realized rather than reversed during Coleman Young's five-term tenure.

By the time he left office in 1994, Hudson's and most other retail establishments in the once-thriving downtown area were closed. Worse yet, the dream of full integration symbolized by the little black girl and white girl playing together in his campaign commercial had been twisted into raging black racism followed by stark white flight.

The police department and many of the other city agencies operated by black managers appointed through Coleman's political patronage were rife with corruption.

Congressman Conyers was in Washington calling for a study to determine whether reparations and a separatist state for African Americans were in order to remedy the ills of slavery, which were more than a century old.

I knew that Detroit would suffer a final round of white flight fueled by fear of black people when I read in a wire story in 1991 that two black-trash teenage girls, known to police and prosecutors as the "terrible twins," had attacked a white suburban woman at the July Freedom Festival on the city's riverfront.

When I read further that there was a real possibility that black Detroit police officers had refused to protect this woman and her daughter, my heart sank. I knew that Detroit was finished.

I felt compromised and disillusioned by Mayor Young, who had once been a hero to me and to many other citizens both black and white. I held him, along with his entire gang of political cronies, responsible for killing the city.

Today a people mover runs from Detroit's Renaissance Center to the Millender Center, a building complex named for the man who I believe must have died with a broken heart as he watched the sorrowful outcome of his lofty dream of seeing his people become political leaders in America.

Whitey will pay.

That is the overriding political platform of many black urban politicians, the ones whom I have dubbed poverty pimps. They stake their political careers on knowing that whitey will pay because of his guilt and because of his fear.

Poverty pimps are the grossest beneficiaries and purveyors of the Myth of the Hobbled Black. In fact, they probably should be held accountable for actually creating the myth that black people can't get ahead in America because white people have kept—and continue to keep—them down. That notion is what generates the guilt that produces the dollars for their districts.

Fear of the random crime that is spreading to mainstream America is certainly a factor in this political scenario, but the fear that these politicians rely upon is more complicated than that. They count on the deeper, more pervasive fear that unless some offering is made to the natives—the natives, in this case, being the African Americans in Dark Town—broad-based unrest will occur.

Bruce, a listener from Memphis, became a lightning rod for horrified callers to my radio show in the spring of 1996 after he described himself as a "nineties nigger." He left little to speculation concerning his intention to intimidate in this dialogue with me:

Bruce: I'm telling you right now that as a black man, I will die before I allow you to take my affirmative action, my food stamps, my welfare. Now, I have the ability to unite with other black men, I have the intelligence to equip devices—

Me: Stop a minute, stop a minute. . . . Your passion is imprinted on me, and if you go much further you're going to get yourself in trouble, and I don't want you to do that. . . . You're threatening mayhem. . . . Let me tell you something. I'm a fifty-five-year-old colored guy, brother Bruce, and the last time I heard that kind of fervor and commitment from people of color in this country was when black Americans were sitting at a lunch counter in Greensboro, North Carolina, demanding full access and entrée to the American system, which we now have. And now you're looking for a guarantee. You're looking for the government to support you through welfare and affirmative action and quotas, and that's insulting and demeaning to the history and the legacy and the spirit of those great Americans who said, "Give me a chance to participate." A chance to participate is not a guarantee.

Bruce: I'm a nineties nigger and I'm not going to take anything from anybody. You're going to give me my affirmative action and my programs or . . . I'm just going to say or else . . . I'll be a guerrilla warrior. I'll come to you. I'll bring that pain. I'll bring a riot and you know what's goin' happen? You gonna give me what I want like you always do whenever we riot. You know you gonna give it to me. I don't know why we got to play these little games.

Mainstream white Americans—and some mainstream blacks as well—get nervous when they hear that kind of talk. They have seen the action it can produce, as recently as 1992 in Los Angeles. They know that urban unrest can swell quickly to capture the attention of the national media, and that the exposure has an impact on the future economic well-being of a city as a whole.

They know that despite police lines—even police lines bolstered by the National Guard—the unrest can spill outside the boundaries of Dark Town.

They also know that those boundaries no longer mark the outer limits of an urban prison camp, as they did as late as the 1950s and 1960s. The ghetto is no longer a ward where blacks are kept in their place by whitey, as it was thirty or forty years ago, when I and other black Americans were confined there, when we were denied the opportunities available throughout the rest of America.

Back then we desperately wanted out.

But today there are black people like Bruce who harbor a fanatic commitment to the ghetto, to their "community." Instead of being confined there, they control and stake claim to this territory, because it represents dollars from the government. They know that, for the most part, whitey will pay to ease his guilt and his fear through taxpayer-supported government programs designed to appease these "nineties niggers."

The politicians I call poverty pimps are the brokers, the middlemen between the government and the people in Dark Town.

I call them poverty pimps for good reason. The white elected officials who are their counterparts must produce pork barrel offerings in the way of industry and jobs to further the economic well-being of their districts in order to retain the support of their voters.

But these politicians have convinced their constituents, most of whom are black trash, to settle for the dead-end political spoils of government welfare. They devote their entire political careers to procuring more welfare and poverty-program dollars for their stagnant districts, and thus I call them poverty pimps.

They have wasted years in office as congressmen and as city councilmen and as mayors without ever creating an environment for healthy business development. And yet when they go to taxpayers to renew the ghetto stipends, they call only for more welfare for individuals and more grants for ghetto businesses that have little or no hope of long-term survival.

After the riot in Los Angeles in 1992, poverty pimps like California Representative Maxine Waters dispensed a lot of lip service via the national media, claiming that all her Dark Town constituents really wanted was a chance to build enterprise and jobs. But the truth is, the real wampum that typically stops a riot is more of the same—welfare.

In fact, the L.A. riots did subside the day welfare checks arrived at the post office. Maybe you remember, as I do, the aerial photos taken from the television news helicopters that showed tired looters standing patiently in long lines to pick up their dole.

In the final phase of political response to the riot, when the L.A. poverty pimps went to work in earnest on behalf of the black-trash rioters, they ended up delivering even more of the same. In this case, it was a campaign promise—never kept—from presidential candidate Bill Clinton for a brand-new entitlement of $1,800 a head.

In order to control their constituents, these poverty-pimp government parasites play a prominent hand in manipulating their own people into embracing the black-trash welfare culture. They help foster the pathological xenophobia that black trash have regarding anything and anyone beyond their Dark Town districts. They advocate that their black-trash voting blocs further estrange themselves from mainstream America by preaching the anti-American doctrine common in these African-American communities. As a result, their constituents live in self-imposed segregation in Dark Town. They lead an empty existence in which the benefits of the twentieth century are unfairly withheld from them.

Despite the best efforts of these poverty pimps, however, welfare as we know it—and as the poverty pimps have perpetually expanded it—is now threatened by welfare reform in Congress. What's more, record numbers of black voters are moving into political districts in the suburbs to join mainstream America. Census figures show that only 16 percent of American blacks lived outside central cities in 1970. The number jumped to more than 30 percent by 1995.

So the poverty pimps are preaching a vicious and destructive form of black racism to their remaining black-trash constituents, blaming whitey once more to cover for their own inability to keep on delivering something for nothing.

With their power waning, these politicians also think nothing of routinely betraying the public trust. They give their unqualified cronies government jobs and contracts. They mismanage, misuse, and even embezzle public funds.

When caught, they cry racism, patently refusing to be judged by the standards of equality that the Bob Millenders of the world fought to achieve just three short decades ago. Instead, they march right down to Dark Town and call a meeting in the street or in a church and preach that they are being pursued and investigated only because they are black. This never would happen, they cry out, to a white mayor or a white city councilman or a white congressman.

Sadly, the bad seeds of this brand of black urban politics were sown with the good intentions of the civil rights movement in the early 1960s.

Back then I was a grunt working out of the Brooklyn office of CORE, the Congress of Racial Equality, in drives to register new Negro voters. Like thousands of other young Americans, both black and white, I believed that the vote was the undeniable equalizer, the final step that would enable us to participate as full citizens in America.

But somewhere along the way, a portion of my newly enfranchised black brethren lost sight of the simple dream to participate as equals in the American political system. Instead, they allowed their voting power to be squandered by poverty pimps, the scandalous champions of today's inner-city Dark Towns.

I have asked over and over on my radio show and in my column for someone to name one major American city that has prospered socially, academically, and economically under black liberal political rule.

When the question first popped into my head, I couldn't think of a single city. It made me crazy. I would think about it in the shower and mumble to myself. There could only be two reasons. Either people who look like me were incapable of governing. Or, as voters, we were making very bad choices at the ballot box.

Then I reasoned that if I could come up with at least one city that had prospered socially, academically, and economically under black *conservative* rule, then the failures couldn't be attributed simply to skin color. Rather, we would have to consider whether they were the fault of the liberal political persuasion.

To date, I have identified at least two cities—Roanoke, Virginia, which thrived under Mayor Noel Taylor from 1975 to 1992, and Kentwood, Michigan, a small city outside of Grand Rapids, under Mayor Bill Hardenew.

Both mayors were black and conservative.

Unfortunately there are many more cities that provide the undeniable evidence of the failure of black liberal rule. The most classic poverty pimp and the most dramatic classic urban failure, by a long measure, are Marion Barry and Washington, D.C.

In March of 1996 a special report on Washington, D.C., was distributed by Knight-Ridder News Service. Here's how it began:

> *Washington — Police have no gasoline for their cruisers. Health clinics have run out of drugs. Six blocks from the White House, firefighters ride trucks with no ladders and buy their own boots.*
>
> *Potholes blister Embassy Row. The decrepit water-treatment plant threatens to spew sewage into the Potomac. Earlier this year, inmates set fire to their cells after the prison ran out of food. . . . The nation's capital is falling apart.*

The article went on about Washington's Mayor Barry, who had been in office for thirteen of its twenty-two years of independence.

> *A charismatic hero to the poor, Barry is also the author of decades of fiscal mismanagement. He spent his first three terms cutting deals with local*

developers and giving away city jobs like candy. He finally drew the curtain on Act I in 1990 with a prison term for possessing crack cocaine.

I wrote a column in March 1994, after Barry had gotten out of prison and was boldly running to recapture his mayoral title. The headline was "Allowing Barry's Candidacy Insults All Honest Citizens."

In the column, I wrote about a man who fits my definition of a black poverty pimp to a T.

When you characterize Barry that way, it's not surprising that he was re-elected in spite of his drug conviction and jail term. To Washington's Dark Town community of illegal black-thug drug traffickers, he was a role model, especially when he declared that the justice system was unfair for convicting him—even after he was recorded on videotape using crack in a Washington hotel room. The fact that Barry had gone to jail was not out of the ordinary for a lot of the black males in his city who also had done time. So he simply played to his constituency and blamed the white establishment, just as they do, for taking the fall.

He knew that when the election came around, all he had to do to win the vote was don his African attire and stroll back into Dark Town, which is exactly what he did.

In 1995, when he had been back in office for less than a year, the city ran out of toilet paper. That's right. According to a May story from the Associated Press, there was neither toilet paper nor paper towels in the thirty-seven municipal buildings in Washington because the city had failed to pay the supplier.

How can it be that these blatantly inept politicians are never held accountable for the cities they kill?

Quite simply, they have learned to play the intimidating race card on two fronts. First, they call anyone who challenges them a racist, and second, they stir up their own brand of black racism among their ignorant constituents.

The poverty pimps elected to office are only part of the dark side of the modern-day black political story, however. They operate in tandem with a legion of unelected community activists who do their bidding in Dark Town. These activists, who are akin to old-time ward heelers, receive political patronage in return for their allegiance. Usually the patronage comes in the form of government dollars steered in their direction to run community social programs.

It follows that they would be cheerleaders for the Myth of the Hobbled Black. In fact, they have become contemporary urban evangelists, practicing the old Reverend Pork Chop style of fire-and-brimstone rhetoric centered on blaming whitey for the misfortunes of Dark Town and coercing white taxpayers to pay for their sins.

They assure the residents of Dark Town that white racism remains a debilitating scourge upon them. They tell their constituents they are so oppressed that it is fruitless to struggle to get ahead until racism is fully eradicated. And until that occurs, these community activists—working with the full backing of the poverty pimps—promise to see to it that the white-run government will provide.

Because I consider myself a member of the mainstream, I know the hard work it takes to stay there—the time and energy it takes to get ahead, the attention that families demand, and the desire I have to make time every chance I can to ride my motorcycle. For that reason, I can't imagine other Americans in the mainstream—even if they are white—tithing 10 or 15 percent of their lives to making minorities miserable.

But that's the essence of what's being sold to black-trash constituencies by the poverty pimps and their sidekicks the community activists.

There is fertile ground for this message to take hold within most every black person, especially a black person exposed only to the narrow confines of Dark Town. We all grew up with some counsel from our elders to be on the lookout for signs of abuse or discrimination from white people. That advice was not designed to breed fear and hate. It was considered practical advice to keep us from being caught flat-footed.

But today's black community activists—New York's Reverend Al Sharpton, for instance—are engaged in an exaggerated and destructive continuation of these lessons, which historically every black child has been taught. Their racial teachings have become so extreme and so outlandish that they are stimulating very bizarre occurrences.

Sharpton has been in the news often over the last decade, always championing the purported racial underdog.

When a white woman jogger was brutally attacked in New York's Central Park, Al Sharpton marched down to Centre Street to defend the black-thug suspects, who by their own admission had just been out "wilding."

Instead of using his powerful community voice to speak out against this senseless and atrocious violence and to draw a definitive line between right and wrong, Sharpton ended up declaring that this white woman, the victim, should have known better than to go jogging in the park in the first place.

Later, Sharpton was a rabble-rouser in the racial showdown in which blacks and whites took to the streets in the predominantly white Brooklyn neighborhood of Bensonhurst, and he was fingered as an agitator in the more recent torching of a Jewish-owned clothing store in Harlem.

Perhaps Sharpton's most famous crusade was in 1987 on behalf of a fifteen-year-old black girl named Tawana Brawley, from Wappingers Falls, New York. Brawley claimed she had been kidnapped and raped by a group of white men who had covered her body with feces and scratched racial epithets into her skin. She claimed that the Dutchess County prosecutor was one of the men.

After months of boisterous public haranguing led by Sharpton, the girl's story was judged untrue by a grand jury. But Sharpton held on to her claims of racial abuse like a bulldog, never fully facing up to the reality that in this case the charges of racism had been out-and-out invented.

The 1990 case of Sabrina Collins attracted much less media attention than the Tawana Brawley incident, but to me it seemed just as significant in illustrating the growing racial division in America.

Collins, a freshman at Emory University in Decatur, Georgia, outside Atlanta, reported to school officials that she had received an anonymous racist letter that threatened her life. Supposedly the letter shocked her so profoundly that she collapsed in fear when she read it. Shortly after receiving the letter, she said, she lifted a rug in her room and found the words "die nigger die" scribbled in nail polish on the floor.

The Georgia Bureau of Investigation was called in and quickly solved the frightening mystery. When the evidence was examined, the culprit was shown to be none other than Collins herself.

The typewriter used to write the letter was the same brand as one owned by Collins. All identifiable fingerprints on the letter—including the ones matching the pattern that would have been left from inserting and removing the paper from the typewriter—were hers. And her habit of confusing "your" and "you're" was evident in the letter.

When confronted, she broke down and cried.

Why? Why would two young black girls, Sabrina Collins and Tawana Brawley, concoct these painful race-based tales?

I contend they are part of a lost generation of black people who have been so conditioned by the Marion Barrys of their world constantly screaming racism that they live in utter fear of coming face-to-face with it themselves.

Tawana Brawley may simply have believed that a cry of racism could be used as a credible excuse for her own misbehavior. Sabrina Collins may have simply been emotionally unprepared to cope with the white world she suddenly found herself in as a nineteen-year-old pre-med student at a predominantly white college.

Even more immoral than terrorizing these millions of ghetto-bound black Americans with fears of white racism, even more immoral than killing the American Dream for them, the community activists, empowered by the poverty pimps, use a new brand of black racism to fire up their community.

This racism emanating today from the black welfare culture has gone dangerously beyond fantasies of being racially oppressed.

In 1993 a thirty-five-year-old middle-class black New Yorker, Colin Ferguson, boarded a Long Island commuter train and pulled a gun. He killed six people and wounded another twenty.

The authorities produced notes written by Ferguson revealing that he harbored an overwhelming hatred of whites, Asians, and conservative Uncle Tom blacks, among others.

I heartily agreed with the late liberal white attorney William Kunstler, who originally took Ferguson's defense case, that this man's act was indicative of black racism.

However, I heartily disagreed with his willingness to buy into the excuse that four hundred years of oppression against African Americans had exerted so much pressure on black people living in a white society that it had driven Ferguson insane and thus he was not responsible for his rampage.

Among the most dangerous of the community activists is Louis Farrakhan, who was by and large dismissed as an isolated extremist until he organized his Million Man March on Washington, D.C., in October 1995.

He failed to mobilize the promised million men, but he did attract hundreds of thousands of African Americans who, at least on some level, were willing to buy into his clear hatred of America and whitey, which he put forth in his racist rhetoric.

On June 18, 1984, my friend and radio colleague Alan Berg was gunned down in front of his home by four white supremacists who hated him because he was Jewish. Eight years later, in a column on the anniversary of his death, I commented on racial hatred: "Bigotry—no matter what group practices it—is a perilous dance with the devil. It's a dance that minority people, especially, should sit out."

The good news is that poverty pimps may die a natural death. Like the dinosaurs, they may simply become extinct.

One reason is that they may be losing their base of voters. While the 1990 census showed that more than 9 million black Americans still lived in nearly total racial isolation, primarily in urban ghettos, it also signaled a historic change in black migratory patterns. Blacks started moving to the economic-growth areas—out of the cities the poverty pimps had killed in the Northeast and the Midwest.

Of course, the poverty pimps and community activists aren't about to let them go quietly.

In 1990, for instance, a study was released by the Center for Poverty at UCLA that showed a 40 percent migration of blacks out of Los Angeles County over the previous five years. A small-time community activist, Californian Tommy Jacquette, head of the Watts Summer Festival, complained that middle-class blacks were abandoning the community.

Jacquette is one of thousands of community activists in dozens of American urban centers who will continue to spout the poverty-pimp platform in an attempt to preserve Dark Town and hold on to their community program dollars.

The other reason poverty pimps may be on their last leg is the U.S. Supreme Court. In 1995, in *Miller v. Johnson*, the Court ruled that gerrymandering—the practice of partitioning electoral districts primarily based on the race of their residents—was unconstitutional.

This ruling marks a turning point for black politicians. In theory, it means that no longer will they be able to isolate ignorant black-trash constituencies and survive delivering only welfare as their pork barrel.

Instead, they will have to answer to a broader base of informed voters and deliver meaningful benefits to them. They will have to embrace mainstream American professional statesmanship.

This can only be a positive turn for black Americans in the political system.

A final note on poverty pimps. In 1996 we are holding the first national election in which the American people have seriously considered that the time might be right to entertain a black presidential candidate.

General Colin Powell, an American hero who rose to the highest military position in this country as chairman of the Joint Chiefs of Staff, adviser to the Oval Office, should be recognized for the self-made black man he is.

But in February 1996, I published a cover story in my monthly newsletter posing the question of whether I could vote an African-American liberal into the White House. My answer was a definite no.

And I firmly believe Powell is a liberal. Despite his declared affiliation with the Republican Party, I believe he has demonstrated that he is one step removed from the poverty-pimp mentality.

His views on affirmative action, in particular, show me that he is not prepared to accept his own hard-won achievements for the true success they represent. He still is uncomfortable as a fully equal American in the political system.

The *New York Times* quoted from his June 1996 commencement address at Bowie State University in Bowie, Maryland: "When one black man graduates from college for every one hundred who go to jail, we still need affirmative action. . . . When half of all African-American men between twenty-four and thirty-five years of age are without full-time employment, we need affirmative action."

As of this writing, Powell had not committed to become Bob Dole's running mate. But he is expected sooner or later to throw his hat into the ring of presidential politics.

Let me go on the record: Electing Colin Powell to the White House would not be good for America. It would be particularly not good for black Americans.

Chapter Seven

Uncle Toms
and Aunt Jemimas

• • • •

*I wonder whether or not after dark you don your KKK uniform and wander
around the local black neighborhoods in Denver and Aurora. I absolutely
believe that, given a chance, you would don this outfit to fly to Somalia
and beat the bones of starving Somalian children and dump them in a
mass grave so that not a dollar of your tax money (which you avoid paying
as much as the next concerned conservative does) won't be spent on trying
to save a life. No matter how much you rant and rave against the black
community . . . our skin is still black and nothing will change that. Cozy-
ing up to the . . . Rush Limbaughs of the world won't help your political
agenda. Truth be known, they are laughing at you behind your back.
"You people" irritate me to death.*

VIA MAIL 12/14/92
E.A.,
DENVER, CO

• • • •

*Have you ever noticed how white people can call your [show] and talk
badly about black people all day long, and you give them nothing but encouragement? But if I call and recount documented atrocities orchestrated
by whites, you get inordinately defensive and become an emotional wreck?*

My great grandmother once warned me "never trust a nigger who is loved by white people." It took my meeting you to truly appreciate what she was saying.

VIA MAIL 12/21/92
M.M.,
DENVER, CO

• • • •

You are awesome!!!
I would walk five miles just to stand in your trash. That is my way of saying that I admire you greatly.
Thanks for having the guts to stand up for what's right, even though I know you must go through a lot of peer pressure. God will bless you for your diligence.

VIA E-MAIL 12/3/95
R.H.

• • • •

You are an Uncle Tom, you put down your own people, call them trash, you make fun of them, you mimic their jive talk, you don't espouse genera-tions of black welfare takers . . . you talk like a "whitie" . . . who do you think you are?
I believe you know exactly who you are, Sir. I have heard it all on your show. I have heard your callers attempt to degrade you and your principles, say despicable things about you, rudely rant and rave as they attack you and what you stand for . . . You Sir, without a doubt, are the most gracious, polite and compassionate talk show host on the air. You truly listen to your callers, give them time to have their say and rarely interrupt them, but your most admirable trait is that you treat ALL of your callers with dignity and respect, whether they deserve it or not.
Brother Ken, of all the talk show hosts on the air, you are truly the most unique; you stand in a class alone and I, just a nonassuming non-colored gal, salute you as First Class #1.

VIA FAX 10/16/95
CAROLYN IN COTTAGE GROVE, OREGON

My daughter never had babies out of wedlock. I never got a call in the middle of the night that my son was in jail. Neither of them has been on welfare.

And I know countless numbers of black families just like my own.

In spite of the disproportionate visibility of black trash and the widespread credence given to the Myth of the Hobbled Black, the fact remains that the great majority of America's black population—from two-thirds to three-fourths of us—go to work every day, pay our bills, keep our kids off the streets, and live above the poverty line.

But tragically, all of the many black Americans who have ascended to the middle class face a personal conflict as a result of the Myth of the Hobbled Black. The conflict arises from the guilt imposed on them based on the premise that no black American has the right to escape Dark Town in good conscience unless, at that very moment, he can take the entire tribe with him.

The wisdom of the ghetto is that for every black man or woman who excels beyond the boundaries of Dark Town thousands of African Americans inevitably fail because they are left behind by indifferent, selfishly successful middle-class blacks.

This kind of reasoning is frequently put forth by the poverty pimps and their insignificant neighborhood activists. It's used to fuel a continuous cycle of anxiety and loathing for the mainstream world and for every black "sellout" who aspires to it.

It's a last-gasp effort by unscrupulous blacks desperately trying to hold on to their eroding base of power in Dark Town.

This same flawed reasoning is used to give credence to the black-on-black oratory that labels the black achiever a double-crosser of his people for the simple reason that he dared to reach beyond the limitations of the ghetto.

I believe the guilt this propaganda generates is the reason we have a silent majority of middle-class black families all but hiding in the suburbs. While the black Americans within this majority may not benefit directly from the Myth of the Hobbled Black, in the end many of them help to keep it alive by their silence.

These black Americans are afraid that the very vocal minority of black trash will challenge their blackness by calling them names that date back to the days of slavery—demeaning names such as "house nigger," "Uncle Tom," "Aunt Jemima," and "Oreo."

The names all imply in one way or another that the black person is either kowtowing to white people or trying to act like white people.

The loudmouthed African Americans who claim to speak for the "authentic" black people effectively use the name calling to silence those blacks who have ventured into mainstream America and learned the truth. The truth that we aren't getting lynched anymore. That we can move comfortably into almost any neighborhood we can afford. That the rewards of mainstream America—which they deem to be only white folks' business—are well worth working for whether you are black, brown, or white.

It's important to the poverty pimps and community leaders to withhold this information in order to keep their black-trash constituencies in check, to keep them isolated in their ghetto political districts.

Since most blacks don't care to be attacked and de-blacked just because they choose to be successful Americans rather than to wallow in Dark Town, the name calling usually works.

I am called demeaning names on a regular basis because I dare to say what all good Americans know is the truth about the black-trash minority, their welfare culture, and the scams they have attempted to work on the American psyche. But my worst sin in the eyes of these African Americans is that I dare to revel openly in the rewards of being a mainstream American.

The first real organized name calling against me occurred when a local television station invited me to moderate a live town-hall meeting to talk about race relations in Denver after the Los Angeles riot in 1992.

Even though I was to serve only as a moderator, black community-activist loudmouths protested that my views did not represent the real black voice of Denver. They threatened the television station with all manner of consequences if I remained part of the show.

"They [the TV station executives] need to talk to our community more," said one black spokesman, self-appointed to protect true black interests, regarding the town meeting. "They make a decision about a forum on racism without even consulting us. Either they're naive or mean."

Later, the same activist, who joined about two dozen picketers outside the hall where the forum took place, went on the TV news and called me "the African-American community's charbroiled David Duke."

Prior to the broadcast, the television station was caught in a Catch-22. Even though they tried to reason that my views were immaterial because I had been hired only to serve as a professional moderator for this program, a couple of black panelists declined to participate, as a show of community solidarity against me.

The station executives had believed they were performing a public service by airing this discussion of oppressed blacks. Apparently they had no idea that they needed to be so selective about which blacks were "approved" to participate in a forum on this heady topic.

Interestingly, when these righteous community activists are challenged publicly, as I continue to do to this very day, lots of other Americans are willing to speak out too.

Chuck Green, at that time my editor at the *Denver Post*, wrote the following in a column on the Sunday morning after the TV forum and all the hoopla:

> *I'm going to ask, precisely, what it is about Hamblin's opinions that black leaders find so threatening.*
> *If you listen closely to Hamblin, he advocates the same values you will hear spoken from nearly any pulpit, black or white, in Denver churches this morning.*

He advocates a strong family structure, condemning black men who don't take responsibility for their children—noting that 62 percent of black children in America's ghettos are being born to single mothers.

He advocates an all-out war on drugs in black neighborhoods, by the residents whose lives are being devastated by the gangs and drug lords who control their streets.

He advocates a greater interest in mainstream education, leading to jobs, for black youth.

He advocates reforms to the welfare system to break the cycle of welfare that has entrapped so many black mothers and children.

He advocates racial tolerance and harmony.

And for all of that, he is condemned and boycotted by black "leaders" in our community. . . . Forgive me if I don't get the point.

The point, of course, is that I challenge the Myth of the Hobbled Black, which keeps these activists and their poverty pimps in business.

In the end, the station stood its ground and kept me on the show, which was aired without a hitch. Between 400 and 500 people crossed the picket line to attend. The only real upshot of the show, which was intended to bring the races together in a dialogue, was that at least one black man in colorful African garb was seen wandering the hallways of the television station for some time afterward. He apparently was brought on board in a conciliatory gesture to serve as a liaison between the station and the "real" black community.

Oh, and another upshot was that the community activist who called me the most names got his own weekly column on the *Denver Post* editorial page—apparently to balance my views, which were deemed by the name callers to be "insensitive to minority issues."

The best bout of name calling against me ended up backfiring against the National Black Caucus of State Legislators.

This group, which is a primary sponsor of the poverty-pimp platform in American politics, held its annual meeting in Denver in December of 1993. Some of their members heard me take them to task on my radio show for making the crisis in Haiti one of their top agenda items. I said that they had bigger problems right here in America's Dark Towns that they should be dealing with on a priority level.

Diane Watson, a California lawmaker who served as spokesperson for the group in this matter, wrote a letter to the radio station where my show was aired, asking for an apology. Ultimately the group wanted me off the air. It threatened to ask the Federal Communications Commission to review the station's license and threatened to call a boycott of Denver as a convention destination unless I was reined in.

Another Caucus spokesman, Kofi Owusu, was quoted in the *Rocky Moun-*

tain News, claiming that I engaged in "minority bashing" and that I was "not serving the public interest."

My response then, as it remains today, was also quoted in the *News*: "If the National Black Caucus wants to take on one person in Denver, Colorado, instead of addressing the murder, mayhem, the high prison rate, the high welfare rolls—if they think that's the solution to their problems, fine. But I'm not going to go away."

I won the local skirmish. I kept my job, which by definition is to offer my opinion—strong as it may be—on the political and social issues of the day. Even some of the liberal-leaning editorial writers in town backed my "right to say it."

And I won the bigger battle as well. A short time after this incident, which had made front-page headlines in the *Rocky Mountain News* and the *Denver Post*, Dirk Johnson, then the Denver bureau chief of the *New York Times*, called and said he might be interested in doing a story about me.

I had lunch with him, enjoyed it, and then promptly forgot about his story . . . until my phone started ringing on January 3, 1994. Johnson's story had run in the *Times* on Sunday, January 2, and coincidentally, my three-hour Denver radio show was broadcast on C-Span on Monday, January 3.

Before that day's radio show was over, I had gotten phone calls from all manner of national, local, and even international media outlets that wanted to fly out to Denver and do a piece on me. I got faxes, phone calls, and letters from a host of literary agents and publishers who wanted me to write a book, from people who wanted to syndicate my radio show—even from some long-lost friends from Detroit and Brooklyn who had either seen me on C-Span or read about me in the *New York Times*.

The rest is history, as they say. I did a few national television appearances and gave a few interviews. I hired a great agent and promptly signed this book contract. My radio show went national about eight months later.

The local community activist who had been dogging me since the TV town meeting gave an interview to one national television show that had profiled me. Once again he called me a "charbroiled David Duke," this time adding that I was a "marquee Uncle Tom" as well.

In retrospect, I guess about all I can say to the Black Caucus is: Thank you, brothers and sisters. Thank you for helping me get the word out.

Although I'm a strong defender of the Bill of Rights, I have always contended that free speech isn't really free. It costs something. Most people give lip service to free speech until their ox is gored.

The poverty pimps are the first in line to take advantage of the protections guaranteed under the Constitution, but they also are the first to throw those protections aside if it will help them maintain a hold on their tenuous empires in Dark Town a little longer. Note that the black legislators ran straight to the government, to the FCC, to change the rules on free speech when they found my candor about black problems offensive and threatening to their power bases.

I am a problem for the poverty pimps because I am a black guy calling their bluff. I circumvent them via the radio and the newspaper to get a message from the outside to the isolated inner sanctum of Dark Town residents.

Clearly I gore their ox every time I have the nerve to say that things are pretty good out here for our kind in the so-called white world. Not only that, but I also call out the poverty pimps and community leaders as self-serving liars for telling their black-trash constituents otherwise.

I also try to send the message to mainstream middle-class blacks that the emperor has no clothes when I proclaim that these name callers have no authority to de-black anybody. All we have to do is ignore them.

But even though these messages make sense, the black middle-class achievers see the vicious fallout that comes from fighting against the community propaganda. They see not only the attacks on outspoken blacks like me but also those on blacks who have risen to some of the highest positions in America, like U.S. Supreme Court Justice Clarence Thomas.

It was tolerable for Thomas to enter the white man's world, to become a federal judge, to marry a white woman, even to live in a white neighborhood, but in the end he was expected to remain in lockstep with what the community told him to do and say.

I believe Thomas realized what was happening to him in the Supreme Court confirmation hearings when he said he was being categorized as an "uppity nigger" because he was straying from the community party line. I'm sure he felt the weight of all the bitterness of the black welfare culture, the poverty pimps, and the community activists coming down on him.

Their message, plain and simple, was "You can leave the neighborhood, but we'll always tell you—Judge Thomas, Dr. Thomas, teacher Thomas—what your obligation is to us."

Clarence Thomas became too independent. He took that momentous step to start thinking for himself.

But I'm even worse than independent. I'm worse for these ghetto intimidators and their cause, because I'm a guerrilla fighter. As unbelievable as it may sound, I am absolutely convinced, as I said on *Eye to Eye*, that I have them surrounded. They'd love to shame me into silence, but I refuse to give them that luxury.

I am not just fantasizing about some idyllic life for blacks in America. Not only do I personally live a pretty good life here, but I know a whole lot of other blacks who live well too. And there are hard statistics to back up my argument that life is pretty good for the great majority of blacks in America today.

There really are lots of us out here. Between 20 and 25 million blacks live beyond poverty and outside the boundaries of the ghetto in America. That statistic alone should diminish the fear that black trash have of venturing beyond Dark Town. If the mainstream were so dangerous or so miserable, would so many of us be here?

The propaganda spread by poverty pimps that racism prevents black people from prospering in the business of America also is a gross misconception.

This notion flies in the face of reality—one slice of which is measured and published annually by *Black Enterprise* magazine.

Black Enterprise has tracked the growth of black-owned businesses for two decades. It lists the 100 top-grossing industrial and service companies and the 100 top automobile dealerships that are at least 51 percent black-owned.

In the spring of 1996 the magazine reported that these two categories of top 100 black-owned businesses posted 1995 revenues of more than $13 billion—an increase of 11.8 percent over the previous year. They employed more than 51,000 people, up 6.6 percent from 1994.

The sales growth in this universe of black-owned business in America outperformed both the Fortune 500 companies, which grew 9.9 percent, and the Forbes 500 firms, which grew 10 percent during the same period.

The largest American black-owned company, TLC Beatrice International Holdings, a food processor and distributor, topped $2 billion in sales in 1995.

This black industry–wide growth was realized, said the magazine, despite an environment of corporate cutbacks and conservative politics that threatened to dismantle affirmative-action programs and policies.

Black Enterprise attributed the success and growth in the black business sector to a variety of innovations from "strategic alliances and acquisitions to launching new ventures and trying different marketing techniques."

Isn't that the way most American business grows?

These hard facts add up to a picture of black enterprise that is much different from the grim claims of black-business oppression that the poverty pimps and community activists carp about. According to them, rebellions like the one in Los Angeles in 1992 are inevitable because of black-trash anger over their lack of economic power and because they don't have a stake in their own neighborhood commerce.

A little old black lady approached me at a gathering several years ago and said, "I know what you're saying is right, but we hadn't ought to be airing our dirty laundry in front of all them white people."

Among other things, she didn't want me to use terms like "nappy hair" in referring to the texture of most black people's hair when I was kibitzing on the radio, or anywhere else within earshot of white people. Apparently she thought that was an embarrassing admission that our hair wasn't as pretty or as good as white people's softer hair.

She epitomized the argument from poverty pimps and community activists—the supposedly true African Americans—that I am racist, that I hate my people, when I acknowledge and speak out against black trash, black thugs, brood mares, and Dark Town.

Do my people really think that white people haven't noticed that there's a crisis in black America? Do they think white folks don't watch the nightly news or read the morning newspaper? Do they think because they don't acknowledge the problem, other than with tired cries of racism, that white people won't notice that cities are dying and their taxes are rising?

Good and moral black people cannot hide from white people any more than they can hide from boisterous black trash and poverty pimps.

It's time for this majority of black Americans to realize that either they're part of the problem or they're part of the solution. And there's no question in my mind that most middle-class blacks are contributing to the problem through their silence.

I consider them silent not just because they refuse to speak out against the horrors, like crime and teen pregnancy, that the Myth of the Hobbled Black has produced, but also because they are silent when they deny their own achievements.

Oh, they know they've made it. And they are happy to have done so. They wouldn't trade their lifestyle for that of a life in Dark Town for one minute. But they insist on denying that fact to the rest of America.

Well, I for one am happy to say I have left those places that so many of my people are afraid to leave. Thank God I had the strength to claw my way out of the ghetto. And I hope God continues to give me the strength to step boldly beyond the shadows—the hiding places where my fellow Uncle Toms and Aunt Jemimas dwell in mainstream America.

Chapter Eight

Quota Blacks

• • • •

Have heard you on the radio a couple of times. You never did hesitate to express yourself aggressively, and it's great that you now have an opportunity to make good use of that quality—both for yourself and for a lot of other people.

VIA MAIL 11/3/95
JIM DYGERT, PUBLISHER, SUBURBAN PRESS
CINCINNATI, OHIO
FORMER EDITOR/PUBLISHER, DETROIT SCOPE
MAGAZINE

• • • •

*I had the pleasure of reading an article about you that was carried in the Grand Rapids Press.
I admire your courage in speaking out against government dependency and the political establishment that pushes that same agenda. I am a female engineer that works with mostly men. Unfortunately, most of the other female engineers I work with talk about the "evil male" and believe they should be given special consideration just because they are women. I do not agree with them and have told them that but I find it difficult sometimes. It is not easy to state opposing opinions when it can lead to being ostracized by your peers.*

Thank you for having the courage of your convictions. It is inspiring.
P.S. My husband agrees also.

VIA MAIL 7/12/94
E.W.,
INDIANAPOLIS, INDIANA

• • • •

I agree with your assessment that Gen. Powell will turn out to be "another
African-American crybaby." I was particularly bothered by something I saw
on a recent C-Span show about the general's book tour. . . . They showed
an excerpt of a radio studio appearance Gen. Powell had made in the San
Diego area in which he was relating a story about racism. He said he had
gone to Dulles Airport on behalf of President Bush, as the president's Na-
tional Security Advisor, to meet with a foreign dignitary. He said he had
arrived in a big shiny limousine with many antennas (implying he was an
obviously important person) and that he was wearing a typically dark
Washington "power" suit. He said he walked up and down the hall several
times looking for the person he was to meet, but, not finding him, the gen-
eral went up to someone at a counter and announced that he was General
Powell and was expecting to meet so-and-so. He said the person was there
all the while but hadn't been expecting a black man as the president's rep-
resentative. The point of his story was that the man was a racist, but I sub-
mit the general is projecting racism where there might not have been
any—he ASSUMES the man overlooked him because he was black, but I
believe the man more likely overlooked him because he was in a business
suit rather than the uniform the man would have expected an Army four-
star general to have been wearing. And the limo with the antennas was ir-
relevant since they were indoors and the man may not have seen the
general arrive! I have a real problem with black people who automatically
assume racism is the reason for anyone disagreeing with their ideas or oth-
erwise opposing them. It's the same as labeling me a "homophobe" because
I disagree with legitimizing gay marriages.

VIA E-MAIL 10/7/95
W.B.

• • • •

Let me ask you something, Ken. . . . Do you think, for one minute, that
you'd have your column in The Post if you used it to tell the truth about the
white power structure and how it does everything possible to keep us down?
Hell, no, you wouldn't! Your "Oh, the whites really love us!" attitude is the
reason you are successful.

If Hamblin was a skinhead or a member of the Ku Klux Klan, his views would, at least, be understandable. But Ken Hamblin is black . . . on the surface anyway, and that is his problem.

LETTER TO THE EDITOR/THE DENVER POST
D.A., COMMERCE CITY, CO

Some of my critics insist my message only gets to white people. They maintain that I say only what whitey wants me to say, that I'm just an old Uncle Tom preaching to the choir.

But I know better. Because I'm one of those rare people who can look through the radio and see what's going on out in radioland. And out there in the tall grass on very still, clear days, I can see the landscape moving. I know then that the black liberals are stirring, snuggling up, and peeking through the grass to spy on me, monitoring what I say on the radio.

They get my message. If they didn't, why else would they howl so when I prick them with a pin to motivate them?

A couple of years ago I decided to turn my radio comment line into the Whiney-Whiney Colored Comment Line. This is a dedicated phone line people can call when they can't—or don't want to—get through on the live call-in lines. They can leave recorded messages that we may or may not use on the show.

I start every show by inviting people to call: "We're the only show in America, perhaps in the world, Mr. and Mrs. America, that operates the you-betcha, 10-4, roger, Whiney-Whiney Colored Comment Line, reserved for at least 400,000 unhappy African Americans. But don't worry if you're not African American and still want to call, because the line is fully integrated."

This was supposed to be a spoof directed at all the people I complain about who have an excuse for their every misdeed and failure and who of course cling to each and every perverse strand of disinformation associated with the Myth of the Hobbled Black.

Amazingly, I built it, and they came. Every day they take the bait. Here are just a few excerpts. The first message came the day after I had been talking on the show about smoking:

• • • •

Tom, this is Dorothy from Corn Lake, Mississippi. You blew it. You committed a cardinal sin yesterday—the sin of script deviation. Stick to the script, boy. You are paid to hate yourself and all black people and expound on that hatred. White people don't pay you for your pain about their habits

*whether it's drinking, smoking, or otherwise. Just read the script they give
you.*

• • • •

*I'm from Honolulu. My name is Jim. I think the Black Avenger is a joke.
Good nigger Uncle Tom wouldn't be where he is if he wasn't criticizing
black people. It's so funny. I happen to be a black businessman and I think
he's just ridiculous.*

• • • •

*Yeah, this is Mack from Santa Maria, California. Brother Ken, that black
businessman from Hawaii that was bad-rapping you is living proof that
same-sex marriages destroy your sense of humor and the added back pressure causes brain damage. I bet you have more white friends than he has
black friends. What do you think, Ken?*

• • • •

*I'm gonna try my darnedest to get Ken Hamblin off the air. I'm gonna to
do everything I possibly can to get that rat off the air. A person like him do
not need to be broadcastin'. He's an idiot, a stone-born idiot.*

• • • •

*Ken Hamblin, you just made a statement on the air that was totally
asinine. . . . There is prejudice within this country, and you might as well
begin to recognize it. It is not the imagination of every black American.
It exists out there. It is real. Colin Powell comprehends it . . . and I think
that you . . . are totally cuckoo not to realize it yourself [Jackie, Honolulu,
Hawaii].*

• • • •

*You know, Black Avenger . . . all you are trying to do is appeal to the white,
narrow-minded ignoramus. That's all you are doing, Ken Hamblin [Jackie,
Honolulu, Hawaii—again].*

• • • •

*Hello, Ken. My name is Ben. I listen to you on KSFO radio in San Fran-
cisco. I also am a minority and I'm really offended—nothing at what you
say, but more so at the people who leave such distressing messages on the
Whiney-Whiney line. I love your show. And what you are saying is very important to America and the future of this country. So keep it up.*

Within the majority of blacks outside the black-trash welfare culture is a group I call the quota blacks, who have just one foot outside of Dark Town. They endorse black-trash back-to-Africa values, and they stand pat in their distrust of and general distaste for America, which they perceive as the white system.

Their endorsement of the black "community" allows them to escape the demeaning label of Uncle Tom or Aunt Jemima. It even allows them to leave Dark Town, as long as they promise to return periodically and always to sing the praises of the community.

Clearly they benefit from the world outside in terms of their housing, their shopping options, their children's schooling, and their overall safety and well-being. But they are very careful not to commit the sin of fully embracing mainstream America.

These are the black people who fill—emotionally and numerically—the "minority slots" in the workplace. Some of them are reporters at newspapers who are always assigned the "black" stories. Some are community activists who derive their living from corporate America's preoccupation with minority relations.

In any case, these quota blacks constitute one of the worst remnants of affirmative action, because they have latched on to a short-term primer program designed to give a group of people fast-track entry to the job market, and they have twisted it into an established division of secondary citizenship in the world of work.

They spend much of their time trying to "get over" in whitey's company or office, just as black trash spend their time trying to "get over" by taking advantage of the spoils of the white man's system—i.e., the government dole.

Quota blacks discount their jobs or their professions as rewarding careers because they are operating in the "white world." Likewise, they are seldom taken seriously on the job, because it's common knowledge they are simply filling minority slots.

Because of their unwillingness to compete on their merits instead of their skin color and because of their self-imposed exile in programs for the disadvantaged, they fulfill their own prophecy that they will never get ahead as their fellow workers do—a fate that, of course, they attribute to racism.

These quota blacks have shielded themselves from any possible criticism from Dark Town by maintaining a powerfully negative attitude about their life in the "white world." They tell themselves that they don't really want anything to do with mainstream America, even though every day they take what it will give them.

Publicly they maintain that what they have—their job, their house, their car, their freedom—is worthless. They abide by the anti-American tenet which decrees that any black man who benefits from this country is a sellout.

These quota blacks have forsaken every black man in the South who was hanged and every slave who was whipped.

They have no allegiance to America because they have convinced themselves that what little they derive from this country is no more than their due in compensation for past sins against them.

The quota black has convinced himself that despite his existence in mainstream white America, he remains true to his blackness first and foremost. He cannot be called a sellout because he has renamed himself in the African tongue. He dresses in African garb. He goes home every weekend and fires up the barbecue, and together with like-minded friends, he denounces America.

Existing in two worlds, the quota black engages in a classic exercise in escaping reality.

But he is not multicultural in any sense of the word, because he doesn't have a true respect for or commitment to either culture. He lives in a twilight world someplace between a cultural heaven and hell.

Secretly he is relieved to be separated, if only by minimal physical distance, from the disorder of Dark Town and the low-class black-trash welfare culture. But he also is uncomfortable in the mainstream culture because, being trapped in the backwash of his own propaganda, he perceives it to be white only.

Nonetheless, the quota black is seen as the liaison between these two worlds. It's as if he has a social pass to cross multicultural borders. White liberals, including heads of corporations and newspaper editors, consult with him: "Tell us. What's really going on in the African-American community?"

Then, after going to the equivalent of the National Press Club and eating caviar and filet mignon, the quota black goes back into the black community, puts his feet up, high-fives with the brothers, and talks jive: "Hey, I went out there, and we got 'em scammed. The white man's a jerk. He thinks I don't know he still hates us."

In essence, he comes back and reflects all of the personal insecurities that he felt while he was sitting at the mahogany corporate table. What he reports back to the black community is not some clandestine information that he has garnered from corporate America, from some dossier documenting racial hatred or discrimination handed to him by some covert operative, like a friendly white secretary or middle-class black executive. He just comes back and downloads his own feelings of insecurity.

It doesn't matter whether the white people at the executive table smiled at him, whether they told him how glad they were to meet with him. He is never comfortable, because he eats dinner on the circuit, he shakes hands, he stands at the lectern, he sits in the audience, always with a sense that these white people don't really want him there.

It's as if he's thinking, No matter how much money you give me, no matter how you welcome me, no matter how much you smile at me, I know that in your heart you despise me. I know that all white people—whether they're blue-collar workers digging coal out of a West Virginia mine or CEOs of Fortune 500 companies—detest me. I know that when I'm not around, you secretly tithe 10 or 15 percent of your life to making minority people miserable. You hate us. As soon as we turn around, you whisper about us behind our backs and laugh at us.

With those insecurities, he remains a quota black. He remains a second-class citizen, paranoid and xenophobic, refusing to accept the full vesting of his American citizenship.

I am the first to admit that there was a time in America when we needed affirmative action programs to open doors that up to that time had been closed to blacks.

In the 1960s before I left New York, I landed a job at the A. B. Dick Company as a 632 IBM card-punch operator. I remember being one of only two blacks in the entire company. They gave me a desk near a window looking out on the corner of Forty-seventh Street and Lexington Avenue.

These were the early "affirmative action" jobs, the ones that put black faces up front—in a window or at the reception desk—to make us highly visible and to preempt any claims that the company was racist in its hiring practices. Of course, this ended up being a form of out-and-out racism. The company knew it, and I knew it. But I needed a job, and they thought they needed me.

Being young and always hopeful, however, I couldn't stop myself from trying to play office politics, which dictated that I continually ask what the future was for me at the company.

Finally my supervisor called me in and was very forthright: "Ken, I'm going to be perfectly honest with you. No matter how long you stay with this company, I don't think you'll ever make more than sixty dollars a week."

He didn't say, "You've got a bad attitude, you're absent from work a lot, you don't do a good job." He just said flat-out, "You'll never make more than sixty dollars a week."

Later I found out that my supervisor made sixty dollars a week, so I guess that was his arbitrary benchmark for me. He was quite certain a Negro sitting in the front window would never make more than he did.

It was a blatant example of how blacks once were regarded as somewhat less than full-fledged employees in the workplace. Either my supervisor was a racist or he was implementing his company's racist policy. I'd say it probably was both.

In the early 1960s, after a number of menial jobs like the one at A. B. Dick,

I pursued an interest in photography and taught myself the basics. A couple of years later I boldly walked into the offices of *Time* and *Life* magazines in Manhattan and asked to apply for a job. They said, without hesitation, that there weren't any jobs for colored photographers.

I lived long enough to achieve satisfaction for my rebuff, however. In 1996 I was in New York to make an appearance on *The Montel Williams Show.* Early one morning my senior radio producer Jake Arnette and I were walking along Sixth Avenue when a well-dressed black man recognized me and stopped to say he thought my message about self-reliance was absolutely correct. As he walked away into one of the Manhattan skyscrapers, like the ones I had fantasized about as a poor boy from Brooklyn, I looked up and realized he had nonchalantly gone to work in the Time and Life Building.

As I have so many times during my life in America, I felt as though good and right had prevailed. This young man was one more tangible example of the rewards made possible by the struggles of my generation.

Back in the 1960s, however, I was still struggling to get started along my own road to success. Even though deep down I knew better, I told myself the problem I had finding the right job might be endemic to New York. So I packed up my young family and headed west.

I was smitten by the stories of opportunity in California and set that as my destination. But I didn't plan the move very well. Our first stop was Detroit to visit my first wife's family. That's where we stayed, because that's where our money ran out.

My in-laws told me the only jobs to be had in Detroit were at the auto factories—and that they were darn good jobs, too.

But after watching the men come home every night zombielike from eight or more hours of hard physical labor, and after taking a couple more dead-end jobs like the ones I'd had in New York, I put my hopes back into my cameras.

I went to the *Detroit Free Press* and the *Detroit News* just before the riots broke out in 1967, and asked to apply for a job as a staff photographer. Same response as *Time* and *Life*: "We don't hire colored photographers."

The *Free Press* picture editor said they were "thinking about it" but they had to be sure the "guys upstairs were ready for it." He was referring to the all-white, all-male staff of photographers whose studio and lab were a floor above the city room.

The riots came and went, and even though I was being kept out of the big-city dailies, I started making a living shooting pictures on a freelance basis for suburban papers and for advertising accounts.

In 1968 a major newspaper strike closed down both Detroit dailies for several months. A guy named Jim Dygert started a newsmagazine called *Scope* to fill the void. He hired me as a staff photographer.

When the big dailies came back, I was concerned, like the other people at the magazine, that *Scope*'s days would be numbered, and we turned our attention to the dailies. Actually, I was quite a bit more concerned than the others were because I had already been rejected by both papers solely because of the color of my skin.

But I guess you could say I got lucky.

My photographic specialty was capturing the street action during the 1960s protests, marches, and riots. The next spring, just weeks before *Scope* closed its doors, I was sent to cover a George Wallace for President rally at Cobo Hall.

There were protesters and picketers outside the hall, and the Detroit police—still fresh from the Detroit riot a little more than a year before—were banging a few heads. I got in the middle of one of the melees and started snapping pictures. I'm not sure who the cops thought I was, but since they knew it was unlikely that, as a black guy, I could be authorized working press, they knocked me out cold.

Here's the lucky part.

Apparently the cops also thought my film was worthless— either because I couldn't possibly be a good photographer or because no one would ever publish my photos—so they didn't bother to confiscate the film in my cameras.

I salvaged the film, and my pictures ran in that week's issue of *Scope* . . . just days after both major daily newspapers had run stories reporting a generally peaceful demonstration— without action photographs to prove otherwise.

In a matter of months the *Detroit Free Press* hired me as its first black staff photographer. It was clearly an affirmative action hire. In fact, I may be the only employee ever hired for the Knight-Ridder newspaper chain who was not required to take the daylong battery of written personnel tests.

They must have presumed I couldn't pass them, and perhaps I couldn't have. I'll never know.

I fully acknowledge, though, that I needed a mandate of affirmative action to get that job.

But here's why I am against the continuation of affirmative action programs today, why I believe that they stop black people from realizing their true power to excel without limitations in the workplace.

The "guys upstairs," the white photographers at the *Detroit Free Press*, apparently were not ready for me, even though the managers in the city room were. I know it was weeks—it seemed like a month—before they spoke to me beyond cursory words. I was shunned, ignored, treated quite frankly as the "nigger" on the staff.

Each one of them had worked hard to become a staff photographer for one of the country's finest daily newspapers. Most of them had graduated from prominent university journalism schools and had worked their way up to the *Free Press* via small-newspaper jobs. At the time I went to the *Free Press*, there were nationally known photographers on the staff like Ira Rosenberg and Tony Spina.

Every photographer at the *Detroit Free Press* in 1969 felt he had earned his job through skill and perseverance. (There were no women there yet either.) Obviously, they all concluded that I had not.

With any affirmative action slot, there is a perception that the employee has been given special dispensation to be there. There is a perception that the person, if required to compete equally with other candidates, would not be qualified to get the job. There is a perception that the affirmative action employee is taking the space of a more deserving employee. The whole concept of affirmative action flies in the face of the American way of winning through competition and feeling good about it and yourself.

Because my specialty was street-action photography and because there was a profusion of those assignments in 1969, I was able to prove my worth by demonstration once I was on the job at the *Free Press*. My photos were published prominently, not just in the *Free Press* but in *Newsweek*, *Time*, and *Life* as well.

One photo of which I was especially proud and which received equally exceptional play was of a Black Panther holding a pistol, sitting on the floor, and leaning against a window with the shade drawn. It was taken soon after the Black Panther Party's Illinois state chairman, Fred Hampton, had been shot by the police in Chicago, and there was growing tension between the law and the Panthers across the country.

I was just getting off from the *Free Press* one night when I got a call from some guys who were part of the Detroit Panther group. They knew my name because of my photo credits in the paper, and they knew I was black because word about me breaking the color barrier had spread through the community.

By the way, back then as now, some blacks thought I was a trailblazer while others thought I was a sellout Uncle Tom for going downtown to work for "the man." On this night, however, the Panther on the other end of the phone was scared and apparently hoped that, whoever I was, maybe I could help them.

He said they were in their headquarters, a house in Detroit's black ghetto, and had spied the Detroit police crawling along nearby rooftops. They feared the worst.

I took it to the city desk, but they weren't interested and said that if I wanted to go, I'd have to do it on my own time.

When I got to the house, the Panthers let me in and, from their vantage point, convinced me the cops indeed were surrounding the house. I told them to call all the TV stations, which they did. Soon after the TV cameramen and reporters started rolling up, the cops dispersed and it became a non-incident.

But I had been the only journalist permitted inside the house, and I capitalized on being in the right place at the right time by shooting only a couple of frames of film, before they told me "No pictures." One picture ended up a year or so later running a full page and a quarter in *Life* magazine to illustrate a Gordon Parks essay on the Panthers.

In 1970 I won first place in the general news category in the Michigan Press Photographers Association competition. But more important to me, I eventually won the respect of my fellow photographers, and many of them remain good friends and colleagues today.

There is no question that many blacks like me were thankful in the 1960s and the 1970s to get into the mainstream job market, even if it meant using special privileges afforded us as affirmative action hires. But, given the alternative of being hired strictly on the basis of merit, I would never recommend affirmative action as the preferred path to building a career.

Even if you prove to be good at your job, the stigma of getting it through affirmative action is all but impossible to shake. About a year after I was hired at the *Free Press*, after I had won the Press Photographers Association Award and after becoming what I believed was a fully vested professional in the photo department, I got good information that I was being paid less money than the paper was paying its summer interns.

I took this information to the picture editor who had hired me, who by then was the editor of the paper, and I asked for parity with the other staff photographers. My request was denied, despite my performance. Apparently my job was slotted as a low-paying OJT (on-the-job-training) minority position.

When I said I obviously would have to find another job, the editor asked me in all sincerity where I could possibly go.

I approached my sad dilemma by drawing upon the fundamental lesson about exploring and utilizing options that I had learned years before at IPCO Hospital Supply. I decided to move into cinematography.

This happened to be 1970, just about the time the Federal Communications Commission, which regulated television and radio, mandated that TV stations hire a quota of black employees in their news and production departments.

One evening after my day ended at the *Free Press*, I was practicing my self-taught skills in cinematography by shooting a protest march at Kennedy Square in downtown Detroit. My footage ended up on the nightly newscast at an independent TV station with a credit to me, Ken Hamblin, as the shooter.

The very next day I got calls from three Detroit television stations and the Ford Motor Company, all wanting to talk to me about a job as a cameraman. Three of them tried to impress me with perks they must have thought I had never enjoyed, like lunch at the Detroit Press Club. Having just been through the shock of learning my real value to the *Free Press*, however, I was wary enough not to be overly impressed by lunch.

Finally I met Jack Costello, the program director for WTVS Channel 56, Detroit's Public Broadcasting System affiliate. When I entered his office, he was on the phone and he motioned me to sit down. He finished his call, stuck his hand across the desk, and said, "Hi. I'm Jack Costello. I gotta hire a black guy." His candor gained my respect from that moment on.

I said, "I'll go to work for you."

In about six months' time, I had maneuvered my way from my post behind the camera to an on-air spot in front of it. Over the next six years I made numerous documentaries and produced and hosted a variety of weekly magazine shows.

At the same time, I produced commercials and short films for political elections and industrial sales and training films for corporations through my own company.

Though I was probably still fulfilling somebody's requirement for federal funding or public relations, I felt I had finally broken out of the affirmative action job slot. Like my first typing job, this meant I had broken through a membrane. From that point on, I was committed never to lose my position as an employee. I would never settle for being a minority employee again.

When I got on the radio, I was committed to being something other than just a black guy doing a public affairs show. I was Ken Hamblin. I had my own opinions about things. I had principles. I stood for something. And that became the springboard for my talk show—not a slice of life from the black ghetto that would fulfill some FCC community programming obligation.

The satisfaction I strive for in every job is to watch my employer realize over time that he or she didn't hire a minority employee to fill a quota, but rather got a fully vested employee, a true participant in the company.

I believe this may be the only developed country in the world that will allow me, as a black man, to reach that pinnacle of full participation—full participation in the business of America. Colin Powell confirmed my belief when he went to England and was asked whether he thought as a black man in the U.K., he could have risen to the highest military rank in the land, as he had done in the U.S. He said no.

But the blacks who continue to pigeonhole themselves as special hires through affirmative action will never realize the confidence of true equality of opportunity or the joys of success in the workplace that are available to them in America. They will never believe that they are where they are because of their own worth. And neither will their fellow employees.

Affirmative action was intended to give blacks an opportunity to prove themselves in the workplace, an opportunity they had long been denied. It was intended to prime the pump with blacks who in the past had been kept out of the colleges, the internships, and the entry-level jobs that could lead to greater responsibility and higher salaries.

It was never intended to breed a class of workers who could submit their Social Security numbers, check the proper race box, and have support for life. It was never intended to become another welfare program.

But the reality is that the quota blacks are extensions of their black-trash brethren who feel America still owes them for the transgressions of the past. They believe they are "getting over."

In their own self-destructive way, quota blacks also are beneficiaries of the Myth of the Hobbled Black.

Like the poverty pimps who will do almost anything to protect their political turf, the quota blacks work hard to maintain their stake in the workplace. Sometimes these two groups even work hand in hand to watch out for each other's interests.

My personal encounters with the far-reaching fallout from affirmative action continue to come from the city rooms of America's largest newspapers.

The predominantly liberal bent of editorial departments is probably responsible for the fact that so many mainstream newspapers are hotbeds when it comes to indulging quota blacks, though I am certain most other large corporations have active quota-black forces on the job as well.

In the early 1990s, soon after I began writing regular opinion pieces for the *Denver Post*, my columns were picked up from time to time by the *Baltimore Sun* and the *Detroit Free Press*.

It wasn't long before I began getting feedback from quota blacks on the news and editorial staffs. They didn't like what I was writing about black trash, black thugs, self-reliance, quotas—all the things I'm writing about in this book.

In Baltimore, the black journalists' association took up my case and began flooding the editorial page editor with e-mail protests about me and my message. They tried to discredit me after they did a search and learned that I had never been to journalism school and that I wasn't a member of any black journalists' association. They called me a racist, a discredit to my race, a dupe for the white man—the usual stuff. Finally the pressure from this black committee—this group of black reporters set up as a placebo for people not in the mainstream game—resulted in the paper dropping my column.

Likewise after I wrote a scathing criticism of their homeboy, Detroit Congressman John Conyers, for backing a bill to study whether reparations for black people were in order, the *Free Press* dropped me as well. In this case, one of the editorial page editors told me I was "intellectually bankrupt."

Obviously I survived these setbacks. My column still runs twice weekly in the *Denver Post*, and it has been carried by the New York Times Syndicate since 1994.

But think about the young black college students today who work hard to graduate in anticipation of joining the American workplace. They work hard to be the best they can be, only to enter a world where quota blacks maintain a stronghold.

Not only are the newcomers subject to the politically correct guidelines of these pockets of race-based bullies, but they become subject to the inevitable and sadly mistaken perception by others in the workplace, often including their supervisors and managers, that all black employees must be tokens.

Besides doing irreparable harm to all black employees, the lingering presence of affirmative action has served to lower performance and entrance standards in many areas of the American workplace. Just as we have muddled the clear-cut traditional standards of right and wrong, we have allowed our standards of excellence to be questioned and compromised by phony considerations such as whether tests are "multicultural."

This consideration usually arises when affirmative action candidates can't pass standardized tests. The fact that the candidates might simply be unprepared for the test or just too dense to pass it is never a consideration. Instead, we allow the quota blacks and their liberal apologists and supporters to throw away the old standards and cry racism.

This convenient excuse for failure boggles my mind. How can they continue to cry racism when today so many of the supervisors who hire and fire them and evaluate their performance are black? Because of the quotas, the concessions, and the lowering of traditional standards of qualification, many young blacks who go through our public education system and come out functionally illiterate feel little pressure. The institution of affirmative action has taught them that all they really need to know is how many people of color the XYZ Corporation is obligated to hire.

Furthermore, it doesn't even occur to them that they might be unfit for a job in ways that go beyond their lack of skills.

No one has ever explained to them that an application for employment is more than a request for a job. It is also a request to join a corporate family. No one has explained to them that part of getting a job is convincing the interviewer that they can get along with their co-workers. No one has ever explained to them that the oral interview is designed to find out whether or not they are going to mesh with the people they would be working with.

Instead, affirmative action has taught quota blacks to be very single-minded. It has taught them to make their job search a black-and-white issue, no pun intended. Unfortunately, sometimes the harder they press their singular affirmative action agenda—"You have to hire me simply because I am black"—the more likely white people at the company are to express racism against them. And so, once again, the quota blacks' worst fears become a self-fulfilling prophecy.

One of the most glaring areas in which standards have been lowered due to the negative impact of quotas is the civil service sector. There has been a fight centered on this issue in almost every city and town in America, particularly over the hiring of police officers and firefighters.

America today has an abundance of black mayors, black police chiefs, black supervisors, and black urban managers, most of them liberal and most of them sensitive to voting blocs of black trash and quota blacks.

As a result, many of these black leaders have bent over backwards to be sure these voters are well represented by black faces in city departments, particularly those departments whose employees are most visible to the community. Black leaders have twisted the original civil rights legislation—designed to prohibit race, sex, ethnicity, or national origin from being used as a criterion for discriminating against, or giving preferential treatment to, someone in hiring and promotions—into a requirement for a certain hiring mix based on quotas.

In an effort to meet the quotas demanded by their black community voting blocs, most big-city police and fire academies have lowered their standards to accommodate black candidates and, in turn, have passed over many better-qualified candidates.

In 1993, while Marion Barry, then former mayor of Washington, D.C., was serving time for dallying with drugs, the current Mayor Sharon Pratt Dixon became so concerned about the city's crime rate that she requested the National Guard be sent in to help protect citizens.

The murder rate at that time was better than one a day even though the city wasn't short on cops. In fact, on a per capita basis, Washington had more police than any other American city.

But a column in the *Wall Street Journal* in November 1993 by Tucker Carlson, an editorial writer for the *Arkansas Democrat Gazette*, recounted an incredible saga of affirmative action.

Carlson began by acknowledging that Washington's police department in the past—in the 1950s—had a reputation as one of the best in the nation.

By the mid-1980s, however, Mayor Barry had instituted incredible affirmative action policies, which one detective who trained recruits said had resulted in some graduates from the police academy being "practically illiterate" or "borderline-retarded."

One of the earliest affirmative action policies was to add points to the test scores of police candidates just for having attended the city's public schools— even if they hadn't graduated. Later the standard was loosened so that a cadet could be expelled from the police academy only if he or she failed two exams. A few months later, wrote Carlson, the dismissal standard was lowered even further to failing six tests.

When even that didn't put enough affirmative action officers on the job, Mayor Barry tried to bring police officers onto the force by lottery. Congress, which still held the purse strings on Washington, D.C., said no way.

So Barry, in his poverty-pimp wisdom, got rid of the academy's final test altogether in 1988.

Meanwhile, the academy overlooked the candidates' juvenile criminal records. In some cases it failed to do background checks at all.

According to Carlson's *Wall Street Journal* column, that failure resulted in 1992 in thirty-six officers being "indicted on charges such as dope dealing, sexual assault, murder, sodomy and kidnapping. In one instance, scores, perhaps thousands, of confiscated weapons (sloppy police record-keeping makes it impossible to know the exact number) were stolen from a police warehouse by employees. At least one was later used in a murder."

Affirmative action never was intended to give a boost to black trash, but clearly black trash has benefited wherever affirmative action policies are firmly in the hands of their sugar daddies, the poverty pimps.

A final graphic example of standards be damned and affirmative action run amok is the case of former New Orleans police officer Antoinette Frank, an African American. She was convicted and sentenced to death for shooting her partner—her partner on the police squad—and two employees during the holdup of a restaurant in 1995.

Frank and her partner, Officer Ronald Williams, moonlighted as security guards in the restaurant. On the night of the heist, Frank encountered Williams working in the restaurant and took him out, along with the two restaurant employees.

Cops have gone bad in the past. But what is amazing about this cop is that she became a cop only after winning a protest against a screening that indicated her police application should be rejected for psychological reasons. The psychologist testified at the murder trial that he had judged her an unacceptable candidate for the police academy.

Part 3

The War of Ideologies
in America

Chapter Nine

Egg-Sucking Dog Liberals

• • • •

Take care and know that you are reaching many people with your intelligence and logic . . . just remember that some of them won't like it.

VIA E-MAIL 1/15/96
M.N.

• • • •

Often I hear true conservatives saying that they are only fiscal conservatives but not social conservatives. This doesn't seem possible, wouldn't the person have to be both?
"The inherent vice of capitalism is the unequal sharing of blessings; the inherent virtue of socialism is the equal sharing of miseries." —Winston Churchill

VIA E-MAIL 1/31/96
T.W.

• • • •

I love your insight, courage and independent thought that persists in being a voice for the people!! For the individual human spirit and dignity. . . . Thank you, thank you! What a succinct, clear summary for why I, too, totally reject liberalism. It has enslaved a welfare class and in the process al-

*most destroyed the intelligence, drive, potential and divine right of the indi-
vidual human spirit to progress, advance, produce. . . . CHARACTER is
what it's all about! Character—goodness, persistence, courage, patience,
wisdom, desire to work, to grow, to overcome, listen and learn, to share, to
serve . . . true character will always succeed—indeed be sought out—irre-
spective of race, age, sex, creed, handicap, sexual preference.*

VIA MAIL 12/10/92
B.W.,
EVERGREEN, CO

• • • •

*As a high school teacher in a predominantly white, middle-class . . . school,
I can tell you that I, a conservative, am surrounded by teachers who claim
to be the high-priests of white liberalism. . . . I read your editorials and . . .
put them in my liberal friends' mailboxes. Of course, a lively conversation
ensues; however, they will not believe you. They can't stand to not have
some poor soul to save from the ravages of a white, capitalistic, imperialis-
tic society. I am amused at their desperation, but I or you cannot dissuade
them from their self-appointed martyrdom. So be it.*

VIA MAIL 1/7/93
P.K.,
LAKEWOOD, CO

• • • •

*When critics roar against you, remember, those who are with you are
greater than those who are against you. . . . Sally forth and slay the dragon
of liberalism. You are a warrior!*

VIA MAIL 7/8/94
G.D.,
GREELEY, CO

• • • •

*Black Avenger,
I enjoy your show on KGEO. Now when my egg-sucking dog liberal friends
call me a racist because I'm not a socialist, I simply tell them to listen to
your show, instead of Ricki Lake! Of course, to them Ricki Lake is an intel-
lectual! Keep up the good work.*

VIA FAX 10/30/95
HALF-BAKED IN BAKERSFIELD

• • • •

Ken, BRAVO. I respect Americans like you . . . who stand up for what you believe. The present Democrats and other liberals are prostituting too many black Americans. I am WASP, but respect the hell out of you.

VIA MAIL 7/5/94
G.K.,
AUSTIN, TEXAS

• • • •

I find myself in agreement with many of your statements, especially regarding the importance of escaping the new socialist agenda, the dependency and hopelessness fostered by the welfare state, the importance of individual responsibility, and the insanity of our current drug laws.

VIA MAIL 1/19/94
L.C.,
SAN FRANCISCO, CA

• • • •

Just wanted to drop you a line and respond to your article . . . about multiculturalists and liberal socialists stooping to the levels of third world countries as opposed to bringing the third world to the level of our great country. As you know this does not stop at language . . . they do the same thing in education. Deletion of college prep courses at the public schools in Gulfport, MS raised more stink than I have ever seen in the community. The board attempted to just "put everyone together so that they may achieve at equal levels. . . ." Needless to say it didn't pass . . . LOWER STANDARDS to achieve equality and appease as opposed to pushing for all you can be . . . yea right.

VIA E-MAIL 12/5/95
G.M.

• • • •

You're a bad joke! You are so cocky and sure that you have all the right answers and that anyone who disagrees is so wrong and wrong because they are evil. It is attitudes like yours that really threaten the greatness of this nation and its ability to evolve, to absorb diverse ideas, and to merge these ideas into better ideas to adopt. For what you want is for only your ideas to be considered and thus adopted—of course this is just what all radicals desire.
Keep up your diatribe and play your games and keep up your chirade [sic] of truth seeking. This country has survived worse than you and you will

*eventually be unveiled and fade off into the obscurity you deserve. . . . A
moderate, who by your standards is a liberal and proud of it!!!*

VIA E-MAIL 1/9/96
M.M.

Like "Dark Town" and "poverty pimps," I coined the phrase "egg-sucking dog liberals" one day in a tirade on my radio show. I'm not sure from what deep recess in my mind it arose, but as I conjured up an image of liberals and began ranting against one of their absurdities reported in the news on that particular day, the phrase just came spewing out.

The vision I had was of a big fat lazy dog sneaking into a henhouse just before sunrise, sucking all the substance out of the freshly laid chicken eggs, and then skulking away. I figured you couldn't get any more dishonest or any deadlier than that.

And that pretty much sums up how I feel about modern-day white liberals and their politics. I believe they are sucking the substance out of the promise America holds for its black citizens—sucking out the energy and the spirit inherent in the American Dream for all people. I'm convinced that these liberals have both practical and philosophical reasons for doing so.

White liberals provide the political alliance with black poverty pimps that is necessary to perpetuate the Myth of the Hobbled Black. They are ready and willing to spread the propaganda that black trash are in their sad predicament only because they are victims of racism and that they are held back by the disadvantages that follow.

White liberals and black community leaders first were aligned in the 1960s during the fight for civil rights and the War on Poverty. A good many of the black protest leaders eventually became today's poverty pimps and African-American community leaders, and a good many white protesters became the social workers and the lawyers who have made thirty-year careers of studying and defending black trash.

These white folks represent the core army of egg-sucking dog liberals.

While I'm not necessarily accusing them of overtly working to hinder the advance of black Americans, it's obvious that their black-trash dependents can realize only so much success or these doting liberals would be out of work. Likewise, these liberals compromise their self-interest if they acknowledge that already there is a capable mainstream black majority who do not need their patronizing assistance. In essence, their livelihood is dependent on perpetuating black trash and the black-trash welfare culture, which, I might add, funds many of them and their programs.

But the liberal social workers and lawyers are only the point men for this political faction. Their cause is augmented by thousands of men and women from all walks of life who are convinced that the American Negro historically has been treated unfairly and that if blacks are still crying out vehemently and loudly about injustice, then that injustice must exist yet today.

They are willing to accept this based on Promethean faith even though they believe in their hearts that they personally are not a party to this injustice and even though they don't observe it much anymore—except as it is packaged by liberal journalists and broadcast on the nightly news.

These liberals also are willing to accept the cries of injustice at face value in spite of growing evidence that it does not exist, at least to the extent that it prohibits advancement, for a growing number of black Americans who are entering the mainstream.

They conveniently overlook statistics showing that black families are moving out of the ghetto and other urban areas into middle-class suburbs. They don't acknowledge places like Prince Georges County, Maryland, a mainstream community with a predominance of black residents.

Instead, by helping to perpetuate the propaganda of victimized black trash, the contemporary American liberal coalition is as big a contributor to the problem of the growing black welfare culture as are the Crips, the Bloods, and the poverty pimps.

But attending to the downtrodden black is only a side issue for most of these white liberals. I believe their underlying agenda is to remake America. And, to me, that seems very anti-American. I believe their socialist agenda flies in the face of every piece of the American Dream that got me where I am today.

If you catch liberals in their own skulduggery by exposing their true political agenda, however, they will never own up to the truth. You can just envision that egg-sucking dog slinking low to the ground with its ears pinned back and its tail tightly drawn up between its legs. Its one aim at that point is to sneak as far away from the chicken coop as possible, off into the morning haze.

Back in the 1960s, I was exhilarated and still today I am greatly thankful for the fact that white liberals were willing to fight side by side with us for the common goal of opening up all of America to black people, of integrating America so that blacks and whites could live and work together peacefully. These were people of conscience, people of ethics, who joined forces with the black civil rights movement to stand up and to say it was wrong when "Bull" Connor turned hoses and dogs against Negroes in Birmingham, Alabama.

White people like Michael Schwerner, Andrew Goodman, and Viola

Liuzzo gave their lives for the cause; I have no doubt they were giving their lives for us.

To my way of looking at it, together we won that war. Civil rights for Negroes were granted. And most of us Negroes, enthusiastic and energized by our new legal powers, went about tackling the tremendous challenge ahead of us to assimilate into mainstream America. We were eager to partake of all it offered.

But here's the rub. Once civil rights legislation passed and Negroes began their new American odyssey, white liberals lost the challenge of one of their most noble causes. Concurrently they lost their Negro wards.

By all rights they should happily have relinquished their paternal position. Of course, some have—or at least they are prepared to do so. But others—the ones I call egg-sucking dog liberals—have not done so yet today, more than three decades after our victory.

I understand that it was natural for them to get warm feelings when they were helping us. But I had no idea that for some of these liberal do-gooders, those warm feelings would become an intoxicating narcotic.

Today they simply refuse to let us go. They refuse to face the fact that it is possible for a black person to get a fair shake—to be truly free and to be treated justly in America. They refuse to admit that we can make it without special consideration and without their special help. They refuse to treat us as equal Americans.

Whether out of principle or out of self-interest, these liberals are willful promoters of the propaganda that we really didn't win in the 1960s. That keeps them in the business of lending a helping hand and feeling good about it. And I believe it also gives continued credence to their long legacy of feeling superior.

When I was a photographer at the *Detroit Free Press*, I was sent on assignment to northern Michigan, where a group of wildlife enthusiasts were picketing to persuade local residents not to feed the bears by leaving food accessible to them in the garbage dumps. These bears were becoming dependent on the convenience of human-served meals, and the protesters feared that in the off-season the bears would be unprepared to forage for themselves in the woods.

In 1991 I drew an analogy between the unhealthy result of feeding those bears and the way we are giving aid to the black underclass, making them dependent on the welfare system. I wrote a column, which appeared in the *Denver Post* and the *Baltimore Sun* with the headline: "Please Don't Feed the Blacks." I've been explaining myself ever since.

Most people agree wholeheartedly with my plea once they understand that my motive was compassion, not mean-spiritedness.

Here is an excerpt from that column:

*Like a brown bear foraging for its sustenance in a garbage dump,
ghetto blacks have lost the need to support their children and fend
for themselves.
Like pampered beasts that have grown bloated living off human relief,
ghetto blacks have become the sluggish equivalents subsisting off liberal
provisions delivered by an endless quota of federal, state, and city relief
programs.
But unlike the bear, which is at risk of being spoiled by a careless human,
underclass blacks have no animal rights network to protect them from becoming victims of human kindness.
In this case, there are no idealistic legions of enthusiastic college students
and housewives willing to post "Please Don't Feed the Blacks" placards at
local welfare centers. Or to picket the originators of so-called antipoverty
programs when social workers decide the best solution to urban black anarchy is to throw more money into the den.*

To this day I have not faltered from my conclusion about the liberal solution of unending welfare and the devastating harm it causes poor black Americans. I believe this patronage, which stems from the liberals' refusal to grant
any black person full equality, may be the one dangerous form of white-on-
black racism left for us to fear and overcome. It puts us at risk of becoming
pets, and to me, that's as bad as slavery.

And so, because I am convinced that American liberal benevolence ultimately could indulge the black underclass to death, in keeping with truth,
justice, and the American way, I again sound the alarm: Please Don't Feed
the Blacks.

Soon after I began broadcasting my radio talk show in Denver in 1982 —
a time when, I admit, I espoused many liberal perspectives — I quickly became the darling of the liberal media corps in Denver. Over the next few
years I was lauded in various critics' columns as "thoughtful, intelligent, and
at times even poetic," as "articulate and well read, a fast thinker, entertaining,
sensitive yet argumentative and opinionated, well paced, persuasive, and
fiery."

I took those accolades to be critiques of my broadcasting ability, not my
politics.

But a few years ago when, as I put it, I started thinking for myself, I quickly
became persona non grata among these same critics, as well as among many
of my colleagues in the radio world and in the city room at the *Denver Post*,
where I write a regular Op-Ed column.

I got the distinct feeling the critics no longer cared much about my broadcasting ability one way or another. Apparently they were appalled at my politics. And the falling-out seemed to be over something even bigger than my opinions.

One critic told my wife he considered himself a liberal and therefore was personally offended by my new conservative politics—and my criticism of liberals. I wondered how that factored into his commentary on my broadcasting skills and how it related to his refusal to acknowledge my popularity or his downplaying of my success in his column.

An editor at the *Denver Post* reportedly dismissed a reader poll confirming my popularity as a columnist because I had "too many white readers." I gathered that in the eyes of that particular white liberal editor, if a black columnist has ideas that appeal to mainstream America, those ideas are deemed invalid and not particularly worthy of publication. His rumored comment made me wonder whether, in his mind, I had been hired with the express purpose of filling the legacy of a token black writer whose ideas were printed on the editorial page simply to appease the minority of black subscribers.

In the end, this cadre of egg-sucking dog liberals have carried their personal disgust of my politics to the point that they literally have blackballed me from jobs and social gatherings.

As of this writing they have succeeded in keeping my national syndicated radio show from being broadcast in my own hometown.*

I believe part of the reason is that they had been enamored with their power to bestow success on me, patronizingly "proud" when they could think of me as their African-American protégé.

But when I began saying things they did not agree with, particularly when I challenged and called out liberal principles that they took pride in, they publicly and privately withdrew support for me, although for a while a few of them called and pleaded with me to come back into the fold.

Then I began succeeding without their help—in fact, in spite of their withholding it. My radio show went national. I was awarded a contract to write this book.

My opinions landed me on national television programs such as *Today*, *Good Morning America*, the NBC *Nightly News*, CBS's *Eye to Eye*, and CNN and CNBC news shows. Articles were written about me and my point of view in the *Economist* magazine and in the *New York Times* and a host of other major daily newspapers across the country.

These were career mile markers that few of my colleagues had reached and probably would never reach. Instead of being happy for a hometown guy who was making it—something all of them had professed to want at one time or another—they developed an even chillier attitude toward me.

---

*As of August 1, 1996, *The Ken Hamblin Show* was picked up in Denver by the Chancellor Broadcasting affiliate on frequency 1280 A.M.

I ran into one honest columnist on the street who told me that I had no idea how many people in Denver's city rooms hated me just because my column had been syndicated by the *New York Times*.

I know there must be a degree of professional jealousy working here.

But I believe it is even more than that. I believe many of these liberals truly cannot accept that a black person, especially one to whom they believe they once lent a helping hand, is capable of standing on his own and succeeding in mainstream America. Or if we do succeed, they believe the only politically correct next step for us is to join them in bemoaning the misfortune of the rest of the black community.

I probably could have stayed in their good graces if I had chosen to live as they do, as limousine liberals—or aspiring limousine liberals. I would have been allowed to reap the benefits of the American Dream both economically and socially without them judging me harshly.

But at the same time I would have had to claim that other people with my skin color, those who make up the black underclass, still were being oppressed. I would have been considered proper if I had constantly played down my own success by adding: "Ah, but how many of me can you count?"

I would have had to abide by their egg-sucking dog liberal denial of the fact that two-thirds to three-fourths of American blacks indeed have stepped into the mainstream. I would have had to buy into their fabrication that a black person making it is only an illusion or an anomaly, not the affirmation of the American Dream that I firmly believe I and other successful blacks represent.

The fact is that I have looked at the black underclass in Dark Town through the smoked-glass windows of the limousine. I had been told what I should expect to see—the squalor, the deprivation, the slums, the American Dream deferred, people loitering with no ambition. And indeed that is the scene I viewed.

But I see the big picture much differently from the way the egg-sucking dog liberals do. For one thing, I see how these supposedly well-meaning white liberals have played a self-serving hand in perpetuating the real tragedy of the black underclass.

I was hurt and for a time I was puzzled by these colleagues whom I once considered friends.

I also got letters and calls from personal friends who reacted harshly to me because of my ideas. They scolded me because I no longer marched in lockstep to their liberal drumbeat.

Some very good old friends from Detroit responded to the first issue of my newsletter, *KEN HAMBLIN Talks with America*, by calling it "appalling."

They went on: "We've always admired your ability to surf the trends. But, more than that, we admired the young, talented people you once were. We know that those people are not dead yet and we miss them. Please come back. You've done it before."

My hurt turned to anger when I found myself engaged in debates with them about whether or not I was living up to the fullest burden of my blackness if I did not share their belief in the Myth of the Hobbled Black.

I found myself in such a debate with a classic egg-sucking dog liberal reporter one Christmas at a party in my home. He stood there drinking my booze and eating my food, partaking of my hospitality, and had the nerve to say to me, with a great display of patronizing patience, something to this effect: "Ken, I'm afraid you just don't understand the struggles of black Americans."

What utter gall!

How dare any white liberal imply that he has a greater insight into being black than I do? How dare these people question the authenticity of my blackness and of my own black experience in America?

I admit that it has taken me a while to free myself completely from my old allegiance to the liberal banner and from the guilt brought about by my lingering appreciation for the role liberals played in the struggles of my people in the 1960s.

But finally I see the egg-sucking dog liberals of today clearly for what they have become—narrow, disagreeable ideologues who refuse to admit the truth.

Even when these liberals are faced with evidence of their own failures—like the ongoing rosters of the poor and the uneducated in spite of more than three decades of burgeoning welfare programs—still they fail to acknowledge that their policies and programs aren't working. They refuse to admit that the things I and others are saying might be right. Instead, tactically, they switch the conversation to why I personally might be saying the things I say.

Some of them try to discredit and deny my message on moral grounds, claiming that I changed my politics and say the things I say on the radio only to pander to current political trends in America. But the truth is that the strength of my beliefs has put me on the air. Being on the air has not shaped what I believe.

I hope this book will explain the evolution of my political perspective and demonstrate the depth of conviction I always have had about what I say and what I write.

But whether it does or doesn't convince them, I would urge these liberals to look to their opportunist president—the one still sitting in the White House as of this writing—for a true instance of a political chameleon, for a prime example of someone who capriciously changes his politics for momentary gain.

. . . .

As they dig themselves deeper into the trenches of egg-sucking dog liberalism, many liberals today are twisting the simple concept of offering a helping hand so that someone can take advantage of opportunity into something condescending and warped, just like today's welfare system.

It is not enough for them to offer a boost to minorities. Instead, they insist on an entirely new definition of fairness, a definition that translates into absolute equality of outcome. They are trying to make "fair" mean "equal."

This is the concept behind the controversial outcome-based education. It is embodied in the idealized doctrine of the level playing field.

When I was a kid I had guppies, and I learned from those fish the lesson of survival of the fittest. For a while I wondered what I was doing wrong when some of my guppies died. But as I grew older, I began to realize that not everything that is spawned survives. Guppies are born in abundance as nature's way of compensating for a relatively low survival rate.

That revelation eventually translated into a basic truth that I believe today about life in general. To me, it means that not every person has a guarantee that he or she will become a doctor or a lawyer or a Rhodes scholar.

The principle of fairness that I—and, I believe, most blacks—sought during the 1960s was a fair chance, an equal opportunity to make it or to fail in America. Like all Americans, we accepted the possibility that we might succeed, we might fail, or we might get to someplace in the middle.

But under the warped fairness mandate of egg-sucking dog liberalism, no one is permitted to fail—particularly the disadvantaged minority. A person may lose the race, but the feeling is that it's really not fair to hurt his feelings or to damage his self-esteem, so we'll give him a consolation prize, no matter what his performance was. Or we'll get rid of winners and losers altogether.

I call this notion the Phil Donahue syndrome because Donahue—in my book, perhaps the archetypal egg-sucking dog liberal—perpetuated this philosophy on his daily television talk show.

I believe, for instance, that according to Donahue it would be unfair not to reward the little nappy-headed black boy who did poorly in the spelling bee because he couldn't read. Clearly the contest didn't take place on a level playing field because this little boy had come from a poor, dysfunctional family and thus had started life with strong odds against him.

My view is that, from a practical perspective, it is impossible and therefore pointless to talk about a level playing field today. Civilization has progressed much too far.

In 1986 I went to Israel on a media trip. While there, I strayed from the standard tour after meeting a reporter from KOL, Israeli State Radio, who offered to take me to visit a Palestinian refugee camp.

First we stopped at the reporter's apartment, where he picked up his 9mm pistol, and then we went to the camp to meet the Palestinian mayor, who invited us into his sparse quarters for tea.

This Palestinian seemed intent on connecting with me, a black American, because of what he believed was our mutual lot in life as oppressed people. But his hoped-for bond quickly turned into an impassioned afternoon-long debate—egged on by several cups of the traditional heavily sweetened tea.

The Palestinian was a determined supporter of the jihad, his people's holy war, despite the odds the world powers had stacked against them. He announced to me with great bravado that his son—who was sitting across the room—and his son's sons, if necessary, would continue the war against Israel until they pushed the Jews into the sea and reclaimed his homeland of Palestine.

I pointed out to him that we were living in the twentieth century. And while the Palestinians might contend that they have rightful historical ownership of this land, today it has been developed by others, with paved roads and modern housing and thriving retail establishments—as modern as McDavid's, the Israeli version of McDonald's.

Furthermore, I pointed out to him that my country was giving his enemy F14s, along with every other type of modern fighting artillery. I asked him if he intended to reclaim his homeland, this property developed by others to twentieth-century standards, from the back of a camel.

The days of Lawrence of Arabia are gone, I continued. His jihad was suicide.

I told him he might as well take his boy out back and shoot him right then because the boy would never succeed in getting Israel back the way his father was instructing him.

The only way to fight Israel now is to learn to fight by the rules set by the powerful, I said. I pleaded with him to send his son to the university and teach him to fight with a pen. You have to participate in this battle with a white shirt and an attaché case.

This is the same message I have for the black revolutionaries who think as we rapidly approach the twenty-first century that they are going to hold America hostage for reparations and a separatist state. Do they plan to send their brothers, the African Zulus, after the American Rangers?

It's absurd to believe that the world will slow down to create a level playing field where the least able and least prepared can be comfortable competing. My message to all underdogs is this: Either learn to participate in today's modern world as exemplified by mainstream America or you're out of the game. Struggling against that reality will do little more than temporarily disrupt the business of America.

So my solution for the little black boy who is unprepared for the spelling bee is to teach him to read. Give him the tools he needs to compete. Don't call off the competition and, with it, his inspiration and his only real chance to succeed.

But the liberals who have become the standard-bearers of political correctness and the excuse generation have turned extenuating circumstances, which in the past were seldom even a consideration, into fully acceptable justifications for not assuming any personal responsibility.

As a result, they are turning the prosecution of black thugs arrested for gang-banging into Sociology 101 by offering their never-ending reasons why we shouldn't hold these sociopaths accountable for their dark deeds. The liberals are championing the proposition that we should at least consider the validity of the thugs' phony crusade for social justice. While all the time innocent people, the majority of them black, are being slaughtered on American streets.

But as I said at the beginning of this discussion, the egg-sucking dog liberals have an even more insidious underlying agenda. I call it their War on Prosperity.

I believe that from the perspective of high-minded socialist liberals—the intelligentsia currently led by the Clintons and their inner circle—open competition, the commerce of capitalism, and the success realized by those who adhere to the American Dream are considered harmful to the evolution of mankind as a whole.

I believe the United States—no, on second thought, the entire contemporary Western world—has been surreptitiously maneuvered into divided socioeconomic camps by this new anticapitalist movement. It is a movement that, like others before it, has initiated a ruthless class war for social, economic, and political control. And as in every military operation or political battle, each side—capitalist and socialist alike—has a hearty appetite for fresh troops committed to storming the political citadels in defense of its ideology.

So these egg-sucking dog liberals help the poverty pimps' cause by endorsing the idea that capitalism—i.e., the American system—always works against people of color. This allows the poverty pimps to fuel the human inferno of social unrest that is easy for them to ignite among their sequestered constituency in Dark Town.

And that, in turn, provides highly visible proof, as documented by the evening news, of what happens when people are kept down and out. The liberal socialists are able to unscrupulously use black trash to provide tangible proof of their thesis. They end up giving credibility to the lowly lifestyle of black trash in order to use this sad segment of people as a component in the modern-day propaganda war between the haves and the have-nots.

In return, this entire sequence of events helps to further the political, xenophobic, and—most recently—racist platform put forth by the poverty pimps to their black-trash constituents.

I believe that the poverty pimps and the socialist liberals together, aided by the liberal mainstream media, have managed masterfully to sway many American people into swallowing yet another myth. This is the myth that capitalism in and of itself is a racist structure and that it is diabolically unfair to black people in America.

In my opinion this makes these egg-sucking dog liberals as anti-American, as philosophically opposed to the American way, as the indoctrinated black trash. Both groups are in complete opposition to our American system built on the American Dream and the rewards of success.

Ironically, this forces the liberals to stand in total opposition to everything they claim to represent. They say they want minorities to be assimilated into mainstream America, but their true agenda is to redistribute the wealth. So when a black American does get ahead—when he becomes successful by pursuing the American Dream—he becomes a problem for the liberals. He is one less downtrodden African American they can point to as an example of the failure of the system they are trying to remake.

Historically, just about every group of people in America today has been down and out at one time or another. But rather than try to incite a revolution, they have used the incentive and the promise of the American Dream to spur them on.

Capitalism and competition are the engines that drive the American Dream. They offer hope to all people for personal success and rewards, even in the face of adversity.

In the early 1980s in America, an economic downturn signaled the first phase of the massive shift from the industrial to the technological age. Americans were uprooted. They migrated in search of jobs from the Rust Belt in the Midwest and Northeast to the Sun Belt in the West, Southwest, and Southeast.

Like the characters in *The Grapes of Wrath*, by John Steinbeck, they moved across the country, camping from the backs of trucks and cars and sleeping in parking lots.

I remember them because when they came through Denver living in those trucks and vans, sometimes they were arrested for leaving their kids unattended in the car too long.

In a place called Clear Creek Canyon in the foothills just outside Denver, officials put signs up limiting the time a vehicle could park in one place to discourage squatters.

The media decried the fact that American families were being displaced. The headlines read that autoworkers from Michigan, steelworkers from Pittsburgh—all the men and women who had vested their lives in the industrial dreams of America—now had become the victims of corporate greed. They were being turned out as America's sluggish industrial giants made the transition to technology in order to compete, in order to survive themselves.

But there was no call for revolution. There was no call for the heads of politicians to roll. No Major MacArthur had to lead troops through any shantytown or city to disperse an angry majority of Americans.

These Americans accepted the loss of their homes in Connecticut and traveled to Colorado. They went from Ohio to Phoenix and from Michigan and Wisconsin to California bolstered by one common denominator: *hope*. They had hope. They had hope in America. They had hope that tomorrow would be a brighter day.

The revolution raged only on CBS and on the front page of the *New York Times*. It did not rage among the American people.

And remember, I'm not talking about a minority of American people. I'm talking about a majority of American people. I'm talking about average white, black, and brown middle-class Americans. They lost their jobs. They had no choice but to give up their homes. They sold their Winnebagos and their snowmobiles. They put all of their remaining possessions into the back of trucks or vans, and they followed the rumors: "Hey, did you hear? They're hiring in Raleigh-Durham," or "I think there's work down in Dallas."

When the greater population—America's mainstream population, the people who have the most vested in the American Dream—continues to push ahead following the path and the spirit of the Oregon Trail, it's clear that it's not that easy to start a revolution in America. It's clear that there is a force at work in this country, molded into the American system, that makes it very hard to duplicate the Russian Revolution here. It's the spirit that repeatedly has driven a rainbow coalition of American people to keep the faith and struggle for a better life.

When you're a liberal socialist, that's bad news. Because it's very difficult to bring about a revolution to remake America with a proletariat who have faith in their political system, belief in their country, and hope for their future.

So, as insidious and unthinkable as it may seem, I believe the egg-sucking dog liberals have allowed some very sad people, who happen to look like me, to be cultured the way you would culture a rare breed of turnip greens or sweet corn. They have allowed these people to culture in a state of poverty and dependency. Black trash are being used as pawns in a massive ideological war instituted by the egg-sucking dog liberals and aided by their lieutenants, the black poverty pimps.

All because these liberals need proof that America doesn't work.

If you listen to my radio show, you know that I put liberalism first and cancer second when ranking the scourges that threaten humanity. I might add that I lost both of my parents to cancer.

. . . .

In October of 1995, I participated in the celebration of the 75th anniversary of the first commercial radio broadcast by sitting on a panel at the Museum of Television & Radio in Midtown Manhattan.

Our session was entitled "Talk Radio's Other Voices." We panelists were described as "alternative voices" in the world of talk radio, which the organizers said was "thought of as a bastion of conservative white males." That description alone should have been enough to make me wary.

But as frequently has happened to me on panels, it wasn't until I got there that I realized I was the token conservative. In this case, I found myself doing combat primarily with egg-sucking dog liberal defenders of and hosts on National Public Radio. Along with a lot of other whining, they were crying about their shrinking audiences. Little did it occur to them that they might be out of step with the American public, who thus were tuning them out.

Based on the following sampling of e-mail after the event, I guess I managed to hold my own. . . .

● ● ● ●

I want to congratulate you for your contribution to the October 26 panel discussion on Diversity and Talk Radio. I was channel-flipping on November 4 and started watching that discussion on C-Span out of idle curiosity. I was about to doze off when you started speaking up, and I enjoyed your opinions so much I laughed, applauded, and stayed on the edge of my seat for the rest of the show. You made that show work, so much so that I stuck around to watch it again when C-Span replayed it two hours later.

It's about time somebody started poking holes in those overinflated, hot-air balloons at NPR. I have never heard such smug, self-important, self-serving conceit in my life as what I heard those insufferable phonies on that panel exhibit. Their procedure of "not offering an opinion" and "hearing all sides" is typical of the standard moral relativism of the day that is rapidly becoming nihilism. They'll accept any opinion—as long as it isn't conservative, of course. What's worse is that our tax dollars are subsidizing their arid hyperbole; their salaries are just another form of welfare. They talk about topics that nobody cares about, and then have the gall to state that they are performing a public service!

I'm reminded that throughout history, so many arrogant dictators with delusions of grandeur erected monuments to themselves in various countries, at great public expense. NPR appears to be yet another monument for the latest crop of elitists. Their message is: "I'm so much better than the rest of you, I shouldn't have to sully my aristocratic hands by actually working for a living! I shouldn't have to sell myself to others," which is what *working really is. These people deserve to have their funding zeroed out; we have a $5 trillion debt and can hardly afford their private little country club at taxpayer expense. If they can't survive in a free market, why should they be on the dole at all?*

VIA MAIL 11/29/95
V.C.,
BURLINGTON, VT

. . . .

I just got through watching you on C-Span, it was a typical group. Six liberals to one conservative. The people from Public Radio were their usual arrogant selves, denying they are liberal.
All of them declaring that they are above opinion.
I was impressed at the way you handled yourself. It is clear that you came from a rough neighborhood.

VIA E-MAIL 11/6/95
K.D.,
SAN JOSE, CA

. . . .

Hi Ken—
I saw the program you were on with those other "talk show" folks. Like she said, YOU set the tone for the whole program. What she refused to realize is that you were flying the conservative position solo. You had to set the agenda, or be walked on by those charity cases that call themselves professionals!
It was great! It was like you turned on the lights and all those little bugs scattered and ran for cover. They couldn't deal with it!
I appreciate that you were NOT interested in their approval, but went anyway. You are truly one of the growing number of gladiators on the air. Keep on truckin'. A fellow rider.

VIA E-MAIL 11/6/95
K.K.

. . . .

Below is an E-Mail I sent to Diane Rehm. I watched with pride your "one man against the army" defense of commercial talk radio in the face of typical Public Broadcasting left vs. right opinion odds. You are one of my champions and thank God for you.

Diane,

I was saddened but not surprised to see reactions by you and your fellow talk radio friends to Ken Hamblin. Mr. Hamblin does not hide his political moorings. He relies on reason and does not base his views on emotional convictions. And Mr. Hamblin refuses to resort to personal insults when debating.

Unfortunately, these traits are not found in most liberals, (as was) glaringly apparent in you and Larry Josephson on this program. The fact is Public Radio/TV is heavily monopolized by people who refuse to admit they are left of center and refuse or are unable to use logic in lieu of emotion when forming their views. And when confronted in a discussion or debate setting, liberal ideology breaks and is too often replaced by personal attacks, insulting remarks, and outright lying. Your belief that Public Broadcasting should not go away is admirable.

If taxpayers were not forced to keep you afloat, why would not your programs survive in a commercial market if they are so needed and popular?

The answer is they would not survive in a commercial setting because most people do not want to support them. The reason is most people do NOT AGREE with liberal agendas in 1995. And we sheep of America CAN and DO think for ourselves and that is why Ken Hamblin is right when he talks.

It just so happens that commercial talk shows, primarily conservative shows, thrive because their voices behind the microphones AGREE with the way Americans think!

VIA E-MAIL 11/6/95
R.H.,
DALLAS

Chapter Ten

The Liberal Void

. . . .

Avenger, To hear your granddaughter singing "America" was a high-proof emotional cocktail. It was great to hear at least one young person who is being raised to revere this nation (we never hear about the kids like her on the news), and also great to hear that song. It was also depressing, in a way, because it seemed to emphasize the number of times and places that we DON'T hear those great old patriotic songs. Our next generation is growing up without the patriotic "glue" that has enabled this nation to stick together for the last 219 years, and that scares me. . . . Keep up the good fight! (Somebody has to!), and keep the faith. Many thanks for your words and ideas!

VIA E-MAIL 12/12/95
S.S.

. . . .

I'm just a white Christian radio broadcaster who doesn't usually hear your program because I have to do my own, but this week on vacation I had occasion to hear your broadcasts on WTDY in Madison, Wisconsin. Thanks for a breath of fresh air in a rather liberal market. . . . I'm sick of being PC all the time, but as a non-commercial (but not "public") broadcaster I work for a company that worries about offending too many contributors . . . so I

have to be very careful not to tread over sensitive areas. I consider you fortu-
nate to be able to express yourself to the extent that the First Amendment
privilege allows. Keep up the good work.

VIA E-MAIL 10/28/95
MUZZLED IN MAD CITY

Oh, say, can you see
by the dawn's early light,
What so proudly we hailed at the twilight's last gleaming?
Whose broad stripes and bright stars,
Through the perilous fight,
O'er the ramparts we watched
were so gallantly streaming?
And the rockets' red glare,
the bombs bursting in air,
Gave proof through the night
That our flag was still there.
Oh say does that star spangled banner yet wave
O'er the land of the free and the home of the brave?

—*Francis Scott Key*

Several years ago I decided to open my radio program every day by playing this country's national anthem. I did so because I was exasperated when I learned that most kids in America no longer start their school day with the pledge of allegiance.

I did it because I am truly proud to be an American, and I wanted to counteract what I perceived to be a slow and insidious decay of patriotism along with the basic values of this country. I wanted to celebrate the good fortune of my accident of birth.

For a brief moment I considered whether playing the anthem bordered on the theatrical. But I decided I was willing to suffer the slings and arrows that would fly, the accusations of being overly dramatic or of pandering, in order to demonstrate my love for America.

In the end, the immediate and overwhelmingly positive response from my listeners wiped out the few doubts I had entertained. Clearly I had tapped into a deep reservoir of patriotism among Americans who were looking for a place where they could join openly with a group of fellow citizens to express their love for their country and to honor it.

Before long I started getting tapes of homespun renditions of the anthem sung by people from all over America. One of the most memorable, which we continue to use from time to time to open the show, was by little Matison Brooke Jensen, only three and a half years old, from Chandler, Arizona.

Her parents, Peggy and Larry Jensen, enclosed a note with the tape: "Our nine-year-old daughter was taught the national anthem by listening to the beginning of your show. Yes, she goes to a public school and they don't teach patriotism anymore. Our three-and-a-half-year-old picked up on the anthem and gets really excited every day when you play it on your show. (She calls it 'her song.')"

Matison's tape was bested only when my own four-year-old granddaughter presented me with a fifty-fifth-birthday present—a recording of her singing "America the Beautiful," which of course I play frequently on the show.

Over the last few years we've received a wide variety of renditions of the anthem from groups and individuals, some awe-inspiring and some not so—but heartfelt nonetheless.

Harold Leake, of Taylors, South Carolina, became a local celebrity when we played his taped anthem. His picture—Gibson steel-string acoustic guitar and all—appeared with a story about his debut on my show in his local newspaper, the *Greenville News*.

Leake was quoted in the article: "Not many shows I know of start with 'The Star-Spangled Banner.' It fanned the flame of patriotism in me."

Same for Krissy Swinfold, a junior high school student from Jackson, Missouri. The *Jackson U.S.A. Signal* carried a headline that her anthem rendition was "featured on nationally syndicated show."

I've gotten more than a hundred tapes of "Oh, Say, Can You See?" including one from a Bedford, Virginia, Elks Club chorus accompanied by a ninety-four-year-old pianist; an arrangement played on a steel pan, especially heartwarming for this West Indian boy; one sung by a hula teacher in Hawaii; and a version played on a Hammond organ by an "unassuming blind guy, seventy years old."

Pam Meline from Chico, California, was the only one to write and proudly challenge my assumption about the lack of patriotism in schools today:

> A short while ago you made a statement that schools do not teach or sing patriotic songs anymore. Blanket statements almost always cause problems.
> Not only do my children say the pledge of allegiance every morning in their public school, Citrus Elementary, but two of my children also sing one of the patriotic songs following the flag salute every morning.
> The tape I am sending you is my son Brent's combination second and third grade class singing the Star-Spangled Banner.

I believe the particularly enthusiastic response from across America to *The Ken Hamblin Show* playing the national anthem is a reaction to the liberal ideology of political correctness, which has sanitized many of the rich cultural values from our country's daily life in the name of multiculturalism and in the name of secularism. Along with those cleansings, political correctness has, for all practical purposes, repudiated pride in the U.S.A.

Personally, I seldom observe the rules of political correctness. But I admit that it most likely was the reason I pondered, if even for only a moment, whether I should play the anthem.

Political correctness is a powerful, ever-present force in American society today, and I contend that it is leaving a dangerous cultural void in this country's value system. It is leaving a dangerous void in our heritage.

I call the void dangerous because there are no empty spaces in nature. You can fill a space with wood; you can fill it with water; you can fill it with sand; you can fill it with dirt. But there is no true empty space. The space you may think is empty is filled with molecules.

So when we leave an empty space by failing to begin each school day by pledging allegiance to the flag, we run the risk of filling the void—in practical terms, we run the risk of filling our children—with doctrines of hate like those promoted by rap music icons who have grown out of the black welfare culture.

These rappers—like 2 Live Crew, Snoop Doggy Dogg, Sister Souljah, and NWA (Niggers With Attitude)—preach hatred of America, hatred of women, hatred of white people, hatred of cops, hatred of any symbol of authority. When we fail to lay the foundation for strong positive beliefs about America, about women, about the opportunities available to people of all races, and about respect for legitimate authority, the door opens for this hatred and negativity to fill the void.

In addition to patriotism, I believe religion is another integral American value being looted by liberalism. In their supposed efforts to be fair and to provide equal status to all faiths, liberals have made it uncomfortable to proclaim any religious belief openly.

By failing to support the virtue of a strong religious base, we leave another critical void and run the risk of filling it with a very ugly replacement.

I am not a born-again Christian; I am a lapsed Catholic. The religious base I am talking about is a basic faith or belief in God. I'm talking about core religious teachings about right and wrong.

It doesn't matter what the particular religion is. It doesn't matter whether you attend a synagogue, whether you are a Reformed Baptist or a Southern Baptist, whether you're a Mormon or a Presbyterian. As long as you fill that space where human values reside with the sense that there is something more potent and more profound than you are, then at least there is a moral foundation to ward off the evil which is omnipresent, always there to rush in and fill the void.

I believe people like Pat Robertson and Pat Buchanan, who are painted as religious fanatics by liberals, represent much lesser threats to this country than the threat we face if we continue to deny religion and patriotism, and if we allow the ensuing void to be filled by hate.

I simply refuse to be pressured by egg-sucking dog liberals and quota blacks into believing that when the pendulum swings back to the Right from the sanitized territory on the Far Left, where the liberals have taken us, we will return to the old hate-filled world run exclusively by wealthy white men.

It is absurd to fear that Pat Buchanan, if he were miraculously to move into the White House tomorrow, could take away all the civil rights we have fought for and won as black Americans. Constitutional amendments, laws on the books, and the moral will of the people are established. Principled Americans, who I contend make up the majority of this country, would not permit that regression.

My position is that these feared right-wing extremists are connecting with mainstream America—at a time when the federal government is out of touch—more because they are speaking to the values we all would like to bring back into American life than because they are pandering to the lowest common denominators of hate and bigotry among us.

And thus I would rather condone them—given the laws we have in place to stop an extreme pendulum swing to the Right—than continue to condone black thugs like the Crips and the Bloods, whom we indulge with a liberal permissiveness that I consider to be the twin social disease to political correctness.

I hold liberal permissiveness responsible for our decaying American society right along with political correctness. And like political correctness, I believe this permissiveness is rooted in the way we address the black-trash welfare culture.

The black thugs of my youth, like Dice, have been allowed to multiply because a good many Americans have been persuaded to believe that kids become gang members only because they are disadvantaged due to their dark skin. They have been convinced that poverty causes crime. For fear of being pegged as racists, they have refused to challenge the Myth of the Hobbled Black.

And so the black thugs are given every benefit of the doubt. As a result, they have spread like crabgrass on a fine lawn—the lawn in this case being America. It's to the point now that white kids emulate them, hanging out in suburban shopping malls.

These rudderless children, both black and white, have established a culture of their own to fill the void left because America hasn't insisted that they be taught right from wrong or held accountable for their actions.

We have not conditioned these young people to believe that they have an obligation to the greater whole. We are allowing them to grow up believing that nothing of worth came before them. We are allowing them to grow up indifferent to God and to country.

In a very slow but relentless manner, like kudzu smothering a country road, this lack of foundation and the resulting void are causing the very pillars of American civilization to crumble.

The decay that started in Dark Town—in the South Bronx and in Bedford-Stuyvesant, in the bowels of Detroit and of Washington, D.C.—is only the leading edge. The trailing edge is spilling into communities like Omaha, Nebraska, and Davenport, Iowa—into little burgs all across the plains of America.

Unbridled permissiveness, like political correctness, is consuming America. And both of these unchecked, perverted social forces are allowing the perpetrators of America's social decay to grow bolder and more brazen.

The result is that our American culture is seriously backsliding into a hellish abyss.

Rampant street crime is perhaps the most visible evidence of social decay stemming from the black-trash welfare culture that is spreading into mainstream America.

Few Americans today would deny that crime is out of control.

National crime statistics can be and are manipulated on a regular basis to show both increases and decreases to suit particular political purposes. But any analysis shows that, as is true of most of the other social decay in America, crime in Dark Town occurs at a disproportionately higher rate than in the rest of the country.

The random, senseless nature of much of this crime, however, presents the very real prospect that unless contained this epidemic eventually will reach out and touch every American of every race in one way or another.

Already, honest, taxpaying Americans can't use their own urban parks and city streets without concern for their safety.

We have lost core downtown areas of once grand cities like Philadelphia, Detroit, Chicago, Washington, D.C., New York City, and Los Angeles as well as any number of great American cities in between.

Liberalism has turned many American neighborhoods into gated, walled citadels designed to hold back the growing barbarism and debauchery.

I am not suggesting for a moment that the black thugs will be permitted to totally destroy America. Before we let that happen, we'll bring in fully armed Cobra gunships to draw the line. But in the interim many more exit ramps on city expressways are closing to you and to me. More and more sections of our cities are becoming off-limits because of the street thugs who rule them. Even the least streetwise among us know where they can and cannot go.

I have suggested on my radio show that city residents should get tax exemptions based on the percentage of their city that is off-limits to them. The current situation is tantamount to taxation without representation.

Think about it. Ask yourself how many places in your city you can't go because you'd be putting yourself in harm's way for the simple reason that your skin is white. If you are black, ask yourself where you can go in Dark Town without causing a ruckus if you're dressed in a suit and tie.

Remember my stroll with CBS into Denver's Dark Town? And remember the thug Michael Asberry implying from under his hood that I wasn't dressed for his community?

My detractors say that I'm insensitive, apathetic, indifferent, slick, sly, corrupt, and that I'm just saying all of these things for a buck. Don't buy it.

I'm angry. I am not just trying to entertain to get high ratings on the radio. I am legitimately angry and passionate about the fact that American women can no longer promenade in city parks on hot summer nights the way they once could.

I'm angry that we have become a nation where you can be told that your Camaro, your Mercedes, your Honda, your Ford pickup truck, your Chevy van, isn't worth dying for.

Americans are not fools. Of course we know a Chevy isn't worth dying for. But do you know what the liberals never take into account while they're conditioning us to passivity in the wake of rising crime rates? When we get into our motorcars, we put our Day-Timers down on the seat. Women put their purses down. We set our attaché cases on the floor. So when we are forced to give up our car, we give up not just the car but also the keys and the address to our house. We give up the safeguards we have in place to protect ourselves and our families. We give up the sanctity of our homes.

The liberals never talk about that part of it. They just tell people like you and me that we shouldn't be so selfish and materialistic in light of the bigger human issues relating to our carjacking. They tell people like you and me — law-abiding, taxpaying citizens — that we should show more understanding and compassion for the criminals. They tell us we must consider the reasons why violent and senseless crime is growing in this country.

They tell us tales from the Myth of the Hobbled Black.

Justifying these heinous crimes that alter our lifestyle is only the beginning of the attempted brainwashing we get in political correctness and liberal permissiveness.

The real tearjerkers are spun in the courtroom when we have the thugs in tow. The princes of Dark Town get cleaned up and put on display while testimony is dredged up from family members or social workers who speak of the thugs' terrible lot in life.

I don't doubt that there's some truth to the testimony. The thugs' lot in life is terrible—from coming up on welfare to being cheated out of an education to usually having poor role models for parents. What I object to is that the testimony inevitably concludes that "he's really a good boy."

No, he is not a good boy. He is a criminal who needs to be punished for his crimes.

By failing to establish what's right and what's wrong even when we get ahold of them after they've broken the law, we are perpetuating lives that are completely devoid of values. We send the message that our values of right and wrong are bogus because we will never hold these guys accountable to these standards. And their homeys who are still out there on the street get our message loud and clear.

When we make excuses for their fratricide, for their cold-blooded murders, and for the utter mayhem they have inflicted on civilized mainstream American society, we are contributing to the sad fact that most of these thugs attach little if any value to human life.

That devaluation of life is reinforced by an increasing number of liberal district attorneys across America, like Bill Ritter in Denver and Robert T. Johnson in the Bronx, who publicly confess their moral opposition to the death penalty. Coincidentally, of course, they seldom, if ever, have sought the penalty on behalf of the people.

The D.A.'s are matched by liberal judges who have created a revolving door through our justice system akin to the one illegal aliens use when they get picked up while sneaking across our southern border and transported back to Mexico, only to come right back across the line the same night.

Liberal, lenient judges keep that revolving door swinging throughout today's American justice system.

The rulings by these lenient judges usually are not given much attention by anyone other than the victims and the victims' next of kin until the thug they let out commits another crime.

One Denver judge's ruling in 1995 made me and a lot of Denver cops pretty irritated at the time she made it, however.

The thug in question was none other than Michael Asberry.

He pleaded guilty before Denver District Judge Lynne Hufnagel to a charge of assaulting a police officer during a traffic stop. The officer testified in court that Asberry had spat on him, kicked him, and knocked out a window in his patrol car. A letter from the same officer to the judge recounted how Asberry had threatened to kill him, harm his family, and rape the four-year-old daughter of a fellow police officer.

Based on Asberry's long career as a menace to society, beginning when he allegedly imported the Crips street gang to Denver from L.A., the prosecuting attorney in the case asked the judge to give him the maximum sentence of six years in jail.

But Judge Hufnagel, after hearing testimony from the usual parade of social-worker stooges, who said Asberry was just mad because he was constantly harassed by police because of his onetime gang affiliation, agreed to grant him probation—on the condition that he leave town.

And where did he promise to go? Back to Compton, California, the primal breeding ground of the Crips, purportedly to help poor ghetto kids.

These kinds of liberal realities in our court system have allowed the street thugs to manipulate American justice to their advantage. If they do go to jail, the sentence is looked upon as a badge of honor—as are the crimes of stealing the cars and killing the drivers.

American kids are getting dumber at a rate that I would be willing to bet is parallel to the speed with which schools have abandoned the standards of scholastic excellence and discipline.

Not only are our young people not being grounded in patriotism at the start of their school day, but they also are failing to get a foundation in academics once the school day begins. I'm talking about the old-fashioned three R's—reading, writing, and arithmetic—not multicultural studies.

Like crime rates, school test scores are manipulated to suit particular political agendas. But in general, the test scores of black students are consistently lower than those of white students.

I don't believe this means that black students are inherently less capable mentally. I think the black group scores are pulled down by students from the black-trash welfare culture who are not encouraged to seek an education as a ticket to get ahead in life and who are deprived of any learning activity at home.

A study for the Department of Health and Human Services conducted by Child Trends, Inc., a Washington, D.C., nonprofit organization, was reported by the *New York Times* in early 1996. It concluded that a group of young black children whose families were on welfare generally are already behind in their learning skills even before they start school.

In a test with questions about shapes, colors, and relationships like "under" and "behind," these youngsters from three to five years old got the answers right only about half of the time.

To make matters worse, when these kids get to school, the Phil Donahue syndrome—the idea that eliminates the concept of "best" students in order to avoid making other students feel they are "second best"—kicks in. As a result, rather than demanding that even the poorest students meet the old minimum standards of excellence, we cite their poor performance as a reason to lower the requirements for the entire classroom. Over time, this erosion of standards has caused the proficiency of all American students to decline.

The liberals refuse to take any responsibility for the fact that many of our kids are coming out of today's public education system effectively unable to read and write.

They call me an Uncle Tom for saying that the administrators and the teachers in the public school system—including a fair number of affirmative action hires—should and must be held accountable for the failure of their students.

If I had a magic wand, I would tackle this problem like all the others I see—at its root. I would fire all the public school teachers on Monday. On Tuesday I would invite them back to take a test to measure their skills—basic skills we should demand that our students be taught, like reading, writing, and arithmetic so they would be prepared to be competitive in America. On Wednesday I would rehire only the teachers who had passed the test.

With my magic wand, there wouldn't be any discussion about whether the test was racially biased.

But the lowering of standards for teachers and students isn't the only negative influence liberals have had on American education.

I remember going into a school in Michigan to shoot footage for a film I was producing in the early 1970s and being shocked when I saw the "open classroom" concept in action. This early liberal tinkering with the institution of education was based on the premise that students should have the freedom to decide what interests them and then study those particular interests. The open classroom got its name from the physical design of the classroom, which was built without walls to encourage students to get up and to wander around—looking for something to study, I guess.

What I observed that day in Michigan was a far cry from the creativity it was supposed to encourage in the children. I saw chaos and anarchy.

Today I realize that concepts like the open classroom and the Phil Donahue syndrome have culminated in the current scholastic atrocity known as outcome-based education.

But at the time, I guess I subconsciously wrote off most of my concerns, suspecting that it was old-fashioned and inflexible of me to expect a school with rules, like the one I remembered.

Which brings up the issue of school discipline, a topic that for me used to conjure up memories of Catholic sisters cracking rulers over the knuckles of students who had misbehaved.

Today not only is corporal punishment of any kind forbidden in most schools, but the tables have turned completely. Students are talking back to their teachers. There even are reports of students assaulting their teachers physically.

Like the thugs who know the ins and outs of the justice system, these bad boys and girls in school know their legal rights, including the limits to which teachers can go when it comes to discipline.

I have talked to teachers on my radio show who are afraid to go to work, afraid of the students for whom they are supposed to be the ultimate daytime authority figures.

I am convinced that this decay in our once-esteemed system of education—at one time believed to be the hope of every American looking to better himself or herself—is emanating from the violent physical world of Dark Town.

I laid out my tongue-in-cheek—but maybe not so far-fetched—solution to the school discipline problem in a *Denver Post* column I wrote in 1990.

After consulting with numerous teachers who confirmed for me that the biggest impediments to a productive classroom are disruptive students and their apathetic parents, I proposed that the disorderly students be tossed out.

"But where would the sorely misunderstood troublemakers go?" was the typical coddling liberal response.

What should we care if they are prohibiting the well-behaved students from getting an education? I thought. But I knew that glib answer would bring a gasp of amazement.

So in the end, I proposed that adult volunteers in a given school district should band together to form a Good Riddance Squad. This GRS squad would be on call throughout the school day to retrieve expelled students from the principal's office and deliver them to their parents—at home or at their place of work.

I even listed infractions that might send a student packing with the GRS: incomplete homework assignments, insubordination to a teacher, fighting in class or on school grounds, theft, gang activity, violation of clothing or hygiene codes, drug use, and any other unnamed disruption of school business.

I believe my tongue-in-cheek GRS proposal got to the heart of the matter—parents being forced to take responsibility for their offspring. And I got a slew of mail like the following applauding the concept:

● ● ● ●

I'm 61 years old. When I was in school you did not remain there if you could not behave. Your Good Riddance Squad (GRS) is the best idea I have heard in years. So many young people want a good education but find it hard when a few disrupt the class. . . . I for one would be a volunteer.

VIA MAIL 10/23/90
B.L.,
DENVER

• • • •

Dear Mr. Hamblin:

AMEN! AMEN! AMEN! Your article ("Two Words For Bad Pupils: 'Good Riddance' . . ." October 23) made those who are ultimately responsible for the behavior of their children accountable. Too bad the GRS won't very likely become a reality.

Isn't it truly amazing how well American parents obey their children? I am dumbfounded at the total state of "helplessness" of the modern day parent. For example, I witnessed a mother sitting on a curb outside a McDonald's weeping while her 3 year old son misbehaved. Between sobs she said how she wished he would just be nice to her!

Unfortunately, "helpless" parents are fast becoming a majority. Their children threaten to destroy every fiber of our educational system. Perhaps these parents are content to allow the problem to rest on the shoulders of teachers and education. But eventually these mismanaged, uncontrolled monsters will enter the workplace . . . Imagine that? Thank you. Your article did this soul good.

VIA MAIL 10/23/90
K.R.,
LAKEWOOD, CO

The next letter astounded me. The author, a teacher, obviously was identifying the precise problem: the negative impact of the black-trash welfare culture on our educational system. But I'm pretty sure he had a much different take on this reality than I did. His reasoning represents to me the epitome of convoluted liberalism eating away at the pillars of American education.

• • • •

There are two obstacles to removing children from schools. The first is due process. Every child in this state is entitled, by law, to an "appropriate" education. Thus to remove a student from the classroom opens the school up to law suits and other legal actions. . . . The second problem are charges of racism. Schools are institutions with white, middle class values. (Even those minorities who become involved in schools seem to adopt the middle class values of the school.) The value of learning is placed over everything, aggression is to be channeled and not to be displayed toward others, backtalk from children is not to be tolerated, and hard work has its reward. These are not always the values taught by some minority groups. As Shirley Brice Heath points out, in Ways with Words, *among some black groups boys are socialized to be aggressive. Thus your argument takes a white, racist point of view. You seem to say that those who have not been brought up to be nice, middle class, white kids should be removed from school. If your program were adopted, the people who would be hurt the most would be minorities, especially blacks. Like it or not these kids get into more fights, talk back to teachers more, etc. than anglo kids. I remember a conversation that I had with a colleague who had been transferred to a mostly black school. She was dismayed at the noise, the attitudes, and the fighting that went on among the students. When I pointed out that much of what she said sounded racist, she paused for a minute and then admitted that maybe it did, "but these kids are so different from anyone else I've ever taught."*

In conclusion, I do not think that teachers are the ones who want to keep discipline kids in their classrooms or schools. We want kids who we can teach. However, removing kids from school has become entangled with issues of due process and racism. . . . In the end the question that the courts and the school administrator will ask is "is it in the best interest of the child," not "what is best for the system."

VIA MAIL 10/25/90
B.C.,
AURORA, CO

The bottom line to the education crisis in America is that we have young people just out of college applying for entry-level jobs in the business world who cannot write or speak effectively. Turning these ill-equipped kids out into the job market is one more dramatic aspect of the social decay in America.

Once again the worst-case examples are the young black trash out of Dark Town who are among the most unskilled, uneducated, and uncivilized in the potential labor pool. Yet they arrogantly proclaim that they "ain't gonna' take a job flippin' no burgers." They contend that these minimum-wage entry-level jobs in the fast-food industry are beneath them.

But the fact is that companies like McDonald's Corporation and thousands of other employers have had to institute their own intensive on-the-job-training programs to bring even their entry-level employees up to a level of usefulness on the job.

Even in the fast-food industry, where starting wages are indeed minimal, the American Dream is achievable, however. In the summer of 1995 the *New York Times* reported the story of three Mexican immigrants who took jobs "flippin' burgers" for the minimum wage of $4.25 an hour. They were unskilled, and reportedly they spoke little English in the beginning. But they took advantage of "Hamburger U"—McDonald's extensive training program—and all three became McDonald's managers making $25,000 to $45,000 annually.

The difference between them and the black trash who complain there are no jobs for them is that these immigrants believed in the American Dream and followed up their belief with a can-do attitude—what we used to call a good work ethic.

The loss of that work ethic is another sign of decay in the American social system, and I personally can vouch for the fact that signs of this decay have spread beyond Dark Town.

Since the early 1990s I have been hiring young suburban kids for my own sub sandwich restaurants. For the most part they are unkempt in their appearance, uncivil to my customers, and reluctant to work beyond a slothlike pace behind the counter.

The general attitude of most of these children bred under the rule of liberal permissiveness is the following: "You, Mr. Store Owner, you must be so rich. You should gimme more money, some time off, a ride on your motorcycle, your season tickets to the Bronco games, a weekend in your mountain house. . . ."

There is absolutely no correlation in their minds between hard work and those rewards. They have adopted completely the socialist premise of something for nothing.

The social decay brought about by the liberal void and rooted in the black-trash welfare culture is turning out a less smart, less motivated, less competitive American workforce. Unfortunately, at the same time we are moving into a world of technological work that values brains, not brawn. We are experiencing the only logical consequence: America does not compete as effectively as it once did.

Evidence of the decay in mainstream America is all around us.

It begins with a growing rate of illegitimate births. It continues with lower standards of excellence in our schools. It yields lower productivity in our workforce. All of these are in complete opposition to the tenets of the American Dream.

Yet all of us good Americans—good Americans who still work every day, who still know right from wrong, who still adhere to the American Dream—are paying for more and more people who are living on the dole and campaigning feverishly against our American value system.

We have today's liberals to thank for the fact that people are not held accountable for their actions, that they don't have to live by the fundamental standards of right and wrong today. We can thank the liberals.

They have anesthetized us with politically correct hogwash while they literally steal our country from us.

I lived in Detroit for nine years. Lately I have thought with great sadness about the majestic Detroit Institute of Art, which today stands in a neighborhood fallen to graffiti, which I sarcastically call the art of the proletariat. This once-great urban neighborhood has been reduced to the grayness of boarded-up buildings and streets too unsafe for most to visit.

There is a magnificent mural by Diego Rivera near the grand entryway of the Art Institute. It depicts the assembly line of laborers who built the American auto industry. It symbolizes the American work ethic, which contributed to the strength of a great city and a great country at the height of the industrial age.

But even the artistic portrayal of our great culture, which is embodied in this mural, is kept from most Americans today. It is being held hostage by the surrounding urban decay and the accompanying threat of crime brought about by the liberal policies that have killed Detroit's center city.

In 1993 I was privileged to visit Cuba, where I was permitted to broadcast the first live radio show back to the United States in more than thirty years from Radio Rebelde in Havana. Cuba was the second socialist country I had visited: the first was Nicaragua at the height of its unrest in the mid-1980s.

While I met wonderful people, my trips to both of these socialist countries only confirmed for me that America is a great country, its political and social systems clearly unmatched in the opportunity they offer for all citizens.

One afternoon in Cuba I was invited to take a private tour of the Museo Nacional de Cuba. The government of Cuba was proud to show me its national art treasures, including originals by world-renowned artists such as Picasso and the works of the great Cuban artists throughout history. The curator explained that many of these masterpieces had been confiscated from private homes after the revolution and now were held by the state—for all the Cuban people to enjoy.

But his story and the socialist master plan had a flaw.

I was in Cuba during the "special period," so named by Fidel Castro apparently to imply a temporary period of shortages after the Soviet Union collapsed and withdrew its aid from Cuba. There was little food, little electricity, little gasoline. The country was running for the most part on rum, sugar, bicycles, and a resolutely proud people.

The Cuban art museum had no electricity for air conditioning. The government was able to maintain only about a quarter of the national art treasures on display, and all of the priceless art was in danger of being damaged from the heat and the humidity. The museum infrastructure, from public toilets to lighting, was in a dreadful state of disrepair. The curator confessed the museum was open to the public for only a few hours a week.

I think there is a strong analogy between the Detroit Institute of Art and the Museo Nacional de Cuba. Both hold national treasures in the name of the people. But in the final analysis the repercussions of liberalism and socialism have actually caused those treasures to be withheld from the citizenry.

The average American or Cuban cannot go to see these national treasures. The people have lost access to a part of their heritage.

I am convinced that by condoning the liberal agenda and the dangerous liberal void it creates, we are allowing the corruption of a political and social system unlike any other in the world. Like a lot of Americans who have experienced the rewards of our American system, I believe that by forsaking our values and proven system, we are doing something terribly wrong.

Chapter Eleven

White Backlash

· · · ·

Hello, for starters my father is a huge fan of yours. He listens to you on your show on KFYI. He referred me to you. Anyway, I'm a 19 year old white female, living in Phoenix, AZ. I have some questions I would like you to answer for me. I guess I'm confused, but everytime I watch tv or talk to Black people all I ever hear is "Feel sorry for me." . . . If a white person or any other race did that there would be a problem. Basically what my point is, is that white, Mexicans and other races aren't out to get the blacks; they're out to get us. I feel cheated that I'm looked at like I did something wrong, (slavery is over!).

VIA E-MAIL 1/8/96
A.F.,
PHOENIX

· · · ·

I am a 24 year old boy from Kansas City. I have been listening to your radio program for about one year. First of all I ride a 1969 Triumph Bonneville. I am very concerned about you not wearing your helmet. I agree that there should not be helmet laws, but I still think the smart move is to wear one. . . .
Secondly, I smoke. I respect your right to not smoke but I never dreamed you would be part of the sissy movement in this country. I bet you have a

windshield on your motorcycle. I guess this is because my father whines about smoking and also has a windshield on his Superglide. Take off your sissy windshield and quit wringing your hands about smoking.

The third point I want to tell you is that you are a great inspiration to me. I went to college at a school called Central Missouri State University in Warrensburg, Missouri. We had a lot of problems with black students there. In fact we were on the national news because of the rioting on campus after the Rodney King verdict. I was at those riots. I have never been in a situation before where the police did not have control. It was a very erie feeling.

I got sick and tired of hearing the whining of black students at my college. Whatever they were doing, they were doing it with someone else's money. We had to hire additional campus police to patrol the dorm where most of the black students lived. There were fights and small riots every year I attended there.

I feel like a racist because I think from my own experiences that the very presence of blacks causes a raise in crime and life as the community knows it is over. This deeply disturbs me because I know in my heart that there are more people like you out there. But when I worked during the summer at a mall here in KC, we stopped playing rap music on the sound system and product theft went down 20%. I think that it is a common fallacy that if you dislike the black culture you haven't had enough experience with it. I find this to be the opposite. . . . I can't say these things to just anyone. You are a ray of sunshine in my life right now. I hope you realize that.

VIA MAIL 8/3/95
J.P.,
INDEPENDENCE, MO

• • • •

My brother is an investigator with the Memphis Police Department. Your radio program is a spark of light for he and his colleagues who are trying to survive in an almost hopeless situation. I'm a white university administrator with many black friends, but in my opinion, only blacks have a chance of changing the attitudes of other "poor me" blacks. Keep up the good work!

VIA E-MAIL 12/21/95
P.D.

• • • •

We are a white conservative couple who are very concerned with the way things are going in this country. One of the things that really worries us is the problems between the white and black races. We find that many black

people have become racists toward whites. We understand that this proba-
bly must happen in order to bring the pendulum back to center . . . but we
wish it would happen soon! We feel that there always have been whites
who only want the best for blacks. And we wish black people would stop
blaming us for all their problems. Not only because it isn't right to demon-
ize us—but also because we truly want blacks to take advantage of what
opportunities there are for everyone. We want to see black people get all the
good they can out of life. It would make their great-grandparents proud.
You are a true inspiration. Please keep up the good work and know that
you are one of the pioneers and leaders for your race and ours. I'm sure it's
hard to be a conservative black. But you will help turn around things for
the black people—they will follow you eventually. . . . thanks for your
courage and for giving us hope.

VIA MAIL 7/20/94
T.K. & D.K.,
CAMBRIDGE CITY, IN

• • • •

I find it offensive that African Americans wear T-shirts and charms with the
African continent on them, or pro-black and anti-white slogans.
If whites complain it is racist and they say it's because they are proud of
their heritage, but if whites do anything of the same nature we are racist.
I'm sick of it! I'm only 23 years old, and I'm already ready to move to the
hills in a small cabin to get away from it all. The only thing that has
stopped me is that I'm afraid the FBI may come and smoke me out.

VIA FAX 1/1/94
ANONYMOUS,
GREENVILLE, SOUTH CAROLINA

• • • •

I heard the second hour of today's show (October 4 after OJ verdict). One
man said he was angry now at blacks. What you said gave me a lump in
my throat. I want to say some things to you.
Thank you for being a good neighbor.
Thank you for answering anger with reason and goodwill.
Please continue to urge responsible people of all races to provide the leader-
ship our country needs now.

VIA E-MAIL 10/7/95
S.R.,
PORTLAND

• • • •

OJ Simpson is free, and I hope the multiculturalists are happy. Their sepa-
ratist ideology has infected our judicial system, perhaps beyond repair. It's
official now, we have two systems of justice and here's how they operate.
Black defendants should be freed in order to "send a message" to a corrupt
judicial system. White defendants, especially if they are cops, should be
convicted in order to "send a message" to a corrupt judicial system.
If this seems contradictory, then you need sensitivity training. And of
course the same poisonous multiculturalists who have done so much dam-
age are ready to help you get your thinking straight.
What are we doing to ourselves? The ideal of a society where color does not
matter has been perverted. The media is fawning over OJ and the "dream
team". A murderer is walking free. Deviancy is cranked down another
notch. And as usual, the victims are forgotten.

VIA E-MAIL 10/3/95
C.T.,
WEST PITTSTON, PA

• • • •

When discussing the [Million Man] march, many leaders, black and
white, have tried to defend participation in the march by seeking to sepa-
rate the goals from the principal organizer, Minister Farrakhan. In effect,
they say that the message is valid in spite of the actions or the character of
the messenger. This strikes me as inconsistent, because many of these same
people have defended the jury verdict in the Simpson trial, using the
argument that the message/evidence was tainted by the character of the
messenger, Detective Fuhrman.

VIA E-MAIL 10/18/95
A.L.

Less than a month after Los Angeles police were seen beating Rodney King on the infamous videotape, 58 percent of Los Angeles residents
polled said they did *not* believe that Police Chief Daryl Gates should be dismissed.

I saw measures of public opinion like that one and the subsequent incon-
gruous outcome of the jury trial in which the police were acquitted as the first
signs of a white backlash against the spreading black-trash welfare culture.

Essentially, Rodney King was just a black speeder who resisted arrest. The
tape showed that a clear-cut injustice was perpetrated against him by these
particular police officers.

But obviously to a great many mainstream white citizens of Los Angeles, King represented a growing black criminal element and a threat to their well-being. This majority of Los Angeles citizens opted to support the police, despite a few bad cops, because apparently after considering the alternative, they believed the cops were their only hope of holding the line between them and the black thugs who were overrunning their city.

My commentaries on the 1992 L.A. riot have been misconstrued more than once. Contrary to what my detractors propagandized, I never have condoned the King beating.

But the Rodney King verdict was proof positive to me that every black person in America risks losing the precious ground we have won if we do not stand up against black trash and the spread of its welfare culture, if we do not clearly separate ourselves as moral, hardworking black Americans from our immoral, menacing black brethren.

One reason this backlash threatens all black Americans is that black people are easy to identify.

Think about it. If there were death squads roaming about targeting gay people, gay people could escape into the closet. If there was a pogrom targeting Jews, Jews literally could change their appearance to pass as Gentiles. While these would not be particularly healthy options, they would be options nonetheless, options that black people—people of the Negro race—do not have.

Although black people are as individually distinct as Jews, gays, WASPs, or any other group, we always will stand out as a group because of our black skin. Therefore, some people—unless we tell them otherwise—always will categorize us as one.

And unfortunately the black-trash welfare culture element among us, though it constitutes a numerical minority and is clearly not representative of the ideals or the lifestyle of the majority of black Americans, is the one most frequently seen on television and in the newspapers. Its voice is the one heard most often by mainstream America.

I personally have felt the backlash against this black-trash culture already.

I have sensed an uneasiness in the eyes of more and more strangers whom I happen to pass, particularly white women who avoid making eye contact with me when I jog by them in a city park. I assume they react this way because my skin is black. Rather than being angry at these white people for reacting to a perceived threat emanating from all black people, I feel great personal sorrow for what we mainstream blacks have allowed to happen to us.

More evidence of the existence of this backlash stemming from fear is in the complaint from some black people that they have trouble getting taxis to pick them up in big cities like New York. The honest cabbies admit they do in fact pass most of us by, citing a rash of robberies and killings, usually by black fares, as the reason.

What was once a prudent decision not to take fares to certain neighborhoods has been broadened by some drivers to a decision to eliminate an entire category of fares altogether.

And then there was the other Los Angeles trial that stimulated a white backlash and proved to me without a doubt how much the entire American black population potentially stands to suffer the consequences. It was the 1995 O. J. Simpson murder trial, which ended in a unanimous not guilty verdict by a black-dominated jury.

Once again the L.A. Police Department played a key role. Only this time the jury decided to stand with the "black community" against the police in the name of victimization, as opposed to the white-dominated jury in the Rodney King case, which decided to stand with the police against a "black community" that it feared.

The Simpson jury overlooked all the evidence against O.J. because of the suspicion that Officer Mark Fuhrman, a lead investigator on the murder case, was a white racist and thus might have been motivated to plant some of the evidence.

The defense "dream team" led by African-American lawyer Johnnie Cochran appealed to the jury to disregard its duty to bring justice in the brutal killing of two people. Instead, he urged the predominantly black jury to bring justice for centuries of black oppression. Astonishingly, the jury complied.

Most white Americans—and a good many black Americans, though they characteristically kept a low profile—believed this trial was a blatant assault against the American judicial system. But an extremely vocal element of black Americans appeared on national television newscasts responding to the verdict literally with glee.

Average white American citizens went into shock. They wrote letters to newspaper editors and flooded the phone lines to talk shows like mine. After years of what they had believed was a time of healing and of getting to know black people on a personal, one-on-one level in the office, in the classroom, and in their neighborhoods, many of these white Americans questioned who their newfound friends really were.

One man who called my radio show epitomized my fears concerning the far-reaching effects of a white backlash.

He said that from the moment the Simpson verdict was announced, he had viewed all black people he encountered, whether he passed them on the street, rode with them in elevators, or sat across the office from them, as one and the same—all cut from the same mold as the black jurors who he was convinced harbored a deep-seated hatred of white people.

His voice quavered when he told me that on that day, though he was embarrassed about his feelings, he had to honestly say that he hated all black Americans.

With this man still on the phone line, I read a fax sent to my show from another listener: "Dear Ken, after seeing the blacks' celebration after O.J.'s verdict, I now think the white race should STAND! And finally exterminate the black race once and for all. If the black race wants a war then let's rumble! We need to take a stand now—in the names of Nicole Brown and Ronald Goldman. We outnumber blacks 88 percent to 12 percent. You blacks want it? LET'S DO IT!"

When I finished reading this diatribe from B.C. of Roanoke, Virginia, I asked the caller whether his hatred had reached the level of this vitriolic call for action.

It didn't surprise me when he responded quietly and sadly that it had not.

The great majority of Americans are good people, people of integrity who carry with them a strong sense of right and wrong. We black Americans who also adhere to basic American principles must identify ourselves. We need to align ourselves with the good folks of America in the name of our common ground of principle. We must stop aligning ourselves with any and every group of black people in the name of a brotherhood based solely on color.

We, and only we, can halt this broadside backlash against us.

I wrote these words in my *Denver Post* column the Sunday after the O.J. verdict: "Today the time is at hand for ethical persons of color to disconnect and dissociate from the notion that, as a consequence of race, they are obligated to stand by the disenchanted African Americans who, in spite of the progress we have achieved in this nation, prefer instead to languish at the emotional trough of racial despair."

I received this letter a few days later:

> *I've worked all my professional life—21 years—in human service programs, championing the cause of those who needed help regardless of who they were or where they came from or what color they were.*
> *Handling "this verdict" has been the hardest thing I've ever had to do philosophically. As one born and raised a liberal democrat, new frontier baby boomer, I felt betrayed.*
> *Your words [in the* Denver Post*] helped immeasurably. You've bridged the great divide that seemed to appear last Tuesday between blacks and whites. There is oneness in the human race. And you emphasized that [when you wrote] "all ethical persons of color."*
>
> D.C.,
> BOULDER, CO

I received dozens of faxes and e-mail messages like the following reactions to the O.J. verdict. To me, they were evidence of the fundamental virtue of American people and their willingness, even their desire, to be discerning if only black Americans would stand up for what's right.

This morning I was so fed up after the verdict . . . that I was feeling the first stirrings of racism. . . . Listening to you I realize that it is a case of them against us, but the "us" consists of all decent-minded people regardless of their race and the "them" are the ignorant malcontents who blame everyone else for their misfortunes.

FAXED FROM CALIFORNIA

• • • •

I was driving through the Jacksonville [Florida] radio area the day after the OJ acquittal, and heard this conservative radio commentator. This guy was saying the same thing my wife and I and our Scottish visitors were thinking.
I had listened to hate mongers like Johnny Cockroach [sic] and his band of liers [sic], with his bodyguard thugs that have more in common with Hitler than a pathetic louse named Fuhrman. It seemed obvious that race relations were set back 25 years in just 3 short days, so he could achieve a personal victory. This causes me great fear for a hope of unity in our country. When I heard you and realized that there was still a voice of reason on the other side of the racial divide, I realize that there is still some hope. I wish you the best and pray your message gets through to the people who need it most and don't realize it.
HOW CAN I HELP YOU???

D.M.,
FLORIDA

Predictably the poverty pimps and their community leaders along with the quota blacks have seized the opportunity presented by the early signs of white backlash to issue a new cry that they are still being besieged by racism.

Aside from the subtle but deadly "welfare pet" racism perpetuated by the poverty pimps and the egg-sucking dog liberals, however, I believe the only real racism that threatens black people today is our own neo–black racism, which is vested in the black welfare culture and which I contend in large part stimulates the white backlash.

These are the dangerous forms of racism as America enters the twenty-first century. These are the ones that threaten to plague my granddaughter, not the old stereotypical racism of carte blanche discrimination and exclusion once practiced against Negroes in America.

The idea of black racism—of blacks hating whites because of the color of their skin—is utterly preposterous to me. It's preposterous because it em-

ple who have fought against this very injustice imposed on
s.

n, practiced by the majority-population race, couldn't with-
he value system of America, how can blacks practicing the
cism presume that they can prevail?

ity and the ethics of Christendom and the Constitution of the
s of America made it impossible to hold my people under the
man's thumb when they were the least powerful group in this country,
en they were chattel, slaves with no economic or political strength, how in
dickens name would it be possible for black people to hold the entire white
population hostage to this neo–black rage?

White Americans will not condone reverse racism, and attempts to prose-
lytize in this area most surely will create a widespread indignant moral backlash, just as there was a moral backlash against black slavery.

Aside from being flat-out morally wrong, black racism is a flawed cause on
a practical level. The math alone tells you that right away. Since blacks make
up less than 13 percent of the American population, the odds clearly are
against blacks prevailing in a battle of skin tones. It is an unwinnable crusade,
a losing proposition.

I contend that black people—black people, of all people—cannot afford
to dabble in this devil's workshop of bigotry and hatred, the kind of blatant
racism preached by Minister Farrakhan.

Every time a voice from this minority black-trash welfare culture fires off
that race-based spark, it is as if all black people have doused themselves with
kerosene and walked into a house to fight a roaring fire. It is not a good idea.

This dangerous endeavor pursued by the vocal minority of black Americans threatens to harm all of us and curtail the progress we have made over
recent decades to become part of mainstream America.

Unless the majority of black Americans reject black racism along with the
entire Myth of the Hobbled Black, unless we unconditionally join the American mainstream, I sadly predict that the backlash could ultimately result in
psychological barriers reading "Blacks Not Welcome" reappearing all over
America.

Occasionally I pose this open question to my radio audience: Are you
afraid of black people?

The initial answer almost always is a politically correct no.

I then offer a scenario such as the following: Assume you and another
driver arrive at a parking space at the same time. Would you press harder for
the space if the other driver was white than if he was black? In other words,
do you avoid everyday confrontations with black people for fear they might

retaliate? Are you afraid they might shoot you? Remember, this is not such a hypothetical question in places like L.A.

Eventually most of the good people I talk to—who in my heart I do not believe are racists—answer that yes, at times they are more afraid to interact with black people.

Sadly, that doesn't surprise me. What did we think would happen when these unassuming white people heard gangsta rappers like Sister Souljah calling for a "day to kill white people"?

The white majority in America might well choose to deal with black racism as a mere irritation if it were not for the fact that black thugs and their racist social crusade threaten to reach out and touch them.

White people know that black thugs—some openly looking to carve a new notch by attacking a white mark—are renowned for their casual killings. They know that some blacks viciously hate "whitey."

So the most identifiable source of the white backlash is fear of the terrifying random and senseless black crime, crime that violates a basic American right to property and a peaceful coexistence, crime that is an assault on our fundamental American right to life, liberty, and the pursuit of happiness.

Because this crime is so arbitrary and generally unprovoked, it's unrealistic to expect all white people to take the time to judge whether a particular black person they meet is a good person or a bad person.

Besides crime, the white backlash also is a response to other characteristics of the black-trash welfare culture which are spreading into mainstream America and challenging our American value system of right and wrong.

Though they generally don't say so outside of closed circles, most white Americans are just as fed up as I am with the welfare rights mentality—especially since they have to support it with their tax dollars. They are tired of hearing excuses for why black trash won't go to work in entry-level jobs when they themselves got started that way. While they once might have been willing to endure inequity in the workplace because affirmative action was meant to correct the old inequity of exclusion, now they are growing weary of "special hires" who don't pull their own weight.

Every night when I put my head on my pillow, I worry that the advocates of the black-trash welfare culture will go too far, that they will push too hard, threaten the American way too much.

I am a realist. I understand that the fabric of American civilization must remain intact; I know we don't want it to tear. I know that the effluvium that ultimately could ooze forth would take shape as groups equivalent to the KKK, the neo-Nazis in Germany, and the Aryan Nations, or as cops the equivalent of Mark Fuhrman.

The only thing that protects the sanctity of my home is the assurance that at the end of three numbers—911—there will be an impartial response from the Colorado State Patrol, the sheriff, or the police. I am terrified that if we allow this backlash to grow, America's social fabric could tear to the point that the security of that response could be taken away from people who look like me.

Don't get me wrong. I am not the old classic Negro who's hiding under the bed fearful that people once again will roam around my front yard with crosses and hoods on their heads.

But I am terrified of the backlash that our children and grandchildren will suffer—of the backlash that will keep them from realizing their American destiny, their hope of being fully vested citizens. I am afraid they will become the victims because for every action there is a reaction. You cannot get away from that. It is a scientific fact.

We emotionally healthy black Americans who don't hate white people, who don't buy into the Myth of the Hobbled Black, who don't roam city streets killing at random, and who have worked hard to capture the American Dream have an urgent responsibility, whether we like it or not, to stand up and identify ourselves loudly and clearly.

In the early 1970s my wife and I moved into a luxury high-rise apartment building in Detroit, a building that today sadly is the province of drug dealers and pimps. We had a corner apartment on the eleventh floor, overlooking downtown Detroit and the section of the Detroit River that runs by Belle Isle, where the hydroplane boat races are held every summer. There were a swimming pool, tennis courts, and a doorman on duty for both security and courtesies.

It was the first place I had ever lived where I felt that I was truly realizing the benefits of my hard work in America.

Though both of us had fairly high-profile media jobs at that time, we agonized like a couple trying to buy their first house about whether or not we would qualify to rent this dream apartment.

In the days—which seemed like weeks—while our application was being processed, we would drive to a McDonald's across the street from the high-rise, buy a cup of coffee, and gaze up at the very apartment where we might be lucky enough to live.

Finally we were approved, and we moved in.

Just as I had done when I maneuvered myself out of the shipping department and into my job as a clerk-typist years before in New York, I promised myself I would never slip backward from this new lifestyle I had achieved.

Frank Manning, one of the Detroit black rat pack I had met when I moved from New York, came to see my new place. He looked around, sized up my new digs, and said sarcastically, "Nigger, when the revolution comes, they're gonna get your black ass—"

"When the revolution comes," I interrupted, "the doorman will stop them."

Even back then I had figured out the real meaning behind the slogan "The business of America is business."

I didn't get that message from middle-class parents who mentored me in the way of the corporate world. I had to put it together the hard way. I had to look around, scan the horizon, and learn from what I saw.

I had just seen the Detroit riots and the 1960s antiwar protests. From them I had learned two things.

One was that when a citizens' protest is deemed valid by America, change is instituted in the name of the inherent virtue that ultimately prevails in this country.

The second thing I learned, however, was that it was just as important to institute that change in order to restore order and get on with the business of America.

This is the practical side that makes America what it is.

I am not discounting the fact that there is an underlying moral objective behind making change. I have said repeatedly that I believe that the grand majority of Americans are good people. And I still do. History is rife with exceptions, the people who are not good, and when such people surface, the country moves collectively to speak out against them.

But I often ponder just how big a part the practical need to get America back to orderly business plays when change is instituted.

I think it's important to know, for instance, that the civil rights legislation that came out of the 1960s was as much about order as it was about poor black people suffering discrimination and nice white people stopping it. It was a way to stabilize American society in order to get on with American commerce.

Likewise, we changed the rules in the office so that the stereotypical sexist and bigoted white male managers could no longer stand around the water cooler fantasizing aloud about the size of a woman's breasts and exchanging racist jokes. There is no question that there is virtue in the new rules, but I contend that a big reason those rules were changed was that the men's outspoken prejudices against their co-workers disrupted the office and thus were not good for business.

I also learned in the 1950s and the 1960s that when a citizens' protest was deemed invalid by the greater majority of Americans, it could and would be contained by force—also in order to get on with the business of America.

When southerners gathered on school steps in Alabama to protest integration of blacks into the all-white classroom, when Alabama governor George Wallace literally stood in the schoolhouse door to bar Negroes, we sent in federal troops to override and, if necessary, to overpower the protesters and to restore order.

The bottom line is that it's bad for business when black people riot and interfere with the hum of American commerce. Likewise, it's bad for business when the Ku Klux Klan marches down Main Street. It's bad for business when sexism or racism is tolerated in the workplace.

Eventually either the people in America who represent the greater good will stop what they are doing, join in, and institute change, or force will be used to quell the disturbance in order to resume business as usual.

Either way, it's an undeniable truth that the business of America requires stability and order.

With anarchy in America, with burning cars blocking the highways, with snipers operating from rooftops, business is halted.

When there is anarchy, riots, or mayhem in the streets, people don't get their morning newspapers. The garbage doesn't get picked up. Food doesn't get delivered to the grocery stores.

In the 1960s my generation thought what was good for business meant only what was good for General Motors or General Foods. Today I know that most businesses in America are small entrepreneurial companies spawned by the large corporations.

Think about how many truckers it takes to deliver parts to the Fortune 500, how many cups of coffee the drivers drink between California and Michigan, how many times they stop for gas, how many waitresses sling hash at the truck stops, how many mechanics are on duty to change tires and fix breakdowns, how many guys it takes to deliver the diesel fuel to the pumps, how many people deliver the sunglasses, the cassette tapes, the candy bars for sale along the way.

The business of America is an endless consuming machine. Someone has to make the paper cups for the truck drivers' coffee. Somebody has to deliver the cups to the truck stop. Somebody has to stand in the store all day to sell the cups of coffee. That person usually has an entry-level job.

And that entry-level job is the epitome of opportunity in America because it represents a foot on the first rung of the ladder, the opportunity that you can't find in places like Nigeria and Nicaragua.

I know now that there's nothing wrong with business in America. It provides the infrastructure that allows the riches of mainstream America to flourish, riches that we all can and should enjoy.

Likewise, we all should have figured out by now that civility is good for America and good for us. It doesn't matter what motivated the majority white population to act on our behalf.

I don't care how they came to the conclusion that they should let my people go: "Why, we can't keep holding those Negroes down. They're really very angry, and we're becoming so much more genteel than they are. You know, they've been working that back forty like the dickens, and pretty soon they'll be able to overpower us."

I don't care if it was self-serving on the white man's part. We are here now. And now we have an obligation as grandfathers and grandmothers, as fathers and mothers, as sons and daughters. We have an obligation to look to the future, not to yesterday.

I am not suggesting that we become brain-dead and forget where we've come from, only that we honestly look ahead to savor what we have to gain.

There is no just reason for the black-trash welfare culture to try to undo this American system, to undo what most black people—along with the vast numbers of good Americans of all races—have worked so hard to achieve.

There is no reason, because the business of America continues to offer a good life for anyone willing to get on board. It doesn't matter whether somebody thinks you're a dirty Jew, a shit-faced nigger, or a knife-wielding wetback, once you take a step to get into the business of America, once you become part of the greater whole, the potential is there for you to prosper. Success is what America is all about.

Clearly, it wasn't always that way for black people. But thanks to the moral protest that the people of my generation made about the old unjust system, today blacks like any other citizens can get their piece of prosperity from the American mainstream.

The black poverty pimps and community leaders are promising their black-trash constituents a new revolution in America. But America cannot simply be taken by force, not by physical force, not by psychological force, and especially not on a platform of hatred and racism.

The attempt by these misguided African Americans to do so clearly is bad for business, and that's just one more reason—maybe even the most important reason—why at some point their ill-conceived revolution will be suppressed.

Either the greater majority of black Americans can stand by quietly and be swept up in the backlash this folly generates or they can set a clear course for success in this great country by openly supporting and embracing American mainstream values and the American Dream.

Part 4

America Works!

Chapter Twelve

The Black Avenger

* * * *

Please keep up the good work. U are an excellent translator between the races. I stand tall as an American with YOU! THANK U.

VIA E-MAIL 1/16/96
C.L.

* * * *

Just read a couple of your pieces from the Denver Post, sent to me by my relative from Castle Rock. Sir, may I say that you should run for President in the place of Colin Powell. . . . Discrimination would vanish of its own volition if all black people would just follow your excellent example. There is no way I can look at you sir, except as my human equal. Your philosophy on rights, responsibility, fairness, government, people, issues are none surpassed. You amaze me, and I love to read you. Keep up the good work—and maybe somewhere down the line all people will see your wisdom.

VIA MAIL 9/16/95
R.C.,
COMANCHE, OK

* * * *

Thank you for who you are and all you represent. I am a 52 year old col-ored man who is also proof that the American Dream is alive and does work. I have received my certificate of absolution. You have validated the things I believe in. Please keep up the good work.

VIA E-MAIL 2/3/96
L.C.,
JACKSONVILLE, FLORIDA

• • • •

Just a quicky to let you know that you have a fan, 42 yrs, White, Southern (S.C.), college educated, long haired, biker-type, conservative, veteran, home owner, gainfully employed ($50,000+), family man. I believe in God and country, prayer and patriotism. I believe a man is a man regardless of race, creed or natural [sic] origin. I respect or despise a person based on himself not others who look like him.

VIA E-MAIL 11/21/95
M.C.,
GREENVILLE, S.C.

• • • •

Having grown up a racist, but having been dealt with by God on that and other sins of pride, I think American radio listeners are indebted to you and your distinct apologia. Referring to yourself as a Negro and [an unassuming colored guy], disarms white people and, in my opinion, allows thinking people to venture past facades and to probe issues.

People in our generation are racists—more than we need to be for ethnic pride. But you are accomplishing something that's hard to believe—becoming a kind of ad hoc opinion leader for populist southern white people who are not reckless in their love of other races.

Your pride . . . is healthy. It was acquired by earning your way and overcoming racism.

VIA FAX 10/26/95
P.S.
HAWAII

• • • •

I live in Eugene, Oregon and listen to you on KPNW radio. I'm a 43 year old nondescript male. (Except for my premature gray head). I have a beautiful wife, 4 kids. I've worked hard all my life to keep my family afloat. Put two kids through college. (Haven't made it there myself). Enough for the demographics.

I want you to know that you have inspired me to once again be proud to be an American! Your down to earth logic is awe inspiring. I live in a medium size community (120K) where people take care of their own needs. No one owes me anything! Isn't that the way it's supposed to be? The problems of the inner city seem a million miles away. We moved from Detroit to Eugene 11 years ago to raise our children in a healthy environment, but the buffer zone seems to be closing in.

Please keep up the good work knowing you have become my mentor! If you need a quota white as a sidekick, let me know!

VIA E-MAIL 11/20/95
CARL,
EUGENE, OREGON

• • • •

People like yourself really are beginning to piss me off. I am beginning to just hate conservative black Americans. Brown, Yellow and Red Americans, that are Conservative are also on my list. It would be so much easier if you MINORITIES would just get together and ALL become Liberal Socialist Lockstep PC Nazi's as Jesse Jackson, Anita Hill, Ron (Dum Dum) Dellums, Kwazi Enfumi (sp?), Reverend Al (SHE WAS RAPED BY WHITEY) Sharpton and the list goes on ad nauseam, have done. If this were to happen then I could just become a racist and a bigot with no problem. For then all minorities including black people would be the same instead of just a vocal minority of your race being stupid enough to believe the lies issued daily by the likes of Sharpton, Jackson, and the rest of them.
But NO you have to be intelligent and a free thinker, like Clarence Thomas or that Representative from Oklahoma, who's name I am ashamed I cannot recall. Though if you minorities were all to adopt the idiocies of the failed left I guess I would not be a bigot or a racist, rather I would be the same as I am which is an Angry White Male. Angry about the last 30 years and what these people and the Kennedys and LBJ and Foley and more recently, Gepheart and Clinton (Mr. and Mrs.) and for those same 30 years the Main Stream Media has been forcing down our throats . . . Socialism and a new world order. Well I guess I will not become a bigot or a racist and I hold you, Ken Hamblin, to blame for this . . . you and all decent hard working law abiding Black, Brown, Yellow, and Red Americans, no matter where your ForeFathers and Mothers came from. I will try not to hate you too much.

VIA FAX 10/6/95
D.B.,
ALAMEDA, CA

• • • •

It is an absolute honor to listen to you everyday on WOKV, Jax., Fl. God bless you in all of your endeavors and never back down from your stance.

VIA E-MAIL 1/16/96
B.S.,
JACKSONVILLE, FLORIDA AREA

• • • •

Ken, saw you on C-Span. You are great—like a breath of fresh air.

VIA MAIL 7/6/94
K.Y. & J.Y.,
TACOMA, WASHINGTON

• • • •

We've seen and heard you on tv maybe 2 – 3 X. You're our kind of guy and talk show host—terrific on C-Span yesterday. . . . This world and our country need people who think and speak like you do!

VIA MAIL 7/7/94
B.K. & A.K.,
BISMARCK, ND

• • • •

Had to let you know how much I enjoyed your appearance on C-Span the past week. It's refreshing to see and hear someone who has logic and clarity and good sense in their values. Keep up the good work.

VIA MAIL 7/10/94
H.P.,
NEW ORLEANS, LA

• • • •

Ken, just dropping a line to say a few of my co-workers and I just recently found your show on 1320 AM, in Richmond, Va. We love your show and what you have to say. We're detectives with the Richmond Police Department, so if you're ever in our City, we've got your back! We've been spreading the word about your show and hope you'll gain more Richmond area listeners. I've even got my husband and sons hooked. Keep telling it like it is brother!

VIA E-MAIL 10/27/95
DET. J.M.,
"THE UNASSUMING WHITE, FORMER MARINE, WOMAN COP,"
RICHMOND, VIRGINIA

• • • •

Just wanted you to know that I've followed your career with interest ever since I saw you profiled in Destiny magazine, and I'm so thrilled and proud to be represented by someone like you. . . . You perform an invaluable public and social service, and I hope you keep going strong against

*the riptides that would like to pull you down to a lesser, but more danger-
ous, wavelength.*

VIA E-MAIL 10/24/95
D.M.

*Here comes the Black Avenger
He's riding out from his Colorado Rocky Mountain Cave.*

*He stands for truth and justice
A real American Hero
The Black Avenger always saves the day.*

*Just an unassuming black guy
Stamping out liberal egg sucking dogs.*

Here comes the Black Avenger. . . .

— WRITTEN AND PERFORMED BY DOUG HOOLEY

PRODUCED BY EMERALD PRODUCTIONS, DEXTER, OREGON

Broad brushstrokes have been used over the last couple of years to paint a simplistic picture of the serious grievances emanating from middle America.

This picture painted and broadcast by the mainstream media is far different from the complex white backlash that I see and fear, however. The mainstream media have reduced nearly every political and social phenomenon I have written about in this book to a simple sound bite and a three-word headline: "Angry White Men."

The premise is that the black race and the white race are moving farther and farther apart because these angry white men are coming together in a collective backlash against the benefits afforded blacks through civil rights over the last three decades.

The evidence frequently cited is that these men, who for years held an unfair advantage in the workplace and in society in general, now are attacking programs such as affirmative action, which were designed to give minorities the edge to compensate for the years they were not treated as equals.

The predominantly liberal media report that these white men make up the core of the growing conservative audience of talk radio. As a nationally syndicated talk radio host who is on the air for three hours five days a week, I guess this means that I should be among the first to hear from these guys.

But in actuality, that misconception is shattered regularly on *The Ken Hamblin Show.* The most interesting evidence against the stereotype comes in call after call, day after day, from white men, white southern men in particular, whom I hear crying uncle in this tired debate about race.

They are not crying uncle in the sense that they are rolling over.

What they are saying is: "Look, I personally didn't do it. I've gone through the family Bible. I haven't found one instance where we owned slaves. But I'll admit that at one time in America an injustice was committed against people of color—against black people, African Americans, Negroes. And as a white person, I am willing to atone for that."

In January of 1994 my local Denver radio program was broadcast live on C-Span and then repeated several times over the following week. On that show I addressed this guilt factor among white Americans and, as a spoof, offered to send my listeners and my viewers a copy of my very own "Certificate of Absolution."

Some months earlier, a man had called me on the air, identified himself as white, and told me with candor and some degree of desperation that he was tired of feeling guilty about "my people."

That prompted me to come up with an official pardon in the form of a certificate, which only a clear-thinking black American would be authorized to issue. Soon after that, a Denver printer named Rex Kniss, who listened to my show, called and said he would be willing to print the certificate.

Rex added some "certificate" language to my thoughts and we ended up with the following:

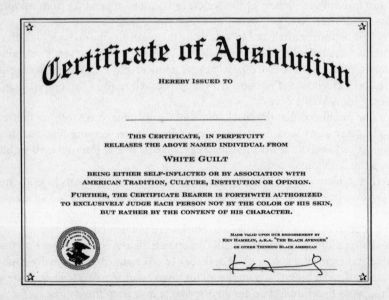

I signed the Certificate "The Black Avenger," a moniker that I use particularly with my radio listeners. The idea behind the name was that I wanted to avenge the lies and the disinformation that more than thirty years of liberalism have brought about in this country. More to the point, I wanted to present myself as living proof that America works for black people too. As the Black Avenger, I was a living, breathing challenge to the well-honed Myth of the Hobbled Black.

"The Black Avenger" caught on among my fans in 1993 while I was on a local Denver radio station that also carried Rush Limbaugh. Limbaugh was hyping his newsletter by promoting an appearance in Colorado after one of his callers from Fort Collins, a man named Dan, said his wife wouldn't let him spend the money to buy a subscription. Limbaugh said he'd personally come out to Fort Collins if Dan would organize a bake sale to raise money for the subscription. The result was "Dan's Bake Sale," which drew Limbaugh fans from all over the country and raised money not only for Dan's newsletter but also for charity.

My local station got behind the event by lining up buses to take our Limbaugh fans fifty miles north to Fort Collins.

Meanwhile, I had just gotten back into motorcycles—a couple of years late, I might add. As I tell my wife and all of my male friends circa fifty years of age, it's a male rite of passage to buy a motorcycle when you turn fifty. I was fifty-two, pushing fifty-three, and hadn't ridden one since I had a Honda 150 in the late 1960s.

A fellow motorcyclist called my show and said he didn't want to go to Dan's Bake Sale by bus, but that he and I should go on our scoots. That prompted a lot of on-air bravado, and I ended up leading a cavalcade of some forty bikes in front of that many more buses to Fort Collins. On the ride, I was dressed in black leather from head to toe and wearing a black helmet with a tinted face guard—exhibiting some resemblance to Darth Vader or—you got it—the Black Avenger. After that trip, the Black Avenger moniker stuck.

Over time, when asked why I called myself the Black Avenger, I must admit I started answering a bit flippantly, mocking the comic book characters of my youth: "Truth, justice, and the American way . . . honey."

I added "honey" after a black caller, in all seriousness, challenged me, claiming that "truth, justice, and the American way" were not "black" values because these American principles weren't afforded to black people. He further insinuated that I was trying to "act white." Of course, I stood my ground.

I am an American first, I replied. Don't ask me to choose between this Republic and the color of my skin. If you're a Pan-Africanist or a black nationalist, you won't like that answer.

After thinking about the absurdity of this man trying to discount blacks as beneficiaries of the American Way, I decided to add "honey" with an ethnic ghetto drawl for the sole purpose of messing with self-righteous African Americans like him who still feed off the Myth of the Hobbled Black.

As a result of my appearance on C-Span, I received nearly 8,000 pieces of mail, more than 5,000 of them requesting the Certificate of Absolution. To this day I hear from people from all over America who remember the program, and my staff continues to fill orders for the certificate every week.

Needless to say, it warms my heart to know that so many white people are sleeping better at night, no longer writhing in pain brought about by their white guilt.

All joking aside, the extent of white guilt in this country is immense. It directly correlates with the endless depiction by the mass media of the profound pain that black people purportedly still suffer as a result of the years they were excluded from America's mainstream.

The constant reports of this pain and suffering that are broadcast through the media, combined with the "blame whitey" syndrome that emanates from the black-trash welfare culture, have caused some white Americans to suffer such a high degree of guilt that they have an almost fanatic desire to undo the injustices of slavery, perhaps beginning with guilt about not having delivered the forty acres and a mule promised to every Negro after the Civil War.

The greater majority of white Americans have passed on a nagging sense of social obligation from one generation to the next. After four or five generations, however, mass amnesia has set in. The people who are haunted by this guilt—the white majority, mainstream Americans obsessed with undoing this injustice—have forgotten exactly what their crime was. In fact, they have no idea what their particular crime was.

As is the case with my southern callers, most Americans can't trace their family tree back to the equivalent of Tara, the fictitious plantation in *Gone With the Wind*, or to the ownership of slaves. So the guilt no longer arises from having once personally owned slaves, be they black people or indentured Irishmen. The guilt now is imposed just because of a lack of melanin in their skin, just because they are white. Simply by virtue of the birth of a white child, another guilty American is created. It's as if we were talking about the burden of the national debt. That baby inherits the guilt of slavery, the guilt of an injustice of long, long ago.

Because of this guilt and the ongoing stories of black oppression, white people have been conditioned to accept just about any level of black rage and the illogical demands resulting from it.

All of which brings us back around to modern-day African-American revolutionaries like welfare queen Dorothy King.

Despite her crassness, in some ways King is very sophisticated. She knowingly touches a little secret in white people who have been conditioned by years of hearing about black hardships—the little secret that they are glad, they are relieved, to have been born white rather than a disenfranchised minority. These white middle-class citizens—especially the thirty- and forty-something crowd—have been inundated from the cradle with news reports about the dreadful burden of being black in America—reports of suffering the hardships of poverty, racism, and second-class citizenship.

While going through college, these white folks saw liberal administrators and professors excuse low test scores from black students because of these inherent hardships. They felt sorry for affirmative action students who obviously must have been scared, because they refused to compete. And though clearly this discrimination was self-imposed by the blacks themselves, they watched black students segregate themselves at all levels of campus life—from African-American studies to African-American student unions to African-American graduations—in essence implementing a post–civil rights version of "white only" and "colored" sections.

These white people graduated, got married, and began family life in comfortable suburbs . . . and bingo! They see Dorothy King on the nightly TV news, cataloging all the black hardships they have been conditioned to believe exist.

So when King makes absurd demands, like "give me" a house, these guilt-ridden white people shy away from standing up to her with what should be the logical American response: "Heavens no, we won't give you a house. Go out and work for it."

Nope. They stay out of it. Because they fear that X-ray vision might discern their little secret—the secret that they are eternally thankful they are white, and just having that thought makes them racists.

I have heard white Americans express so much racial guilt that, being the old Catholic that I am, on some days I feel as though my radio show has become a confessional.

Because of the earnestness with which these people come to my show, it has dawned on me that if we as minority people, as black Americans, can't cut a deal with these average white Americans who are sitting at the table apologizing for the past, then we are a flawed and a lost people.

Or we are a disingenuous people who demand to prolong the negotiation with no intention of ever ending the strife and the separation, with no intention of ever doing our part to fill up the moat between the races or of getting on with the business of continuing to build a strong America that will benefit all of us.

I have a bigger, more selfish reason for wanting to avenge white guilt, however, a reason that goes beyond relieving the strain on white America. Guilt almost certainly inspires pity for the injured party—in this case black Americans. I contend that we can never stand tall as a people and expect to be treated as equals so long as we allow ourselves to be patronized in this fashion.

I also hear from white people across the country who call my radio show and say essentially, "Get over it."

They respond to the poverty pimps' demands for more and more reparations for black people by asking what credit they get for all the taxes they have paid to support decades of Great Society programs that benefited black recipients. They want consideration for the years of affirmative action that gave black Americans a pass to automatically step to the front of the employment line.

Those kinds of queries undoubtedly contribute to the notion that there are angry white men. And I am certain there are, in fact, some white men who are angry, perhaps even racist. But the truth is that, as a black man, I ask some of the same questions, albeit from a different perspective.

When will black people recognize that we are able and willing to stand on our own? When will we acknowledge that we are able and willing to stand side by side with other Americans to compete for jobs and our piece of the American Dream? When will we get over that ugly and unjust period in our American history and evolve into healthy citizens of this great country?

I don't perceive that the majority of white Americans I talk to are saying "Get over it" sarcastically in order to dismiss the subject or to lobby for a return to the days of yore.

Rather, I think they are saying to black Americans: "Get over it, because even if we haven't paid the bill in full, we certainly have made enough of an effort to make amends that you should acknowledge some sincerity on our part."

Personally, I heartily second the call to get over it.

I am absolutely convinced that if we black Americans unequivocally throw in our lot with mainstream America today, we have much more to gain in the future than we have lost in the past. We have more to gain by putting our energies into the pursuit of the American Dream than we have to gain by continuing to whine about being compensated for having been kept out of the game in the past. We have an opportunity to realize all the benefits of being an American in the name of all of those who came before us, those Negroes who were kept unfairly from the full potential of this great country.

I would go so far as to say that we *owe* it to our forefathers to seize the opportunity that they helped to make available to us by their own stalwart faith in the American Dream. I know that all of my life I have felt I owed it to my mother and her sisters to make something of myself, to achieve the level of success that they only dreamed would be possible in their new homeland.

Today mainstream America has opened its full society and culture to us. The white majority has supported legislation that makes the American Dream truly accessible to all black citizens.

Oh, sure, there's still the old-guard club or the snooty neighborhood where the members or residents may look down their noses at black newcomers. But I would wager that those scenarios are few and far between.

And I am also willing to bet that in most cases the feelings of discrimination and exclusion are self-imposed by xenophobic quota blacks.

In fact, some of today's cries of racism have become downright ludicrous.

I wrote a column in the *Denver Post* in the summer of 1994 about a group of Denver area black women who claimed that a white shopkeeper in a Western Slope mountain town "stripped away our dignity, making us feel frustrated and powerless" by making an offhand remark when they walked into his store.

It seems one of the women was complaining about the heat, and the shopkeeper responded, "Hey! Watermelon's not served until one o'clock."

When he realized the ladies were seriously offended, he reportedly tried to make light of the situation, but alas, the oppressed travelers bustled out the door and followed up by writing a critical letter to the editor of the local newspaper.

I wrote that had I been presented with the watermelon-serving schedule, I promptly would have inquired about the cantaloupe.

I don't doubt there are some angry white men. I'm still unconvinced that this shopkeeper was one of them, however.

More important is the fact that I am one black man who refuses to be shamed or made to feel powerless anymore by white bigots and racists. White folks can no longer intimidate me. I know better.

What I am constantly amazed at is how thin-skinned, how delicate, and how utterly afraid the beneficiaries of Dr. Martin Luther King's proud march for liberation have become.

Furthermore, as a black American, I am shamed by the Myth of the Hobbled Black. I am shamed that so many of my people have allowed themselves in one way or another to become part of the sham.

Someone must have the courage to kill this myth. Someone has to be embarrassed that, with the opportunities available to us today, so many black Americans remain in a declining state of existence in Dark Town. Someone has to be embarrassed for the great number of middle-class black Americans who live in seclusion, apparently afraid to celebrate their success as educated and sophisticated Americans.

Someone must speak out to avenge the mythical disability of the Hobbled Black, and I think it's only logical that successful middle-class black Americans take the lead to meet this challenge.

White liberals won't do it because they continue to feed off the myth in order to further their own political and social agenda. White conservatives who speak out about ending the welfare culture have no credibility. They are summarily labeled racists.

And so I have lobbed a loud salvo by declaring myself the Black Avenger, standing tall to dispel the Myth of the Hobbled Black. I am standing up to put an end to the decades of liberal propaganda which deny that today opportunity exists for any American man or woman willing to pursue it.

I fully understand that it's not easy to be black and publicly refute the

Myth of the Hobbled Black, because the quota blacks, the poverty pimps, the African Americans, will do all in their collective power to try to de-black you: "You ain't black no more. You don't understand the pain and suffering. You forgot your roots, boy."

But their admonishments have nothing to do with pain and suffering. The real reason they are trying to de-black me and people like me is that we are telling the truth. And the truth is that being poor and black does not give you an excuse to gang-bang, to ruin a city, to make parks unsafe, to terrorize senior citizens, and to denounce the American Dream.

I am not a mean person. But I have run the gauntlet of ghetto life, and I have survived. I understand the value of life. And I understand that being poor is never an excuse to become a mugger or a killer.

Like a lot of black babies, I started out on the lowest social rung. I was raised by women. I grew up on welfare. I lived on the toughest streets of New York.

But I was not raised to be black trash or to be a victim. I never went through a drug rehab center. I have never been a guest of the government beyond my enlistment in the service. I have never believed—because I was never told—that because of the color of my skin I could never get the fullest measure of opportunity in America.

When you are poor, you may be so busy trying to survive that you miss the opportunity to smell the roses. You may miss the pure joy of watching your children grow up. But none of that gives you a valid reason to disregard what's right and what's wrong.

I am one American who is saying no to the myth that all people of color are weak, illiterate, potentially violent, and substandard in their expectations for themselves and their children as contributors to the community.

Despite the attempted intimidation emanating from the black-trash welfare culture, every day I hear from more and more healthy black Americans—and guilt-free white Americans—who are joining the crusade to tell the truth about black people and their good fortune to be Americans.

My personal adventure in America is at its pinnacle today because I am able to talk every day on my radio show with so many people from coast to coast and from all walks of life. I hear personally from hundreds more Americans off the air every day through the Internet and via letters to the editors of newspapers that carry my column.

And every day I am reassured that the heartbeat of America remains strong. I am reassured that the great majority of Americans maintain the true American spirit, the spirit that ultimately will make it possible for us to prevail.

I draw my strength from that heartbeat of America; it gives me the power to be the Black Avenger.

Chapter Thirteen

Fully Vested Americans

. . . .

*I have heard people in the media refer to you as a black Rush Limbaugh.
Of course to them it is the biggest insult they could heap on you. It should
be worn as a badge of honor. To these people black conservative is an oxymoron. It isn't. In fact . . . I always knew there were many blacks who were
conservative and who shared my values. I guess because of the liberal bias
in the press, that black conservatives were literally a silent majority.
Knowing there are many blacks who are indeed conservative, is encourag-
ing to say the least. Mr. Hamblin, people like you will do more to help race
relations in this country than all the civil rights leaders combined. . . . People like you make me feel as though there is still hope for this country.
Keep up the good work. We need more people like you out there in the
main stream press.*

VIA E-MAIL 1/22/96
R.B.,
AKRON, OHIO

. . . .

*To: Program Director, KSFO
San Francisco, CA
Thank you for including KEN HAMBLIN: THE BLACK AVENGER in
your programming. He is just great. I love this guy!*

I'm a Bay Area native. I was for civil rights in the 60's, against the Vietnam war in the 70's, and a recycler and energy saver from the 70's on. I still believe in those things but, being intelligent I have made observations and conclusions over my forty-four years. I've seen the ACLU sometimes tie the hands of courts, parents, and educators in an attempt to preserve rights of minors who cannot be fully responsible for their actions. I have an educated view of the economy and understand how government social programs often promote what they are designed to cure. Our country was built on individualism. That means self-reliance and government restraint. Opportunity here is still proven today by immigrants.

But I am still a closet conservative! I'm embarrassed to be linked with loud mouth conservatives who do nothing but spew nasty exaggerated claims about conspiracies in government services to intentionally undermine the stability, freedom and success of this country for their own twisted purposes. I can't listen to their hateful tone of voice and nasty innuendoes with nothing to back them up but a warped perspective of the world. They do nothing constructive to enlighten judgments or opinions. I consider those talk show hosts to be a national problem in their own right.

BUT—Ken Hamblin is different. He is reasonably polite and not nasty to those with differing views. He shows white Americans that all blacks are not prejudice against us. He has intelligence, thoughtfulness and humor on issues the media makes us believe are all our fault. He shows us not all blacks think the deck is stacked against them more than ever and that all blacks don't have a chip on their shoulders. He is an example of a successful, responsible family man, the kind of man to be exemplified by the Million Man March.

THE BLACK AVENGER is one conservative talk show that is good for the country and not frustrating to listen to. Thank you for having the insight to carry him. I might even wave the conservative flag if you get rid of some of those others.

VIA FAX 11/13/95
V.C.,
CORTE MADERA, CA

• • • •

Greetings from a "so called pointy headed" academic from Iowa (an ex-liberal who cut his liberal teeth in Boulder during the "70's" and has finally grown up into a responsible conservative).

I have heard your show . . . and I was bolstered, indeed, that I finally heard a voice of optimism from a black leader on the air. Perhaps your voice combined with those of Powell, Clarence Thomas . . . will reach enough black citizens to reach critical mass and bring about real confidence and hope in

the black community rather than continued victimization and dependency.
Love your show!

VIA E-MAIL 12/27/95
C.H.,
CEDAR FALLS, IOWA

• • • •

I am a 21-year-old Black female who listens to you regularly. Although
sometimes I think you fly off on a tangent, I agree with many things you
say. I never really paid attention to politics and just let my views be formed
by others. I voted for Bill Clinton just because he was a Democrat and in
my house we were Democrats. Over the past four years I have started really
paying attention to events in this country and abroad and I found that my
views are very Republican. I have to live with the fact that my vote in 1992
helped to put a man in office who says so many contradicting things I can
hardly keep up. This administration is involved in so many shady dealings
and I truly believe that he has little or no conscious. I will not make the
same mistake twice. Shame on any American who lets themselves be fooled
or should I say duped by Clinton once again in 1996. I love this country
and would rather be there than anywhere else in the world. My parents
raised me and my sisters to believe in God and ourselves and to know that
we could achieve anything we wanted. I will always believe this and will
pass that on to my children. I guess I just wanted you to know that there
are some young Black Americans out here who don't feel we are owed anything but a chance to rise to our full potential. The only check I want is the
one that comes after an honest day's work. Keep the faith and keep standing for what is right! God Bless you and your family.

VIA FAX 11/30/95
J.H.,
OKLAHOMA CITY, OK

• • • •

Subject: Ted Kopel [sic] Town Meeting
EXAMPLE: A white woman was expressing her view on how children in
her school are taught to a color blind society. Then a black woman said
children do not need to be color blind. They need to be taught to respect
those of color.
Mr. Hamlin [sic], at this point I turned the T.V. off. A person earns respect, I do not care what color you are.

VIA FAX 10/5/95
A.C.,
YULEE, FLORIDA

• • • •

Your show is the greatest proof that TRUTH knows no boundaries of color or race. I really enjoy your commentaries and have shared them with many people that I come in contact with. Keep up the good work of chomping up liberalism.

VIA E-MAIL 11/8/95
A.W.

• • • •

Success in this world is not a result of being black or white; it is largely a product of individual achievement. In the case of many prominent men and women of color who have achieved success, their accomplishment was not a result of someone needing a "token." They got where they are because they spent a good part of their lives preparing themselves to seize the opportunity that presented itself.

There is no question that there is hardcore, intransigent racism in our society today. That's a fact of life. It is also a fact that that meanness is not always and only directed at blacks. Indians, Orientals, Hispanics, and even whites suffer under the scourge of such wasted energy. The wise man, however, will not waste effort trying to change the hearts of people portioning such meanness (only God can change the heart). The wise man will work to change their minds!

I just finished reading the life story of Chappie James, this nation's first black four-star general. Permit me to offer some extracts . . . words that are just as relevant and important today as they were when they were spoken back in the early '70s. . . . "I am a citizen of the United States of America and I'm not a second-class citizen. No one here is a second-class citizen until he thinks like one or performs like one. . . . And if I stopped to challenge every man who called me a nigger, I wouldn't be a brigadier general today. I wouldn't have time. I'd still be on [some] corner, poor as a churchmouse." . . . This book ought to be required reading for all high school students . . . and their parents! If black kids aren't motivated for success, it's not always the fault of something or someone else. Opportunities abound. But they are there for the taking!

VIA MAIL 3/16/91
J.W.,
AURORA, CO

• • • •

Great job, thank you for keeping the world in perspective. Judge a man not
by his color, but by his duty to family and community.

VIA E-MAIL 2/2/96
B.C.,
SAN RAMON, CA

• • • •

This is probably going to ramble but bear with me. I'm a 35 yr old white
male ex-con. Yeah, I did it. I'm lucky I didn't do more time for what I did
(armed robbery), 5 yrs in prison was more than sufficient to get my atten-
tion. I'm on parole until 2001. . . . Anyway I went to prison a cocky Liberal
that thought the world owed me a living. I came out a true conservative be-
liever, with a work ethic you wouldn't believe. I work 2 jobs, my wife works
one and we both do as much volunteer time as possible at our little girl's el-
ementary school (I never miss a cupcake sale or a PTA meeting). . . . So,
keep up the good work. I did my time, but the only way I can really repay
society is to raise my little girl to be the good citizen I was not.
P.S. To all the Law Enforcement Officers out there. Keep it up. It's worth it
and even I thank you. Probably saved my life.
Thanks.

VIA FAX 10/20/95
J.B.,
CALIFORNIA

• • • •

Ken Hamblin, I have listened to your program for about a month now, and
I must say that you have one of the best radio news/talk shows I've ever lis-
tened to.
Your unique perspective allows you to tell it like it is without being con-
cerned about racism, and I respect you for taking your views to the limit.
I listened to you on 10/25/95 and was extremely shocked/elated just how far
you will go to express your views on the air! I am referring to your discus-
sion on why there's nothing one can do to appease a person who is from a
minority group who continually complains about our great country.
I am a conservative Hispanic/Latino/Mexican-American (whatever), and
even though I don't agree with everything you have to say, it's OK, because
for the first time in my life, because of you and Rush, I am beginning to
talk about my political views, and asking more questions, and challenging
people to explain their points of view and analyzing more ideas.
I want to thank you for your excellent programming, and am thankful
there are people like you that make a great effort to educate and inform us

common folk, and remind us that we do indeed live in the greatest country in the world! God love you, brother.

VIA E-MAIL 11/2/95
E.V.,
BEAUMONT, TEXAS

I have taken the liberty of segmenting the American black population and labeling groups as I see them: black trash, quota blacks, poverty pimps, Uncle Toms and Aunt Jemimas. The only label that has come into common usage, however, is one that is reserved for blacks like me who are making it in America and are proud of it.

We are called—usually with some disdain and, at a minimum, with some curiosity—the "new black conservatives."

The conservative label was first applied to me in a January 1994 *New York Times* article in which a reporter mused that I was sometimes called the "black Rush Limbaugh." By the time the article went out over the Times features wire, Times Syndicate editors had changed the reference to the "African-American Rush Limbaugh," apparently adhering to their politically correct stylebook.

An aside on the Limbaugh connection: Not long after the *Times* article, Bernard Goldberg told Connie Chung in their on-air chitchat after his segment about me on CBS *Eye to Eye* that people were referring to me as the black Rush Limbaugh, but he wouldn't be surprised if someday they would refer to Rush as the white Ken Hamblin. I took that not only as a great compliment about my radio broadcasting but also as a sign that black people indeed are becoming equal opportunity citizens.

Before long my name began appearing in articles grouped with other black "conservatives." We were classified as conservatives apparently because we didn't support the black-trash welfare agenda associated with liberal politics and normally spouted by black folks quoted in the media.

I didn't take well to this label immediately.

I had started my political life as a liberal, like most other thinking blacks who suffered racial discrimination and then went through the civil rights era. Back then I lived up to the terms of the classic definition of a liberal—optimistically trying to push forward and change things for the better.

Even when racism was at its zenith in this country—during that time of terror in America when black people found it all but impossible to attain justice in a biased system—I, like the majority of black Americans, still managed to cling to the hope that one day we and our children would break free from the socioeconomic deprivation and the racial hatred practiced against us simply because of our skin color.

We believed that eventually we would be able to participate like other citizens in the promised land of America. We believed in the fundamental tenets and values that had been responsible for building this great country. We simply wanted them to be applied equally to us. We all were striving to be fully vested Americans.

Because of our position as underdogs, our beliefs and struggles were categorized as traditional liberal endeavors. As was customary for liberals, we wanted change as opposed to the typical conservative desire to maintain the status quo.

As I have said over and over on the radio, in my columns, and in this book, I believe that we have won that war. We may not have won it in the conclusive and absolute sense of totally eradicating racism, but we have moved this country as a body politic about as far as a nation can reasonably respond to ensure our equality of opportunity. Now I believe the ball is back in our court.

Furthermore, I know that I personally have succeeded according to the proposition of the American Dream. And my success has made me a confident supporter of our American system and a believer in myself and my own abilities.

Now that I and other blacks like me have realized a degree of success in America and have been labeled conservatives, however, our faith in the proven American system is sometimes confused with the platform of the less virtuous historical conservative standard bearers in America—the Republican Party regulars. I guess that's why we are a curiosity.

In the past, these mostly white men have formed Old Boy Clubs that were closed to people like me and others unlike themselves. They were regarded as robber barons because they gave lip service to the ideals of America and then selfishly husbanded their personal gains within a system only they had access to.

But the doctrine and values that I and other blacks like me have embraced obviously are not those stereotypical conservative—i.e., traditional Republican—values.

Ours are American values: doing the right thing, staying the course, fighting to overcome obstacles, daring to dream, and demanding to be judged by our character and our performance, not by our skin color. Our adherence to those values legitimately should bring us closer to the rewards of the American Dream, just as it does for any other American, and it has.

In the end, I have concluded that if some people think they can demean us by calling us conservatives, when all we are doing is fighting to keep our hard-won stake in America, then so be it.

Because no matter what we are called, the fact is that I can no longer call myself a liberal. The liberalism I believed in as a young man has become warped, just as surely as the welfare system I grew up under has become warped.

I became a liberal and a Democrat along with millions of other black Americans who were swept up in the promise of John F. Kennedy. I remember going to huge political rallies for Kennedy in 1960 in Brooklyn and Harlem. I believed in him and in the Democratic Party. I believed they would do something good for black people.

But I can no longer be swayed by what has become a narrow liberal (narrow liberal—now, *that* used to be an oxymoron!) political philosophy that, in essence, guarantees some people a free economic ride. I cannot stand by idly while this political agenda is bringing about the moral and physical decay of a faction of black people who today are living like pets in urban zoos.

The litmus test for the liberals of today is that they have had more than three decades to pursue their programs, and today things are worse. Anyone in his or her right mind would know that something's wrong and that we have to change our approach to solving the problem of poverty and its dreadful by-products.

In 1992 I voted for George Herbert Walker Bush for president because I could no longer stomach the patronizing and decaying agenda of the Democratic Party.

I could not continue to march under the liberal banner because I no longer liked what liberals stood for—gun control, outcome-based education, endless affirmative action. Not to mention that they were soft on crime and stalwartly anti–capital punishment.

I took a lot of heat for my vote . . . at home, on the radio, among my friends. The people around me were incredulous: "How could a black guy possibly vote Republican?"

But I saw my vote as part of my birthing as a fully vested American citizen. I can think for myself, thank you. I don't need to abide by the party line just because everybody who is purportedly just like me does so.

I wrote a column for the *Denver Post* in the spring of 1992 that carried this headline: "A Democrat Gears Up for the Big Switch."

I explained that I had made a vow the year John F. Kennedy was elected never to forfeit my hard-won right of access to the ballot box. I reasoned that by continuing to vote for candidates and policies I now believed were wrong for this country, I was in essence forfeiting my vote.

Someone sent a copy of my column to President Bush, and he sent me a personal handwritten note.

In it he said, "I will continue to try to merit your trust."

I am not ashamed to say that, given where I and my family had come from in America, I was especially touched to be acknowledged as a valued voter and American citizen by the person holding the highest office in the land.

Like so many of the truths and values instilled in me, the "it's all right to think for yourself" notion was probably planted early on by my aunt Merle. In spite of our overwhelmingly liberal Democratic immigrant household, I distinctly remember seeing her wearing an "I Like Ike" button prior to the 1952 presidential election.

Seeing that button obviously planted a seed in me, a seed that remained dormant until I began asking some very hard questions about federal programs instituted out of Washington by the liberal Democrats. The money for those programs, which in theory was to trickle down to revitalize black inner-city ghettos, too often was becoming entangled in the net of corrupt black politicians and community leaders.

The War on Poverty, the Model Cities Program, local projects like New Detroit—every city in this country had a scam to help the disadvantaged blacks and their pitiful ghettos. But where were the results?

I defy you to name a single ghetto that was shut down, other than by bull-dozers.

Being from New York I was inherently cynical with regard to politics, and there was a time when I would have attached no hopes or expectations to tax-payer-funded projects.

The politicians would always say, "We're going to build this toll road, and when it's paid for, we'll shut down the tollbooth."

Right, I thought. Show me a tollbooth that's been shut down, and I'll believe you. As an East Coaster, I couldn't think of a single toll highway or bridge where that had happened.

But then I moved to Colorado, and I found out that Highway 36—the Boulder Turnpike between Denver and Boulder—was once a toll road. And sure enough, when it was paid for, the tollbooths came down.

That one public works case history changed my entire perspective on my tax dollars and the state-run programs they paid for. I began inquiring about the results of some of these programs.

I am not saying I don't want to pay a toll anymore. What I am saying is that it is possible for a road to be paid for. It's possible for results to be seen; it's reasonable to ask for those results.

It's also possible, and sometimes prudent, to admit that a particular path leads nowhere, and to turn to a new one.

But the Democrats seem to regard poverty and the underclass as continuing, endless problems, with no expectation of closure. There is an assumption that a certain number of dollars will always be set aside for poverty programs and for the disadvantaged—and minorities as a group are automatically considered disadvantaged.

It doesn't seem to occur to anyone that the funding never closes down a ghetto, that the hard-core underclass of the black community never seems to aspire to get out of the ghetto, and that lots of minorities clearly are not laboring through life "disadvantaged."

In keeping with my resolve to think for myself, as of this writing I have not officially joined the Republican Party, though I have met and felt a common bond with a great many Republicans since I voted for George Bush in 1992.

I joined the grassroots political revolution of 1994, voting a straight Republican ticket. By doing so, I broke ranks not only with my traditional party but also with a friend who had been my state representative. That friend was a Democrat and a black man. I felt he no longer represented my best interests on the floor of the Colorado State Capitol Building.

This man, a retired army lieutenant colonel, had been elected to several successive terms in the statehouse from his district, and mine, which happened to be a predominantly white, mountain community.

One morning I awoke to see his picture in a Denver newspaper arm in arm with the African-American state representatives who hailed from Denver's Dark Town. He was pledging to stand with them on a vote for gun control as an antidote to crime in the city.

I called him up and asked him how he could betray his own constituents, who I firmly believed were independent spirits when it came to gun control. Many of my neighbors were living in the mountains in large part because they were outdoorsmen and hunters. Our district, I pointed out to him, had a low crime rate despite the fact that it wasn't at all unusual to see guns in racks in the back windows of pickup trucks.

In essence, his response was that he was a black man, implying that this was a black issue that commanded his support based on his skin color.

I told him: "I will vote for a candidate who is black—I will not vote for a black candidate."

His reply was that he would always be black first.

Apparently I wasn't the only voter who felt this politician had betrayed his public trust. He lost that election and hasn't held public office since.

In spite of the mandate given Republicans across the country in 1994, however, I predict that the Republican Party of old, whose members have roots far different from mine and from those of a lot of other new conservatives, both black and white, will have to make some fundamental changes in order to capitalize on the great opportunity it has to become the new broad-based party of the people.

I am not suggesting that the party overtly try to solicit a new black voting bloc, however. I believe such a move could easily become patronizing.

I am committed to being a fully vested American citizen—not one brought into mainstream politics under an affirmative action program.

But if the Democrats no longer serve my interests and if I'm not sure the Republicans are ready to embrace me as an equal voting citizen, then how do I and other black Americans become fully vested participants in the American political system?

One fundamental step we can take is to move to communities where competitive candidates canvass for our votes.

I cannot tell you the number of middle-class black families I know who are living in a political limbo. They have yet to commit themselves entirely to America and to what it can offer them and their children. So they live on the fringes of Dark Town, where gunshots routinely ring out in the night, in neighborhoods that long ago were given over politically to the poverty pimps.

Most of these citizens discounted the ghetto rhetoric of those politicians long ago. Even though many of them fit precisely the profile of the voter that the Republicans want in their party, however, the party doesn't reach out to them because they live where Republicans seldom field viable candidates. Essentially these citizens have disenfranchised themselves by their addresses.

It's like this. All my life I have heard about the Welcome Wagon. I waited for the Welcome Wagon to come to my house. Only recently have I come to understand that you've got to live in a neighborhood where the Welcome Wagon operates.

My prescription for black Americans to become fully vested voting citizens is embodied in a simple civics-geography lesson: Move to a healthy community, speak to your neighbors, take your kids to the community center to see Santa, go to the political rallies.

Don't get motivated because you're a black person with a black agenda that takes precedence over all else. Get motivated as a citizen of your community. Seek out and support political candidates who represent your values, not the ones who simply happen to match your skin color.

Go where there's quality schooling and then work to maintain that quality. Join the block association. Support neighborhood peer pressure to maintain a strong, healthy community—from clean streets to well-kept houses and lawns. Join the community effort to keep crime out—which, by the way, is not an effort to keep black people out, as is rumored by the quota blacks.

My advice for the Republican Party and its candidates: Don't target me with special treatment because I am black. Target me like anyone else on your hit list—because I represent a political vote in your district.

I want the Republican Party to reach me through its candidates, particularly the candidates at my community level who eventually will come to my door to ask for my vote because I have a vested interest in their districts.

Those candidates must speak to the issues I'm concerned about. I don't care whether a candidate is white or black, male or female, Republican, Democrat, or Libertarian. If that candidate isn't a neo-Nazi or a member of the Ku Klux Klan—which would give me strong reason to suspect his or her motive—I am prime fodder for their vote.

Whatever party label we decide to wear, we have reached a time in America when we all can and must come together as we did in the 1960s to take the moral high ground to stop the decay of this great country and its value system.

We must address the decay at its sources, namely the black-trash welfare culture and its enabling arm, the liberal socialist contingent.

Middle-class blacks need to come together with other good Americans in a united front against these ideological scourges.

Here is my own preliminary political agenda:

- Clean up the black urban ghettos once and for all.
- Campaign to vote the poverty pimps out of office.
- Do what's necessary to stop the breeding of brood mares.
- Use any and all means necessary to stop rampant crime and terrorism by young black thugs.
- Get black kids back into good schools with the highest standards, even if that requires booting out minority teachers and administrators who don't uphold high standards.

I want full participation in national mainstream politics. But I am convinced that the first political step all blacks must take as fully vested American voters and fully vested American citizens, is to clean up our own house first.

After the new Republican Congress was elected in 1994, the liberal Democrats had to come to grips with the fact that their ability to continue to pull the wool over the eyes of upstanding American voters was waning.

They attributed—rightfully, I believe—much of the get-out-the-vote effort for that midterm election to conservative talk show hosts, primarily Rush Limbaugh.

In their efforts to respond to this new political threat, the Democrats and their political strategists undertook two major retorts, both of which failed miserably because they grossly underestimated average American people.

The Democrats' first tactic was to get their own people and propaganda on the airwaves. If talk radio was such a persuasive medium, if a host could dictate to or brainwash voters—and they believed that brainwashing was the only explanation for what happened in the 1994 congressional election—then they too would make talk radio one of their media strategies.

After all, how hard could it be to be a talk show host?

They soon found out.

They fielded dullards like Mario Cuomo, still licking his wounds from losing his bid for reelection in the New York gubernatorial campaign. There was talk of pairing him with Ann Richards, who had just lost the governorship of Texas. Former California governor Jerry "Moonbeam" Brown launched a syndicated radio call-in show, which ended up running only a short time in

Denver for a couple of hours on Saturdays. They even threw up a trial balloon for Hillary Clinton just after she fell flat with her health care reform plan.

The American people proved more discerning than the condescending liberals gave them credit for. In less than a year, that great equalizer of the radio business—ratings—had all but nullified the liberals' intended talk radio takeover.

When Plan A failed miserably, they moved to Plan B: Lash out at the lineup of popular conservative talk show hosts and attempt to discredit them and their followers.

Perhaps seeking a personal vendetta against Rush, who rides the president interminably and mercilessly, Clinton led this attack himself.

Soon after the bombing of the federal building in Oklahoma City in the spring of 1995, Clinton insinuated in a Minneapolis speech that this sick crime had been motivated by conservative talk show hosts fanning the fires of discontent among certain unstable American citizens—namely the most extreme of the angry white men. He leveled a broadside attack that denounced pretty much the entire institution of talk radio and its listeners.

I personally was offended. I felt the need to think and speak for myself, as a fully vested American and a talk show host. So I wrote a letter directly to President Clinton. My radio staff made sure that my letter was hand-carried to the White House and reviewed, if not by Clinton, then at least by his closest personal staff. The word came back that he was in "no way" interested in continuing a dialogue on this issue with me and my listeners.

So I filed the following open letter to the president in my New York Times Syndicate column:

• • • •

April 27, 1995

The President
The White House

Dear Mr. President:
When you spoke out against the "purveyors of hate and division" in this country during your speech in Minneapolis last week, most Americans presumed you were pointing at conservative radio talk hosts, such as myself. I respectfully wish to respond. And most importantly, I would like to invite you to join me one day soon on my radio show to talk one-on-one with my proud American listeners.
Let me say I do consider myself a conservative. But I, like the overwhelming majority of the millions of conservative and liberal citizens who listen to

talk radio, want nothing to do with hate or division. In fact, I consider the open forum of radio to be a tool for bringing Americans, especially those who hold differing viewpoints, together.

Perhaps if I tell you something about myself you might understand how I came to my conservative perspectives.

I am a fifty-four-year-old first generation American born to a West Indian immigrant mother who, along with her sisters, spoke to me and my siblings about what it meant to be lucky enough to become American citizens.

Mine is a typical story of a black boy born into poverty, raised on welfare and toughened to survive life on the streets of an American ghetto—in fact, one of the worst: Bedford-Stuyvesant in Brooklyn, New York. My father left home when my brother and I were small, and my mother raised us and three more alone. There was no pride in our poverty. I know because, as the eldest, I frequently accompanied my mother when she went to beg for credit at neighborhood groceries. I experienced homelessness during a time when it was not acceptable, least of all trendy. We moved as many as four times some months, and once rode the subway all night with nowhere else to go. I remember being mortified when my mother made me wear her own laced shoes to school one winter when mine wore out because getting an education took precedence over embarrassment.

Mr. President, through all the hardships of my youth, I honestly cannot say that I recall my mother ever telling us we couldn't achieve because we were black or that the American Dream didn't apply to us.

Yet when I joined the U.S. Army at seventeen, I was horrified to find "Colored" and "White Only" signs near my base in Fort Campbell, Kentucky. When I came home, I joined the legions of blacks and whites, Christians and Jews, men and women who worked together through the 1960s to change that bigoted system. We took down those signs, and we finished making the American Dream, which my mother had sought, available to all people.

In 1969 I was the first black photographer hired at the Detroit Free Press, clearly a beneficiary of affirmative action. I worked hard to prove to myself and to my colleagues that I deserved the job, hard enough to be awarded honors by the Michigan Press Photographers Association.

Today I feel that I am living proof that America works. But I, like many other hardworking Americans who believe in the American way, see cracks in our very foundation. And I am working desperately to repair them for my children and for my precious four-year-old granddaughter.

If that makes me conservative, so be it. But I hardly think that makes me a threat to the country I love, certainly not a purveyor of hate.

Every day I talk to people from all walks of life and from all corners of the country, and many of them are indeed angry about a myriad of issues from

gun control to taxes to crime. But we conduct ourselves as proud Americans
who are intent on preserving, not destroying, the best our country has to of-
fer—not the least of which is free speech.

In 1984 my friend and colleague Alan Berg, an outspoken talk show host,
was gunned down for his views. But he left me and his many radio listeners
with a fitting legacy in his analogy of talk radio as the "last neighborhood
in town."

Mr. President, I urge you on behalf of my listeners to experience that vi-
brant, not violent, American neighborhood firsthand. The welcome mat is
always out at The Ken Hamblin Show.

> *Sincerely,*
> Ken Hamblin

I can remember being absolutely, totally frustrated one time because I
couldn't figure out how to raise $10,000 to buy video equipment that my wife
and I needed for a mountain cable television station we were operating. We
were en route to the Eisenhower Tunnel, returning home from a trip to Denver, and it was all I could think about.

What am I doing wrong? I thought. This is absurd. There is a solution to
this problem. I just need to find it.

In retrospect, I realize that I didn't waste time attributing my dilemma to
the fact that I was colored or that life was unfair. From the moment the need
for money materialized as a problem, I took it as a challenge.

Both of our parents probably would have looked at us and said: "Ten thou-
sand dollars! That's a half or a third the price of a house. Who do you think
you are, getting so agitated and annoyed because you can't see how to get that
much money? That's a lot of money."

But once again I didn't blame the fact that I couldn't immediately solve
this problem on my upbringing in poverty or my lack of sophistication concerning money matters.

I know today that my frustration was typical of the setbacks that all Americans experience from time to time when they reach out in earnest for the
American Dream.

Maintaining a can-do attitude in the face of inevitable obstacles will ultimately help you succeed.

It's the exact opposite of the self-defeating attitude: "Hey, they ain't never
gonna give me nothing 'cause I'm black."

If you don't have a can-do attitude, I am truly sorry. I don't know with certainty where you can get one. I don't know whether you can get one at Harvard or at Yale or by working in the Peace Corps or from your mother because

she always told you that you could do anything you set your mind to. I don't know if you can get one by walking through Manhattan and looking up at tall buildings.

But I suspect you might be able to get a can-do attitude in any one of those places if you open your mind to it.

I know for certain that I am thankful to have that attitude and that I see lots of other Americans who have it too. I also know that you need some degree of curiosity and willingness to explore uncharted territory to go with the can-do frame of mind. And I know that acting upon those attitudes will eventually help to build self-esteem.

Developing self-esteem is a lifelong endeavor. I did not always believe in myself the way I do today. But I remember always being curious about what else was out there.

I remember sitting next to the open door of a C-130 transport plane as I was about to make my cherry jump at Fort Campbell, Kentucky, about to become a member of the army's 101st Airborne Division. At that point in my short teenage life, I hadn't even been up to the top of the Empire State Building.

The jumpmaster saw me stretching my neck to see out the open door. He confronted me by barking the number painted on my helmet and asking: "Are you looking out of my airplane?"

"No, Sergeant."

"Don't you lie to me. Get up and stand in the door."

We were at about 1,500 to 2,000 feet above the ground. The plane was descending to about 1,200 feet, the height from which we would jump.

I stood in the door, the wind beating against me. I was a kid from the streets of New York. The panorama before me was unlike any perspective I had experienced from rooftops in Brooklyn. It was a clear, clear blue-sky day over Kentucky. I saw a big orange ball out there, and as far as I could see — it was amazing — light from that ball touched the earth. At that moment I realized there were things that were bigger than me. But instead of fear, I felt an insatiable curiosity.

Being blessed with curiosity and a can-do attitude yields a certain excitement about life. You come to realize that if you want to have fun today, you'll have to learn how to do certain things — like jump out of airplanes. If you can gather up enough curiosity and gumption to do it the first time, it becomes easier and fun the second time around. And after a couple of jumps, the experience becomes part of who you are. One day you can call yourself a paratrooper. You are building your self-esteem.

Besides learning how to do things and acquiring new skills, sometimes you have to venture into the unknown to build self-esteem. This too is a lifelong process. You don't conquer all the unknowns as a kid scurrying through dark subway tunnels in New York City.

I am a scuba diver, and I admit I sometimes dive alone, mainly because my wife won't dive.

For a number of years, we used to take our twenty-four-foot Bayliner boat to Lake Powell in Utah and Arizona. Being new to diving and gung-ho about it, I was determined to descend into this artificial lake with a mostly silt bottom.

I didn't really expect to see anything. I knew Lake Powell wasn't a diver's paradise with colorful fish and coral reefs like the Caribbean. But new divers will dive anywhere—from swimming pools to cold mountain lakes with no visibility to blue holes no more than ten feet in diameter.

So I suited up and slipped off the swim platform into Lake Powell, visibility about forty feet. I went down to about sixty feet below the surface at which point everything below me dissolved into this abyss, this black inky place that I had absolutely no desire to explore.

Being a new diver, I had all the gear, including a speargun, which I had fired off—quite ineptly—at a few carp. When I surfaced, I did a very stupid thing.

The speargun sinks when it is armed and floats when it is not. As fate would have it, when I surfaced near the back of the boat, I became preoccupied with getting my gear off to climb aboard and I nonchalantly laid my speargun down on the surface of the water. At which point it promptly sank.

About that time, my wife came to the stern. "Good dive?"

"Yeah."

"Where's your speargun?"

"I lost it."

"You what? You paid a lot of money for that speargun. You should go back down and find it."

"It's not important. Let it go."

"Don't be silly, just go get it."

She had no idea that my speargun had fallen into that place at the bottom—that dark, ugly place. I did not want to go down there, but of course my male pride would not let me tell her that.

That afternoon, she still hadn't forgotten the gun, and neither had I. We had about eighty feet of line on board, which I tied together. Then I fastened one end on the cleat and dropped the other end off the side of the boat.

I suited up again, and I slowly began to descend down the line. How bad could it be? I thought. Even if it's murky, I'll just hold on to the line with one hand and feel around for the gun with the other.

But the line ran out.

As I descended hand over hand along the rope, I reached the end of the line before I could touch bottom. It was still totally black beneath me.

I hung there, off the end of that line, in dark murky water, a young diver *alone*, thinking how ridiculous I would look to anyone who could see me. You've got the picture: I looked for all the world like a baboon hanging off a vine in the jungle.

It seemed as if I hung there forever. I knew I had two options. Either I could work my way back up that rope, tell my wife I couldn't find my gun, and always know I had stopped short. Or I could let go and face the unknown.

For what seemed like hours, I repeatedly would gather enough courage to let go of the rope with one hand and quickly grip it with my other hand.

Eventually I let go of the rope completely and began to descend into the dark. I could hear my heart going *boom-ba-boom-ba-boom*. I thought I might possibly die down there. But then, as I began to sink into the blackness, I realized that God did a pretty good thing with pupils, because when necessary they open up to take in more light.

As my eyes adjusted, I began to see the bottom of the lake ever so faintly. I groped along the lake bed, floating in and out among petrified trees with their gnarled black branches looming up in all manner of contorted shapes.

But none of my worst childish, nightmarish fears materialized and before too long, I spotted my speargun. I picked it up and ascended back up to the sunshine and my boat and my wife. I'd be a liar if I didn't admit I was a little bit cocky when I placed the speargun on the swim platform with a great sense of accomplishment.

For some black Americans, taking a step out of the ghetto, outside of their community, must be a hundred times more intimidating than my dive to the bottom of that murky lake.

I have black friends and acquaintances who have given me all manner of excuses, but the bottom line is they will not leave Denver to visit me in the mountains because they harbor old-fashioned fears about traveling through areas where white people outnumber them.

They are afraid of the unknown, and their fear prohibits them from indulging a curiosity to explore America beyond their self-imposed urban barricades.

Self-esteem comes from knowing where you are, determining you don't want to stay there, and then mustering the gumption to explore what might be, the courage to face the unknown, and the can-do attitude to move mountains if that's what it takes to change things for yourself.

The seed of self-esteem is planted when you feel in your heart and in your gut that you know what it takes to change things. That's a hard trait to acquire when you are exposed to poverty pimps and black community leaders preaching about how stuck and oppressed you are because of white people.

As poor as we were, though, I never felt that worthless. I just remember being somewhere I didn't want to be—which is not as negative as it may sound. It can be as simple as finding yourself on the wrong side of a river or having the bus let you off a mile or so short of the place you wanted to go.

It's very American not to be satisfied with your current position in life and to continuously look ahead to your next opportunity.

A black person builds self-esteem exactly the same way any other person does. Contrary to what some liberals believe, black self-esteem does not come from handouts or from trying to make poverty less uncomfortable or less embarrassing. It does not come from trying to turn things topsy-turvy by declaring that poor people and unwed mothers have a right to the same things that those of us who fought our way out of those boxes deserve.

Self-esteem does not come from using your handicaps to jump to the front of the line. Real self-esteem comes from overcoming your handicaps and winning your rewards fair and square. That's the American way.

Getting my affirmative action job as a photographer at the *Detroit Free Press* didn't give me self-esteem. Proving to my fellow photographers that I could take pictures did.

The only way to acquire self-esteem, the only way to achieve the next and final step as fully vested American citizens is for black Americans to live up to mainstream American standards and values and demand to be judged by those standards and values.

By doing so, we can effectively stop the white backlash and open the floodgates to receive all that this great country has to offer its citizens.

Near the beginning of my career as a talk show host in the early 1980s, I had a regular slot on KOA radio in Denver from midnight to 5:00 A.M. five days a week. Lousy hours, long hours. But I was happy to get on the clock as a full-time regular host.

Besides, KOA was a 50,000-watt AM station with a signal at that time of the night that reached into thirty-eight states and sometimes beyond, to old Mexico and Canada. It was like having a national show—the dream of every talk show host.

One night just a few weeks into my new overnight shift, a woman called me and said something like this: "Ken, I need you to help me win a bet. My friend says you are black, but I bet him that you aren't."

It was a call I knew would come eventually. While I never tried to hide the fact that I was black, I didn't do a "black" show, billboarding myself as a black talk show host dealing only with black issues. I considered myself a mainstream American even back then, even though my politics were left of center.

We kibitzed back and forth for a few minutes and finally I said to this woman, "Well, I'm afraid your friend won the bet. I'm black."

"You're kidding. You don't *sound* black. Ken, are you putting me on? Are you really black?"

"Yes," I said.

"Then say something black," she responded without skipping a beat.

After a moment of dead air brought about as I was trying to regroup, I said in my warmest radio voice, "Ken Hamblin."

She laughed and hung up, and we took a break for commercials.

Throughout my radio career, my phone lines have stayed lit up pretty much all the time I am on the air, because I always have made callers a big part of my show. It was no different on this particular night—until that call came. During the few minutes of the break, the flashing lights that indicated callers were on hold waiting to talk to me on the air went dark one by one.

It was about 12:30 A.M. I didn't get another phone call all night. I hadn't planned to have any guests on the show that night, so for the next four and a half hours I did a monologue. I realize today that my memories of Jean Shepherd's radio monologues probably helped to pull me through that night, the longest night of my radio career.

I walked into my bedroom about 5:45 that morning, exhausted but determined not to lose this battle.

The next night I left for work loaded down with books—books of poetry, books of philosophy, books about current political topics. If I ran out of steam doing my monologue, I would read to my audience—who, by the way, I was convinced was still listening.

But I didn't need the books. I opened my show . . . and before long, the first call came, then the second, then the third, and then all the lines were lit up once again. A couple of callers talked guardedly about my being black. One man said he didn't think I should have my job. When I asked him who he thought should be behind the mike, he said, "a white man." But by the end of that second night, things were pretty much back to normal.

Did I experience racism on my night of the monologue?

Of course I did.

Was it racism in the sense of wholesale hatred of black people?

Perhaps, in some cases. But my guess is that most of my listeners were like a great many talk radio devotees who enter into an intimate relationship with the host. They consider the host to be someone they know personally. Listeners at that time of the night in particular may consider the host among their few true friends. My being black may understandably have been perceived as a secret that I unfairly had kept from my friends in the audience.

I am not denying that their shock to the point of silence nonetheless represented some degree of racism.

But whatever form of racism I and my fellow black Americans experience from time to time, there's a bigger question to ponder than whether there is still racism in this country. That question is whether we can become fully vested Americans as long as racism still exists in the United States.

Of course we can.

The unique thing about America is that there is room for racists—even for the extremists who hate blacks, who hate Jews, who hate gays, who hate any-one unlike themselves.

You don't have to like black people, but in America you cannot lynch black people with impunity anymore. You don't have to like Jews, but you cannot sneak up to a synagogue and paint swastikas on the door with spray paint.

There is racism in America, just as there is racism throughout the world. But I no longer would say that I am victimized by it, though admittedly I am touched by it from time to time.

Back in the 1970s, on one of my adventuresome trips to Atlantic City, Wyoming, my friend Mike McClure and I pulled off the highway and went into the Rock Shop, a combination bar, restaurant, and retailer of local rocks and gems. Lined up on stools the length of the bar was an assortment of dusty cowboys and miners, most of whom cut their eyes at me when I came through the door. I read into their scowls a big "Niggers Not Welcome," the same message I had gotten in that café in Clarksville, Tennessee, in 1958.

By this time, however, I had a fair share of those good-old-boy attitudes under my belt. I also knew by then that I had the law on my side if I wanted to order a beer, which I did.

Later, when we walked out, Mike, a Wyoming native, leaned over and said: "Hamblin, I was backing you up all the way. I figured you'd be okay, though, because you've had a lot more experience dealing with them than they've had experience dealing with you."

He was right. In addition to having the law on my side, I was considerably older than when I went into the army in 1957. And I'm even older and more experienced today. I've seen racism before. I can smell it coming, I can guard myself against it, I can brace myself for it, and I can scold myself for getting caught flat-footed because of it.

With age, I have learned to evaluate racism. I realize that I am the one now who has the options about how I will or will not respond to it.

I think another question is more pertinent than whether racism still exists in this country: Can a person ever be a fully vested African American? Or Irish American? Or Italian American?

I think not.

Can a white woman who is fully accepted by the black family she marries into ever *not* be white at an NAACP gathering? No.

Can a dog be a giraffe? Can an Asian be an Indian? No.

But we all can be Americans. We all can be fully vested Americans.

We all can demand and receive unconditional participation in the success that is available to all of us via the American Dream.

I am going to be black until I die. I was born black, and am comfortable being black. I use a number 2 suntan lotion, and there's nothing I like more than to kid those people who supposedly are so "superior" when they burn from too much sun.

I feel a part of the deal. I may never feel as much a part of the deal as Neil Bush is—because of his money, because of the work his daddy did.

But can I be a fully vested American? You bet I can. And I intend to continue to fight for that status every day I'm alive. I intend to fight for that status for myself and for the legacy I will leave for my grandchildren.

Historically, America has dealt with black people commercially through slavery, then brutally by discrimination. Now, as we near the beginning of the twenty-first century, aside from the potential of broad-based white backlash against the black-trash welfare culture and its own brand of black racism, there is only one kind of racism that truly threatens black Americans.

This subtle racism is frequently veiled by pompous good intentions. But it nonetheless threatens to reduce black people to little more than welfare pets. This condescending racist attitude is applied not just to black welfare recipients but to all blacks.

It is an attitude that is perpetuated through political agendas such as affirmative action, through acquiescence to excuses for obvious wrongdoings, right down to an insistence that black people cannot think for themselves politically.

The only possible conclusion that can be drawn from this attitude is that black people are not fully capable and therefore cannot be fully equal citizens of this great country.

I learned very early in life that you can never be the full measure of a man when you are on welfare. I didn't learn that about being black. The very essence and substance of this country, the Constitution, taught me that it didn't matter what color I was or what region of the country I came from. Our Constitution taught me that I could dare to reach for something better, that I could dare to fulfill the will and wishes of my mother and her family before her.

Black "conservatives" like me are continuing to push the envelope in our search for true equality, for total vesting as Americans. Unfortunately, we have to push that envelope the hardest within factions of our own race. And we have to keep exerting uncompromising pressure on the egg-sucking dog liberals who refuse to let us stand and fall on our own merits.

But we cannot lose sight of the fact that we are the leading edge of a generation of black Americans who are establishing themselves as able and willing to think and compete autonomously, a generation that can and most certainly will become the first fully vested black Americans.

Chapter Fourteen

Stand Up for America

••••

We simply MUST take our country back from those who would seek to destroy it from within. I stand with you Brother Ken. Keep the faith.

VIA E-MAIL 1/19/96
G.G.,
DeQuincy, LA

••••

Brother Hamblin,
Thank you for the picture. I enjoy it and have it framed above my PC. I still listen to your show and wish that you instead of Louis Farrakhan had led the "Million Man March." You are a better messenger and say the same things he did but with more veracity. You would've been great!

VIA E-MAIL: 10/20/95
K.T.

••••

I'm a 47 year old white male that listens to your program every day. There is no way I can tell you how much I enjoy your program, and keep it short. But let me say this. America needs more people with similar attitudes and ideas like yours. Keep up the great work. People might just get the message that integrity and honesty combined with hard work and sincerity will work for them also.

VIA E-MAIL 12/27/95
J.S.,
MONTGOMERY, AL

• • • •

I just want to take a few moments to encourage you to continue to be vocal concerning issues that impact the quality of life for us all. It takes courage to take a stand for that which is morally and ethically "right." Many aren't willing to risk personal attack for that which they believe in to make a positive impact—you have and I respect you for that.
There will always be controversy, but you challenge my thinking and force me to take a serious look at my own opinions. I pray God will provide you with wisdom and to use your visibility for his greater purposes.

VIA MAIL 12/31/95
J.A.,
LITTLETON, CO

• • • •

You are a credit to the human race. Keep fighting the good fight. After 40 years of liberal democrats, it's time for all persons who value family, hard work and independence to regain control of our great nation—the best nation in the history of man. I'm solidly behind you and Rush—as are millions of others who make this country work.

VIA E-MAIL 12/10/95
J.M.,
FLUSHING, MICHIGAN

• • • •

Thank you for being the only one on radio today (and I listen to A LOT of talk radio) to remind us all of Pearl Harbor. My Father was USMC—wounded in Guam and scheduled to be in first wave in invasion of Nippon. If it had not been for the A-Bomb I would most likely not be here. God Bless America. God Bless Brother Ken. God Bless & Watch our Men in Bosnia.

VIA E-MAIL 12/8/95
T.T.

• • • •

*Your themes of self responsibility, work and clear statements of right and
wrong action are welcome and I support your opinions.*

VIA E-MAIL 12/11/95
L.N.,
ST. LOUIS AREA

• • • •

*I'm sorry to admit that at one time I was a liberal and in fact I voted for
Willy Boy much to my regret. Now I've "seen the light" and I truly have
you to thank!! I'm a single mom—have been for eight years—and I've
never been on welfare (wouldn't know how to go about getting on it), never
begged on street corners, never had food stamps, etc. I am encouraged on a
daily basis by your commentary and common sense approach to our problems here in the U.S. and around the world. Keep on believing and standing up for what you believe in, and I will too.*

VIA FAX 10/9/95
D.C.,
PHOENIX AREA

• • • •

*My Brother Ken,
I applaud you for your unwavering convictions. I am a relatively new listener to your broadcast and have been pleasantly surprised to hear a man,
such as yourself so confidently express his views concerning the plight of
the black man, and the oppressive policies of the established welfare state. I
am similarly pleased to hear the stand you take against the organization
known as the NAACP, which at one time may have been genuinely concerned for the welfare of the black man, but as of late is singularly concerned about the continuance of its own existence. . . . God love ya.
Airborne. (Just for the record, I am of Mexican and Hungarian descent—a
Hungry Mexican.)*

VIA E-MAIL 2/1/96
J.L.,
COLUMBUS, GEORGIA

I started playing the old Sly Stone cut "Stand" as bumper music on
my radio show in 1995. It has been my way of saying to my radio audience—
to America—that we need to get back to the basics that made this country
strong.

I am trying to encourage people, black and white, to absorb the strength and the character of their heritage as Americans.

I'm trying to make them remember the strength it must have taken to resist the attack on Fort Sumter, the strength it took to survive the Bataan March, the strength it took to endure as a POW in the Hanoi Hilton.

I want them all to understand what it took to be the first black Union soldiers in the Civil War, soldiers who were fighting for America but knew full well that if caught by the Confederacy they would be treated not as POWs, but as chattel. They most likely would be summarily executed.

I want them to comprehend the spark of adventure that necessity turned into a grueling commitment on the part of the pioneers who forged ahead on the Oregon Trail to explore and settle this great country.

I want people to remember the black men at Tuskegee who wanted to fly but were denied that privilege. I want them to remember that these black airmen ultimately were recognized as exemplary war pilots.

I want them to remember the struggle for civil rights led by a true rainbow coalition of Americans who stood up for morality and justice.

I want them to think about the white boy in Vietnam who soiled his pants the first time a bullet whizzed by his head. The white boy who turned to his buddy—to his black, his Hispanic, his Jewish buddy whom he may have seen in a different light before the war—and drew strength.

All of these historical events illustrate the strength of character that I believe is unique to the melting pot of blacks and whites, men and women, Protestants and Catholics, who believe in America. It's a melting pot of character that I want Americans to draw from today. I want them to draw the strength necessary to say one thing to the dissenters in our country: "Good-bye."

I want us all to stand and say unanimously to the dissenters of color: "It is time to get over the injustices of the past, lest we forfeit the future. Now it's time to celebrate your good fortune that you are Americans. No one is going to breast-feed you anymore. No one will coddle you any longer."

I want us to say to the socialist liberal dissenters: "America is about competition and striving to be number one. America is about everyone having the chance to run that foot race. It's not about calling off the foot race to shelter the losers."

I am trying to get the boss, faced with an incompetent employee who happens to be black, to reach the point where he can look that employee in the eye and say, "You are not cutting it here, so I am going to give you a bad report."

If that person believes the report is based on racism instead of an honest judgment of performance, then so be it. The important thing is that the boss find the strength to take a stand for excellence, which used to be the American way.

I am trying to get the black men and women who graduated from medical school solely on their academic merit to employ the strength of the American spirit to walk away from people who try to discount their achievement because of some convoluted notion stemming from the Myth of the Hobbled Black. I'm trying to help these successful black Americans find the strength to transcend the envy and hatred of the black-trash welfare culture so that they can enjoy the fruits of their honest efforts.

My prescription for America is to rekindle the positive energy that has made this country great.

We must once again put forth role models who believe in the American Dream and all of its promise. I believe that simply respecting the men and women who stand up for the clear-cut American values of hard work, right and wrong, and well-earned success will go a long way toward preventing the black-trash welfare culture from spreading further into mainstream America.

It's especially critical that we blacks who have become fully vested American citizens speak out about our stake and our success in America. We must stand up and be counted among the revitalized American role models.

But I urge *all* Americans—be they white or brown or yellow or black—to stand up for the clear-cut values that have always guided us to right wrongs and to build upon what's right.

We should begin with the simple courtesies that demonstrate the value of respecting the rights of others. Like nodding hello in an elevator. Saying excuse me when you inadvertently bump into someone. Greeting a bank teller or a grocery clerk with a smile. These wonderful pleasantries should be a part of routine living in a civilized society.

I'm not the first pundit to call for a return to family values. However, my message is short and simple in this regard. I want to return to the day when it wasn't acceptable for our young daughters to get pregnant before they were married.

I want to return to the time when you weren't labeled an extremist or a right-winger because you proclaimed your love for this great country. And I want to protect the symbols of our patriotism.

That includes continuing to fight for a constitutional amendment to outlaw the desecration of our flag. Too many Americans have drawn strength from Old Glory on battlefields throughout the decades to allow it to be reduced today to an object of contempt in the name of ultraliberalism.

I believe that preserving the true meaning behind the colors today will help to see our children through the challenges that they inevitably will face as Americans.

I want to restore the value of a human life in America. That means getting rid of every liberal-minded prosecuting attorney and judge. Let them operate out of the public defender's office or a social worker's clinic where they can legitimately work as advocates for thugs and predators.

I get thrown off of juries in my hometown because I am so adamant about crime and punishment. The judges and the lawyers know from reading my columns in the *Denver Post* that if the defendant gets on the stand and says, "Well, I stuck up that old boy because my kids at home were hungry," I'm going to send him to jail. And if, by chance, he ended up killing the old boy, I'm going to demand his life in return.

I believe we should return to the clear-headed notion of celebrating our success in this great country, not apologizing for it. Success is the driving force of the American Dream.

Don't kid yourself. Without the motivator that some call greed, most of you reading this book wouldn't be where you are today. You would not be able to carry on those little friendly debates: "No, no, no, no, no, I insist. Let me pick up the lunch tab." You wouldn't be able to send those checks off to Junior at college. You wouldn't be able to say to your wife "Let's buy it" when the two of you agree that your granddaughter would look adorable in a new dress or hat or coat.

It meant a lot to me to be able to write the check for my daughter's formal wedding. It means a lot to me to write a check for my granddaughter's school tuition every fall.

Greed in the sense of working hard all your life to get ahead is not a bad thing. I have been working hard all my life, and I believe I deserve to savor my rewards.

But all of us who have achieved a degree of success in this country are constantly bombarded with the ideology of the liberal socialist camp. That has caused many of us to feel ashamed and guilty about our success. We are told we are bigots. We are told we are selfish and insensitive to the suffering needy just because we have been able to achieve some of our goals.

This assault from the liberals has caused some Americans to lose faith in themselves, to lose faith in their commonsense ability to distinguish right from wrong. At a minimum, it has made them hesitate to intervene when they see obvious wrongdoing.

How many times do you avoid "getting involved" in a misdeed because you fear being chided that what you are observing is just a "black thing" or a "poor thing"? Well, I think we need to return to the time when we made judgments based only on whether an act was right or wrong. No more special concessions for being black or being poor.

I don't think anyone has anything to fear from the moral code of that kind of America. One of the things my fifty-plus years of life has taught me is that, overall, America is a nation of fair and just people. In the final analysis, we believe in doing the right thing—skin color and economic bracket notwithstanding.

• • • •

By standing up for what is right, for success and for the American Dream, I am not putting down poor people. My detractors may tell you that. But I'm not insensitive. I'm not insensitive at all. I'm just not running for anything. And more important, I'm not running from anything.

The truth is that what I learned firsthand about poverty is that you don't settle for it. You *do not* settle for it.

That's what splitting rails and reading by lamplight were all about, and I am a descendant of people who grew up with kerosene lanterns. I know that I wasn't unique in my climb from poverty. I was part of something greater, part of a whole. Knowing, or at least imagining, that there could be more to life was what made me refuse to settle for being poor.

Today, when I am asked how I would solve the problem of black welfare babies—the innocents who are bred to suffer—I respond that I'll meet any-one halfway. But I won't go back and drag them out, kicking and screaming, denouncing the hope of America. If they drag their feet or tarry, I will move on. I won't try to save everyone in Dark Town. They must have some inkling of the concept of opportunity in America. They must also understand that there is no free lunch in America—or anywhere else.

I cannot walk on water. I cannot flap my arms and levitate. I'm just an unassuming colored guy. I make all the same gas stops as anyone else. I check the air in the tires. As I get older, I probably throw away tires that have more life on them than I would have when I was twenty or thirty years younger— just to be sure I won't ever have to bend down along the side of the highway and jack up my car to fix a flat.

I say all of that because I have come to realize that, like any other human being, I have only a certain amount of energy and a certain amount of time. So I have learned that we all have to make choices about how we disburse our energy.

That realization has led me to the hard reality that we likely won't be able to save all the people languishing away in Dark Town. But this is not Chech-nya. This is not the Soviet Union. This is not Fidel's Cuba. This is the United States of America. All anyone has to do in America is to take the first step, and there are any number of good Americans—including me—who at that point will extend a helping hand to them.

So I urge all good Americans to stand up for America, the American way and the American Dream.

But don't void or minimize the time you have to share with your children or with your community worrying about those who do not believe in these tried and true principles of America.

Do not buy into the liberal agenda that would have you conducting safaris into places where people do not want to be liberated. Don't go out and buy a long rope and start whirling it over your head to catch the homeless, the needy, and the disenfranchised. You cannot do what the government of the United States of America has not been able to do in more than thirty years of liberal handouts.

We commit ourselves to a lifetime of work when we deal with children, when we deal with family, when we deal with our American community. Nobody has the energy to make good on those commitments and then run down the road to capture people who don't want to be caught in order to bring them into twentieth-century America.

I contend, however, that by making a positive public recommitment to America, we will be doing the very best thing we possibly can for those lost souls. We will be setting an example, offering a road map, showing once again that anything is possible in America.

Then it will be up to every individual to make a commitment for himself or herself to step from the mud below toward the sky above.

Young black people will have to decide for themselves whether they will be winners or losers. They will know that choosing a path of pregnancy, welfare, or gang-banging no longer will be rewarded.

They will have to understand that a spark must be ignited in their souls if they are to travel a winning path. Once they decide they're not going to be losers, nothing—not the KKK, not the white citizens council, not any group of bigots, not the old laws of apartheid in South Africa—nothing can stop them because they will be able to dig deep in their souls to acquire the strength to carry on. Welfare and liberal indulgence can never offer that kind of can-do attitude.

I believe that spark is innate in every human being. But the people who don't ignite it will die just as surely as an errant moose going across the tundra in Alaska. If it lags behind, a wolf pack will cut it off from the herd.

I care about the person on the sinking ship who can't swim but refuses to stand on the deck and quietly go under. That spirit has brought humankind to where it is today.

The crime is not trying to swim.

I would ask America to respond only to the people who understand that the mouth-to-mouth resuscitation this country offers them in the economic and educational arenas is a two-way deal.

I have always believed, and I continue to believe, that our country has an obligation to meet the needy halfway. But I also believe the needy have an obligation to meet the country halfway. When the contract is not met by either side, the deal is null and void. Because many modern-day welfare recipients are not doing their part, I believe the obligation to them on the part of taxpayers has been voided.

If it were up to me, I would follow up the civil rights movement of the 1960s with a civil obligation movement today.

We have won our freedom. The America of today can work for everyone. Now we must fulfill our obligation to the people who struggled on our behalf by participating in America as fully vested American citizens, committed to listening to the moral conscience of this country. We must fulfill our obligation to the whole.

I have determined that my mother's American Dream was authentic because I have realized it.

And now I refuse to keep this truth a secret. I refuse to go along with the party line, to quietly adhere to the Myth of the Hobbled Black.

There are those who have said that my message has similarities to the fundamental message of self-reliance that Minister Farrakhan and his cohosts preached to the 400,000 black men who participated in the Million Man March in the fall of 1995. But I would beg to differ.

My message, while demanding a degree of self-reliance as a strategy, is a much bigger message about a return to the principles and a rekindling of the positive energy of the American Dream. Further, my message is aimed at all of America, not just black Americans.

But if I stood before an audience like the Farrakhan audience, I would raise my hand like the pope and give absolution to the many successful black men in that audience who still carry the burden of guilt for their achievements.

I would say, "Look to the man on your right and on your left; look to the man in front of you and behind you. They are men who have earned the right to be fully vested American citizens. All of you have earned the right to be successful in America.

"Going back to the first black man who landed on these shores in bondage, to the first black man or woman who ran north to freedom, to the first black person who said no to the back of the bus, to the first black boy who marched for his freedom and his right to education, to Martin Luther King who stayed the course when he was shouted down and called a nigger in places like Cicero, Illinois. . . . All of you are products of that proud heritage.

"That heritage has earned you the right to look at the man next to you and determine whether you want to be his friend, whether you want to live next to him, whether you want to live with his values or challenge him to live with yours.

"You have earned your freedom, not just as black men but as fully vested Americans."

I would challenge those men to stand up to anyone who tried to reach into their pockets or their psyches, because no one has a right to steal their hopes and dreams, the things they are trying to put aside for their children.

I would say that this is a great country. If they need proof, all they would have to do would be to turn to their left, walk to the National Archives, and look at the Constitution of the United States, which serves us all. They could gaze at the Capitol Building, where the American people have seen to it that civil rights laws were passed to make us truly equal citizens. All they would have to do would be to walk straight ahead to the U.S. Supreme Court Building where our stalwart battle for black civil rights has been challenged and won time after time.

From this point on, I would say, the burden is now their own.

Then I would tell them to look around again. I would tell them that no one in the crowd could save them from their failures. Others can only inhibit them by trying to make them feel guilty about their success.

What would I say to the black thugs who I know were in the audience as well?

Nothing.

I would say nothing to them. Because what I would have said to the successful black men would have been applicable to the whole. If that message didn't fit for the young thugs, they simply would not receive it. Because you cannot be something you have not prepared yourself to be. You cannot spend your life as a drug dealer and a gang-banger and expect to become a tenured teacher at a university, living the life due the black girl or boy who cracked the books instead of hanging in the hood with the homeys.

You cannot devalue another man's hard work and achievements simply by commandeering the results of the sweat of his labor. You can't take another man's rewards just because you were a young black thug who went through a rehab program and now you are too old or too tired or too burned out to run with the dope dealers and the gang-bangers the way you once did. You can't just come in out of the cold and be granted automatic credibility, full parity with those who worked hard and aspired to the mainstream.

So I would say nothing to them. They need to become part of the whole. They need to embrace America before they are even in the game.

As for the quota blacks, I would tell them that they are thieves who steal the nectar of accomplishment from the people who have run the gauntlet, who have met the challenge of racism head on, who have stayed the course against all the dirty looks, all the obstacles that had to be overcome in order to become fully vested American citizens.

I would tell them that they no longer can become police officers or accountants or federal workers strictly based on numbers, on a minority quota system. The time has come to compete fairly and squarely.

I would repeat the words about affirmative action spoken first by Booker T. Washington and more recently by Justice Clarence Thomas. Washington, a former slave who founded the Tuskegee Institute in Alabama, said: "No greater injury can be done to any youth than to let him feel that because he belongs to this or that race he will be advanced regardless of his own merit or efforts."

And from Clarence Thomas's concurring opinion regarding the 1995 U.S. Supreme Court ruling against excessive implementation of affirmative action: "These [affirmative action] programs stamp minorities with a badge of inferiority and may cause them to develop dependencies or to adopt an attitude that they are 'entitled' to preferences."

Both men were speaking about universal truths concerning the true source of self-esteem and self-respect.

Thomas's words speak to the fact that with between two-thirds and three-fourths of black Americans established in the mainstream middle class, it is now time to let go of the notion that we as a people need special preference to compete. It's time to allow us to stand or fall on our own two feet. That is the true test of equality. And it is the very principle that establishes that America is not a class-conscious society. Everybody has a chance to reach for the moon.

But as I said, my message is not limited to black Americans. It is a call for all Americans, without regard to their skin color, to all Americans with the same positive mind-set about America and the American way to unite against those who would tear America down. I want us all to take a united stand against the perpetrators of the Myth of the Hobbled Black. I want us to call out the poverty pimps, the quota blacks, and their high-minded conspirators, the egg-sucking dog liberals.

Taking this stand will be good for all blacks who are ready to take that final step to become fully vested Americans. And taking this united stand will be good for all Americans.

Once upon a time I believed that when my kids were grown, I could count myself out of the game. I knew I would have to continue to be a good citizen, obey the law, and go to work every day. But I thought I would no longer have the overwhelming responsibility of caring about the bigger universe of social and political concerns.

Then my first grandchild was born, and I realized that no man can isolate himself. You may think you can drop out. You may think you can waltz away. But then your kids have kids, and you're right back in the game.

In fact, as a grandfather, I have come to understand that old folks like us who have experienced life's challenges as well as its offerings are even more obligated to care about future generations.

I had hoped I would be able to turn with the baton of life in my hand and be able to firmly slap it into the hands of the good folks who followed me. The day came when I was prepared to hand off that baton.

I was smug. I knew that my generation had done a pretty good job with this country. We had gotten people on the right track. People were talking to one another. We had corrected some clear injustices. A lot of us black Americans had gotten ahead in America, thus proving that we had been worthy of being given equal opportunity.

But the sad fact is that when I turned to pass the baton to the black children behind me, I found almost nobody there. The next generation had been mugged. They had been mugged by Louie Farrakhan in Washington, D.C., by Charlie Rangel in New York, by Maxine Waters in California, and by John Conyers in Detroit.

While I was busy looking ahead to the future, they were snatched up by the poverty pimps and the African-American pseudo–community leaders who had stolen the legacy of the accomplishments of my generation. I did not like that.

Speaking as a fully vested black American, I ask these questions again and again: When and why did those people walk away from the hopes and dreams of America? When did they abandon the hopes and dreams of moral leaders like Martin Luther King, whose simple hope was that his children might "live in a nation where they [would] not be judged by the color of their skin, but by the content of their character"? When did they lose sight of Dr. King's plea for equal opportunity and replace it with a demand for eternal reparations?

We are talking about the final stage in the liberation of a people, making black Americans fully vested citizens. The first step is to free each man and woman so that all African Americans can stand on their own and be judged as accountable, capable Americans.

Then we must determine what obligation these individuals have to the whole.

It's at this juncture that I depart from those who uphold the Myth of the Hobbled Black. Because I believe the obligation to the whole is not encompassed in looking back with reverence to the stagnant community that the African Americans define as the ghetto and that I call Dark Town. I believe our obligation to the whole is what all Americans, black and white, owe to America. And I believe we must all stand up for that America.

Chapter Fifteen

Pick a Better Country

. . . .

I like so many great Americans share the dream of equality, opportunity, comfort, good kids, a friendly community, and a safe, unified country, under GOD (as so proudly proclaimed by millions each day). I would like to commend you for being a champion of yourself, your family, your community, and the distinguished people of America. You are a hero of mine. I am a 17 year old, white Catholic girl living in the south, who sees (I am not blind!), but disregards the color of one's skin. . . . Is it not a wonder that I am a poster child for the NAACP or white, bureaucratic liberals who are "for the movement"? Don't they claim their objective is to have an American that judges others not on the basis of their skin tone, but on their content? I am going to stick my neck out and say . . . THEY'RE LIARS! . . . It's ok to say America isn't a utopia. She's not. It's ok to say that this and that is wrong with her, but being Americans, we must not continue to indulge ourselves with this pathetic whining. Instead, we must follow up on our dissatisfaction with real action. That's what this magnificent country was founded on. That's what we call TRADITION. That's what WORKS. I, with you, implore all the Americans who are guilty of this crime against America to cease calling people "African-Americans," "Jewish-Americans," etc. Just drop the "ishs" and "ans" and just be Americans. In doing so, we demonstrate our unification and solidarity as the great country we are to

the world and more importantly, we show our commitment to one another.
We are Americans . . . the standard of the world.

VIA E-MAIL 2/1/96
C.T.,
JACKSONVILLE, FL AREA

· · · ·

I seem to recall an article in the Post sometime back about how economi-
cally deprived blacks in Haiti sell their female children into bondage to af-
fluent black families where they are forced to serve at drudgery.
Those African Americans who feel they would be better off if their ancestors
hadn't been imported to this country as slaves should be afforded every op-
portunity to return to Africa. It would be less expensive for the government
to repatriate these people than to maintain them here with their con-
tentious and divisive attitude.

VIA MAIL 12/10/95
A.O.,
ANYWERE AVENUE, LALA LAND, USA

· · · ·

Brother Ken,
A country was formed in the mid 1800s for freed black slaves from the U.S.
It is known as Liberia. Just tell Louis F. and his gang [that] Delta is ready
when they are.

VIA FAX 1995
BROTHER MARK,
ANDERSON, SC

· · · ·

To all distinguished contributors to the "CONSERVATIVE
CHRONICLE" . . .
A very special thanks to Mr. Ken Hamblin. If nobody else does, he surely
grasped the meaning of the American Spirit and the depth of its possibili-
ties. Does anybody have to be any color, nationality or religion? I certainly
do not call myself a Germo-American. Having come to this country forty
years ago at the age of thirty, I never thought of myself any other than
"American" and oh so proud of it am I.

VIA MAIL 12/6/95
B.P.,
HESPERIA, MICHIGAN

• • • •

Ken, I'm a VERY ASSUMING white guy who has been listening to your show for a number of months. You mentioned you are not "a man of letters." I hereby give you the following letters:

> *A – for Astonishing*
> *B – for Bodacious*
> *C – for Cool*
> *D – for Devastating (to Liberals) and*
> *E – for Excellent*

Furthermore, I get really nervous when a black guy does as good an Irish accent as you do. And I know Irish accents. When I couldn't take New York City anymore in 1970, I took my Irish wife and American infant daughter and went to live and work in Ireland. Seven years later, in an effort to escape 30% inflation per year and an experimental social-welfare state, I returned to America with the same wife, the same daughter and three Irish-born sons. I had eighteen hundred dollars to my name and thought that in America anything was possible. Five and a half weeks later, I had a job at $19,800 a year and had bought a three-bedroom house with "nothing down." Yeah, it's true that I'm still a computer professional and doing very well, but I never would have been if it wasn't for the support of two guys in a major New York bank that thought I was worth promoting first into Operations and then, into Programming. They thought my skills and hard work overcame the fact that I didn't have a high school diploma, so they blew my horn for me, and put their reputations on the line to help advance my career. I hope I made it pay off for them. See, Charlie and Fred were both black, and in the sixties in New York, things weren't any better for black guys than they were for white guys with no High School diploma. Tell your black brothers, Ken, that they, and you, and I have found the promised land. It's called America! Ain't it great to be here?

VIA FAX 11/3/95
BRIAN IN EL GRANADA

• • • •

. . . I'm sure you must have received a ton of mail congratulating you on your thoughts and stand regarding the current moral level to which our country has descended under the liberal philosophy in current fashion. You, Sir, are a breath of fresh air. . . . We, indeed, are all Americans—period. Of course we ALL come from different and varied extractions, but if that ancestry is so important and paramount then it behooves one to return to the source of that ancestry. Not since the early 1800's has anyone been

forced to come here.... For those who think they have it so bad here they
should be invited to GO where they think it is so great.
Thank you ... just for being you, hopefully the breath of fresh air herald-
ing a gale.

VIA MAIL 7/14/94
R.W.,
OCALA, FL

• • • •

Brother Ken,
Yesterday (Wednesday, 25 Oct 95) you took a call from Brother Michael
who is a citizen of Nigeria. Brother Michael is typical of liberals in Amer-
ica and worldwide.
Brother Michael said you were blaming all black people, worldwide for all
the social ills prevalent in today's society. Obviously Brother Michael does
not listen to your show. You do not hold black people responsible, but liber-
als ... like Brother Michael.
When you asked Brother Michael why he was in the United States instead
of helping his people in Nigeria, all Brother Michael could come up with
was there are Americans in Nigeria. He steadfastly refused to answer the
question. Wonder why?
I have a challenge for Brother Michael. Ask ten of your liberal friends to go
to Nigeria with you. Each of those ten liberals should ask ten of their lib-
eral friends to go also. Each of those should ask ten and so on and so on.
This will be the greatest thing that ever happened to America. The only
problem is that as soon as all these liberals get to Nigeria and look around
they'll want to come back to the good old USA.
Let's not let them back in.... oh well, just a nice thought.

VIA FAX 10/26/95
BROTHER R.A.,
JACKSONVILLE, FLORIDA

• • • •

I always looked upon anybody who said that they are whatever American
that they're first loyalty was to whatever nation they said and not to Amer-
ica. All they did was just live here but that won't be for long.

VIA E-MAIL 12/7/95
R.A.

I am not a world traveler. I have never been to Africa, the land of milk
and honey that is revered by those hyphenated Americans who cling to the

Myth of the Hobbled Black. But I read newspapers and magazines, and I watch television news broadcasts.

I have seen the reports of famine and of deadly diseases like AIDS and Ebola, which are widespread on the Dark Continent. I am aware of African racism that goes beyond black-versus-white to long-held prejudices and discrimination based on tribal affiliation and geography.

I reel in utter horror at the fact that even as I write these words slavery is being carried on in North Africa in Islamic countries like the Sudan, Mauritania, and Libya. Africans with features like mine are being captured by Africans with keen Arab features. The women are being chained and auctioned off as concubines while their children are pressed into servitude.

Khalid Abdul Muhammad, a former top aide to Louis Farrakhan, didn't speak of this immoral practice by his own people when he lashed out at Jews as the "bloodsuckers of the black nation." Louis Farrakhan himself clearly has turned his head away from these centuries-old atrocities while he cozies up to the modern-day slave masters. Maxine Waters and Jesse Jackson are noticeably silent about this black-on-black matter. To the best of my knowledge, liberal Colorado Congresswoman Patricia Schroeder has never so much as squinted about it publicly.

I have spoken to Africans on my radio show who have come to America, many to partake of this country's bountiful educational opportunities. More than one of them has marveled at the misconceptions that so-called African Americans have about their ancestral homeland today. They say these blacks should count their blessings that they were born American citizens. They speak of the lack of human and civil rights, of the harsh and unjust dictatorships prevalent on the African continent.

While I cannot report firsthand about Africa, I have been to Haiti. In fact, my experiences in Haiti marked a significant turning point in my personal evolution. They helped me to grow as a human being, as a black man, and as an American.

I saw Haiti as a young man in the early 1970s during a time of adventure in my life when I was making frequent pleasure trips in my own airplane back and forth to the Caribbean. On my early trips to Port-au-Prince, even though I was flying a tiny single-engine Cherokee 180, I nonetheless felt like a jet-setter on the couple of occasions when I parked next to Jackie O.'s private jet at Duvalier International Airport.

My daring flights to the Caribbean in my little airplane reached their zenith whenever Haiti was a destination. It meant that I had to leave the relative security of hopping from island to island down the Bahamian chain. I had to venture out over the deep blue—out of sight of land for more than an hour—to head south to Haiti, which makes up the western third of the island of Hispaniola.

There are many little proverbs and maxims that pilots historically have traded in airport coffee shops. Like the saying that there are only two kinds of pilots—those who have landed with their gear up and those who will do so one day. Or the proverb that says there are old pilots and there are bold pilots, but there are no old bold pilots.

Some pilots consider it unsafe to fly an airplane with only one engine under any circumstance. These guys think you would be nuts to fly single engine over water, especially offshore beyond the range where you could glide if your engine stopped. According to this group of pilots, no matter how well your plane's been running, how well maintained it is, you're sure to have a rough engine when you leave sight of land.

And sure enough, just about every time I flew to Haiti, I spent most of my time on that last leg over the deep blue adjusting the fuel mixture. I monitored the purr of my Lycoming engine, straining to reach the fullest possible limits of my senses. I don't know whether I heard my buddies' voices ringing in my ears or whether I truly heard my engine missing, but I know I heard something.

I remember the first time I landed in Haiti as if it were yesterday. I touched down and taxied off the active runway to a parking area, where, with the prop still whirling, the plane was surrounded by a sea of little Haitian urchins, some I would guess to be no more than seven or eight years old. I had this image of them being chopped to pieces by the propeller, and I thought to myself that this was indeed a foreign and uncivilized place. Even in the Caribbean islands to the north, I had observed more order than I saw here—in this place where children ran unfettered about an active airport.

When I cracked the cabin door, they hit me with a dozen languages, vying for the chance to tote my bags and wash my airplane. First Spanish, then French, German, English. When I didn't respond immediately, they tried patois and dialects I couldn't begin to recognize.

At that moment my Haitian education had begun.

Here I was, a poor black kid from the streets of New York. I had arrived at a point in my life where I was feeling pretty smug about myself. I had flown in my own private airplane to this exotic Third World island country in the Caribbean. I had money and credit cards in my pocket. I was eager to see this black-ruled nation for myself. Because my ancestors hailed from the West Indies a bit farther south, I guess I even imagined this to be part of a journey back to my roots. But I was smacked in the face with unexpected realities.

My first jolt involved those kids and the perspective they offered as to just how far I had come in the world. Here I was—Mr. Hotshot, a film documentarian, television personality, accomplished photographer—standing on the wing of my airplane face-to-face with children who clearly had had little or no official schooling, but who already had learned the essence of survival in the concepts of "can do" and competition. These peasant boys, the wretched of Haiti, realized that in order to stay alive, in order to survive, they would have to qualify as efficient beggars on that airport tarmac. They had to compete to be there. The qualification was that they had to be able to communicate. They had to be able to ask for the opportunity to work in every language they might possibly encounter.

I was proficient in only one language. So my initial reaction to meeting these young Haitians was how ill equipped I was to function outside the boundaries of English-speaking countries, which at that point in my life were the only countries I had ever visited. Simultaneously, I felt like a world traveler and a provincial unsophisticate.

Today I think of those children in yet another light. I think about how they had made an effort to equip themselves to survive, even given the extremely limited resources available to them in that pathetic country. And I think about how comparatively ill equipped the black babies being spewed out of America's black welfare culture are today. At least those Haitian youngsters had tried to better themselves. Their drive had not been deadened by an expectation—an expectation always met—of the government dole.

Eventually I was rescued from this swarm of hyperactive youngsters by Paul, a Haitian man who became my guide on that and every one of my subsequent trips to Haiti.

This was during the rule of the Haitian dictator Jean-Claude Duvalier, known as Baby Doc. Paul, always in dark glasses and Western attire, clearly stood out as a former member of the Tontons Macoute—the ruthless private army that had operated under the direction of Baby Doc's father and predecessor, François Duvalier, known as Papa Doc.

During more than a half dozen trips that I made to Haiti over a couple of years, Paul showed me a Third World country up close—a black-run Third World country. It was a land worse than anything I had ever seen in my life for people of color. It was so wretched that places like Harlem, East Saint Louis, and the South Side of Chicago seemed like resorts when compared to the squalor and the human misery I saw there.

Human waste and sewage literally ran in well-worn ditches alongside some back streets in Port-au-Prince. People swarmed about the streets of the city from sunup to sundown. A friend of mine, a wacky white Canadian professor who was taking his students back and forth from Toronto to Haiti around the time I was going there, aptly described the economy and the workforce in Haiti as 90 percent unemployed but 100 percent busy. On one trip into the mountain village of Petionville, I saw men sitting along the side of the road pounding rocks with miniature hammers in order to grind them up to make concrete.

On another trip I met a South American photojournalist whom I accompanied into the countryside one night to attend a voodoo ceremony. Minutes outside Port-au-Prince, the roads fell into complete disarray from the jungle overgrowth, and the world went dark. There was no electricity. In the village I met the only overweight people I ever saw in this country of malnourished peasants—the obviously corrupt voodoo priest and his wife.

Of course, all of what I saw in Haiti flies in the face of years of propaganda from the black poverty pimps and the egg-sucking dog liberals who blame all the failures of their black constituents and wards on the fact that America is an oppressive environment for minority blacks because of majority white racism. From their perspective, which they adamantly preach to their black communities, it is presumed that if only blacks could gain ruling power, they would thrive.

According to them, a black-ruled country most assuredly would offer a model setting for black prosperity. Haiti is the oldest black republic in the world, the second-oldest independent country in the Western Hemisphere.

The slaves on the French colonial island, led by Pierre Dominique Toussaint l'Ouverture, rebelled and gained control of the colony in 1791. When Napoleon I dispatched French forces in 1802, Toussaint was tricked into captivity, but the blacks ultimately prevailed and declared the country's independence under the name of Haiti in 1804.

Unfortunately, however, Haiti has never served as a model nation in terms of black prosperity; it remains today perhaps the poorest nation in the Western Hemisphere.

Haiti served as a turning point in my life at a time when I was beginning to molt out of the full dress of my black liberal politics of the 1960s.

I was jolted into deep contemplation, in this era of black pride in America, when I met many Haitian peasants who referred to me as a "black white man."

Paul explained to me, quite nonchalantly, that their words had nothing to do with race. They simply were using this reference to indicate my apparent wealth. And obviously, while they connected being white with wealth, they also believed that wealth was attainable for any man in America.

I don't recall exactly on which trip Paul asked to return to the U.S. with me. He said he wanted to work for me in America. He wanted to go with me—the "black white man"—in order to pursue the same opportunity I obviously had taken advantage of in order to be in Haiti as a tourist.

While these incidents planted food for thought, the vestiges of my liberalism still were predominant in my thinking.

On every trip to Haiti I stayed at the Plaza, an old, formerly French colonial hotel in downtown Port-au-Prince. The custom in the open-air dining room situated beneath a gigantic rubber tree was for guests to converse with one another, often joining tables to dine together. As a result, I became acquainted with people from many different places and cultures. I met black

American art dealers from New York, French Canadians, South Americans, and some of Haiti's own elite.

I remember sitting with those people and doing what American liberals, particularly black liberals, were prone to do: bemoaning the plight of the Haitian peasant, the Haitian poor. One night someone asked me: "But, Ken, what would you give them?"

I replied: "All the things we have."

And that person continued: "Well, would you give them telephone bills, car payments, mortgages?"

"Yes," I said without hesitation.

Even then, however, I was unsure of my answer. I thought about that question for years. What will you give a man?

Eventually I began to see my reasoning clearly: The poor Haitians, their lives are so miserable. If we give them all the things that we have, they will be just like us. Their lives will be wonderful. They'll be able to fly to Hilton Head in South Carolina and vacation at the resort on the beach. They'll be able to watch television programs and go to movies. They'll be able to buy the latest cars and clothes.

Somehow I thought that if I gave half of what I'd worked for to these less fortunate folk they would value it as much as I did, simply because I wanted them to.

But life isn't that way. Back then I suspected it wasn't. Today I know it isn't.

It has been probably twenty-five years since I had that conversation under the rubber tree at the Plaza. Yet even today I don't know exactly what I would give to the Haitians.

Today I do realize that you can't simply give a person a dream. You can't give a person the will to walk out of squalor and deprivation and poverty.

You can provide people with opportunity. But you can't make them take advantage of it. Neither government nor foreign aid can mandate that. The dream and the will to chase it have to be nurtured by family; the concept has to be part of the clan. If it is not, then it requires mustering the energy to take a tremendous leap of faith to try to reach for the moon.

If I had the power to affect people's lives in America, I would send young black thugs and brood mares living according to the tenets of today's black welfare culture—hating America, convinced that they are victims—on a ninety-day visit to Haiti. While there have been several shifts in power since my visits to Haiti, I don't believe living conditions have changed substantially for the poor there. And so I would expect these young black Americans to leave Haiti with at least an inkling of understanding of the opportunity that they are privileged to enjoy in America.

I would hope they would see that, contrary to the misinformation broadcast by their African-American leaders, contrary to the Myth of the Hobbled

Black, being an American is far from the worst thing that could have happened to them. I would expect them to come home with a broader understanding of what the Haitians and the Asians and the Mexicans who are desperately clawing at our borders are trying to attain for themselves and for their children. I would expect them to come back with a broader understanding of themselves.

I also would expect them to begin to comprehend the obligation everyone has who pursues the American Dream. I would hope they could begin to see that everyone must contribute to, as well as take from, the whole by believing in and supporting that dream, by working hard, by maintaining the values of right and wrong, and by passing those concepts along to their children.

It would be okay with me if they came back and decided to go to school to become social workers or if they wanted to go to medical school and then join the equivalent of the Peace Corps so they could return to Haiti to make a contribution there. At least they would be adopting a can-do attitude rather than wallowing in the defeatism that controls their lives today. At least they would be saying: I don't like what I saw in Haiti; I want to do something about it.

Lots of Americans have seen things here and outside of our borders that they don't like. I certainly have. And we have adopted a can-do attitude about rolling up our sleeves and finding a way to change those things.

My battle with the liberals is because their agenda has bred generations of people who right now are sitting idly on 125th Street and Lenox Avenue in Harlem or on equivalent corners in Detroit and Watts. These are generations of people who have lost the dream, or may never have known the dream because their mothers and fathers failed to pass it along to them. They have no dream, no active desire to do better for themselves, because they have bought into the myths and the propaganda of hopelessness that have been fed to them.

And so I would expect the black American boys and girls to come back from Haiti with a gnawing desire—similar to that of a fish swimming upstream to spawn—to move ahead. I would expect them to return to America with the knowledge that they can't stop their lives in Harlem or Detroit or Northeast Denver. They would know that there must be another square beyond Dark Town. They would have to go on to see what else there is. They would have to answer some newly formed questions in their lives.

It's one thing to hear about places like Haiti as an inner-city African American who never crosses the boundaries of your sequestered environment. It's another thing to go to Haiti and see for yourself that it is a lie to claim that the antidote to all deprivation suffered by black people is to live in a black-ruled country.

If you live in an environment where sameness prevails—as in a socialist country—you can't even formulate the right questions. And without the right questions, you likely won't ever want to get up off your ass. You won't have a desire to walk into a library. If you don't have questions, you won't ever have the urge to overcome your fear, your bigotry, your racism, your hatred, your xenophobia, in order to walk up to another man and say, "Show me. What is that? How do I do that?"

That's the "how you." That's saying, "Hi, I'm someone. I don't know your customs, the lay of your land. But it would be swell if I could learn."

If you don't know the right questions, you miss the essence of America.

In retrospect, I realize now that I saw some people in Haiti who indeed seemed to have that innate drive to make them dream of better lives and strive to acquire them. Like the little children at the airport who were not content to go hungry on the streets. Like the young people who walked back and forth every night in a lighted park across from the Plaza Hotel to take advantage of one of the few public places in the city with electricity so they could study and read books that exposed them to my world.

I also realize today that the best and the brightest of those Haitians ultimately have struggled to leave Haiti in order to truly fulfill their dreams. And where have they risked their lives to go? Risked their lives in rickety homemade boats over rough and unpredictable seas? They have given everything they have to get to my America.

They have left their black-ruled country—regarded as a utopia by some of their American black brethren—in order to come to America.

They have left their island homeland, which is flush with corruption—corruption very similar to that which is fostered by American poverty pimps—in order to come to America.

Once here, they seek the path to the mainstream, pursuing education and hard work, adhering to solid values of right and wrong, all in order to benefit from the promise of the American Dream.

The same can be said of the thousands of Cubans who have fled from the corruption and the failures of their idealistic socialist society in order to come to our shores. And of the tens of thousands of Mexicans and Central Americans who in some instances have fought literally to the death to get to the United States of America, where, they believe, they can achieve success for themselves and for their families.

Pick a better country.

If by chance you still question the greatness of this country, simply seek out the people who have fled from Haiti, from Mexico, from Central America, from China, or from Vietnam. Ask them about the U.S. of A. To them, America offers everything they need that they don't have. I understand that now. America offers them the opportunity and the freedom to fulfill their dreams.

Occasionally I ask my radio listeners to stop what they are doing, whether they are walking around the house in hair curlers, whether they are out on a tractor in the back forty, whether they are in traffic on the express-way. I ask them to stop for a minute and listen to their heartbeat, take a deep breath, take stock of their lives. Look around and consider an alternative to the America we all know.

I ask them to consider the America that we too often take for granted. The America where we don't think twice about our freedom of movement. The America that allows us to visit countries where people live far below our stan-dard of living and then feel assured that we can come home.

I want them to consider the America where we can get in our cars and go sit on the rim of the Grand Canyon to face the challenges and evaluate the opportunities in our lives. Where we can come back determined to go to school, to learn to fly, to become a better skier, to make it as a radio talk show host, or to go into business for ourselves.

I have stood on rooftops in Brooklyn, I have sat on the tip of Belle Isle in Detroit, and I have perched atop a ridge overlooking a high mountain lake in Colorado and resolved to make good on many personal commitments just like those. Sometimes I was there because I had just lost a job. Sometimes I was there simply because I wanted a faster airplane. But my reason for being there doesn't matter. The total freedom to plot how to get ahead in life is what's so great about America.

That's why I ask my listeners to consider what the people who are trying to destroy America would give us as an alternative.

I'm talking about the people who have a scroll of complaints and are pre-pared to destroy America in the name of those complaints.

"This is not right," they tell us. "That's not right. I'm not getting a fair shake. He's not getting a fair shake. She's not being treated equally. I'm gay, I'm Hispanic, I'm an African American. White people are inherently racist. Not only are they racist, but they are in denial about their racism. Any effort on the part of a white man to say 'I'm sorry' is just part of a big lie. . . ."

The so-called oppressed people will tell you they know things the majority of America's citizens can't possibly know about this country. They recite chapter and verse of historical wrongdoing in America, and they are con-vinced that most people in this country harbor evil in their hearts. In the ver-nacular of the day, they tell you that America sucks.

So what do they want?

They want to remake America. Various and sundry of these special inter-est zealots want to redistribute the wealth, cap the resources each person can have, decide whom you are permitted to marry, determine where you send your children to school and what they should be taught, dictate where you can live, approve the way you worship, and prescribe how much of your life—not just your money—you are supposed to tithe to them, the self-proclaimed oppressed.

That's what I mean when I ask people to consider the alternative. All of the accusations and complaints that this country doesn't work seem to lead to a common end. The radical feminists, the radical socialists, the radical Afro-centrists, are more than ready to knock down the very foundations of this country in their effort to remodel America in their own narrow idealistic image.

But what are they prepared to put in its place? Just daring to ask that question is the point where a lot of good Americans, always willing to give the other person an even break, seem to lose the path. Perhaps they are afraid of being considered insensitive to the less fortunate.

But middle-class Americans must ask that question. They must consider the alternative because it will surely have a negative impact on them. The American middle class and the American rich—the next level to which the middle class wants to go—cannot ignore this ideological challenge to America any longer. They have no choice in the matter because they have the most to lose. The American poor, on the other hand, do have a choice. The liberal socialists have reaped a portion of the wealth from the middle class and the rich to give them a most luxurious choice. They can go on accepting the dole under this America, or they can accept it under a new, alternative America.

But the citizens of the American middle class forgo all of their choices when they allow liberal socialists like those in the Clinton Administration—Democratic Party regulars like Robert Reich, Donna Shalala, and Henry Cisneros—to restructure the quality of their lives in the name of equality and fairness. Those who have gotten into the American middle class by steadily pursuing the American Dream are the ones who must seriously consider how an alternative America will affect them.

For them, there is no option to sit this one out. Saying and doing nothing is the same as seriously entertaining the idea of an alternative America. It's the same as proclaiming that this America is not the best deal for them.

They can concede that they pursued opportunity but didn't quite reach their goal; they may admit that they pursued opportunity and achieved their goal without thinking twice about it; or they can confess to themselves that they were too lazy to earnestly pursue their options at all. Whatever soul-searching they do, if they fail to protest the proposition of an alternative America, in essence they might as well say that this America has failed them.

By remaining silent they are sanctioning the idea that our present America is not their best option—even though this America is not a class-based society, even though it's possible for anyone to move up who seizes the opportunity, even though there is hard evidence that Americans overcome all manner of barriers, and even though both the law of the land and the moral conscience of the greater majority of Americans have in the past caused and will continue to cause good and right to prevail in this country.

If, after considering all of the above, they still allow the idea of an alternative America to flourish unchallenged, then they must realize that whatever alternative to the American Dream they permit to prevail is what they are going to pass on to their children.

So over and over I beseech the man riding on his tractor in the heartland of our nation, the salesperson struggling to close the next deal in Midtown Manhattan, the cowboy rounding up Herefords in Montana, the young soldier, the housewife, and the American mothers and American fathers to consider the alternative.

Because if we allow the fundamental premise of this great country to be brushed aside, we will leave a vacuum that soon will be filled with a completely new paradigm for America. And I don't think the majority of Americans, the majority of Americans of all colors and creeds who have found a way to make America as we know it work for them, will be very happy.

I know I won't. Because I have considered the alternative, and I know in my heart and in my mind that the America we have is worth saving.

Think about what drives you to get up every morning, to feed the kids, to pack them off to school on time. Think about what drives you to go to work, to strive to do your best so that you might get ahead.

It's the old-fashioned American Dream that drives all of us, the same dream that drove most of our parents and in many cases their parents before them. That dream is not broken. It has not failed those of us who believe in it and cherish it. It has not failed those of us who are committed to live by its tenets.

We have no reason to entertain an alternative.

America works. How dare anyone suggest to me that it doesn't work?

I know it works because I am the living proof.

I was born in this country with nothing.

Today I've skied, I've flown my own airplane, I'm a self-taught fly fisherman and a horseman. I've bought and I've sold houses, not as a real-estate agent but as a consumer. I've made money; I've been on the skids. I've jumped out of airplanes. I've loaded my own bullets. I've climbed the Rocky Mountains, trekked their lofty peaks, flown over them by dawn's early light, and slept high atop the tundra. I have been a member of the working press for this country's largest daily newspapers. I am privileged to talk to Americans every day on my own national radio show. I have floated on my boat for days in a secluded, peaceful cove at Lake Powell. I've sailed and dived in the Caribbean. I've visited Nicaragua, Haiti, and Israel—and every time I have been happy to come home. I watched my daughter work relentlessly to become a TV anchor in one of the most difficult and cutthroat businesses I can imagine. I held my son's daughter in my arms when she was just forty-five minutes old.

I am the living, breathing proof that America works. I took lemons, and I made lemonade.

When I went into the army, there were signs posted in parts of this country that read "Colored" and "White Only." I didn't like those signs. But instead of talking about going back to Africa, instead of renouncing my citizenship, I said, "This is my country too."

I went hand in hand with black Americans, white Americans, Jewish Americans, Christian Americans, northern Americans, and southern Americans, and we took those signs down. I am proud to be a member of the can-do generation that made this a better country.

I call myself an American hero.

I am not saying I'm better or different from a lot of other Americans. I am not unique. I am not unusual. I am not a hybrid anything.

I am you. I am you, reading this book. And if I'm not you, I am your father or your grandfather. Like a lot of you, I came from a place where the odds were against me, and I beat those odds with sheer determination and guts founded in the promise of the American Dream.

Like the Poles, like the Irish, like the Germans, like every group of people who ever came from another place, we were taught values of right and wrong and we learned to be tenacious. We never forgot our homelands, but we were taught to derive strength from the opportunity for success and the rewards of contributing to our new country.

I am not saying I'm a hero because of the particular things I have accomplished. I simply have gotten over the obstacles and stayed the course like many before me. I have embraced the American Dream, and no one has a right to take the joys of success in America away from me or any other American hero.

I am saying I'm an American hero because I am tangible proof of what this great country is all about.

Unlike a religious creed, belief in America doesn't require an act of blind faith. If you doubt me, look around you. This country is full of American heroes just like me who started with nothing, watched for opportunities, worked hard, overcame obstacles, and got ahead. They are the men and women— black, white, brown—who have never lost hope, who have maintained faith in the American way.

When the disgruntled hyphenated black Americans and their booster club of white liberals bemoan the racism, the poverty, the low-paying jobs—all their excuses for failure—I issue a simple challenge:

Pick a better country.

They should consult with the desperate refugees who still today are fleeing their countries in hopes of resettling themselves and their families in this land of opportunity.

I think I know what these expatriates would tell them, because I am part of a first generation born an American.

I have said I started with nothing. But that's not altogether true, because I had a strong mother who believed fiercely in America and she inspired that belief in me.

My mother, Evelyn Ford, arrived in New York in 1934 at the age of eighteen with a part of her family. Like others, they came here in small groups, as money would permit.

I grew up listening to my mother and her sisters reminisce about their struggle to get to America. On hot summer nights on the front stoop or in the living room of our Brooklyn apartment, dimly lit by low-watt lightbulbs to save electricity and curb the heat, with curtains fanning ever so slightly from the warm breeze, they talked with pity about friends they had left back home because they had been unable to raise the money for passage to the United States.

As a very young boy I discerned from those lazy evening visits that it cost some people virtually everything they had to become Americans. They spent it all to gain safety, freedom, and the hope of a better life for their children.

While making our way toward the future in America, our family like many others also drew a healthy strength from our lineage. I was mesmerized on those muggy summer nights by stories of life on the island, "back home."

My grandmother Estelle, I was told, was one of eight children who survived hardships from the remnants of institutional slavery. Barbados had a reputation as one of the cruelest environments for former slaves, who lived under the tyranny of a small group of British landowners, among the last in the Western Hemisphere to make their peace with the Negroes' freedom.

I developed a fascination with and an enduring admiration for my grandfather Elias who, determined to reach for more than a life of poverty and oppression on an island, signed on to work as a common laborer during the construction of the Panama Canal.

Once there, he mastered the Spanish language sufficiently to move on to Cuba, where he worked as an interpreter in the courts. And finally he was able to raise passage to begin moving his family to America.

Poor people seldom are granted the indulgence of learning their full family tree. And poor black people have the added impediment of slavery standing in the way of knowing their family forebears.

About all I know about the man who made it possible for me to be an American is that he was five feet four inches tall and weighed 125 pounds. His complexion was dark and his hair kinky and black like my own. He was born in the parish of Saint Philip's on the island of Barbados, British West Indies, on June 14, 1888, fifty-four years after the British abolished slavery in their colonies.

I know that because some years ago my aunt Merle passed on a copy of Grandfather Elias's papers from 1930 declaring his intent to apply for permanent citizenship in the United States of America.

I know that at that time he lived at 111 Washington Street in Cambridge, Massachusetts. He died in Brooklyn, New York, in 1935 at the age of forty-seven.

I know these things because I have his papers. I have them tucked away for safekeeping along with the handwritten note to me from President George Herbert Walker Bush. One day these treasures of my life in America will go to Olivia Christine Hamblin, my firstborn grandchild.

No one will be able to suggest that she does not have a vested interest in America. No one will be able to suggest that she should rightfully take a foreign name. I have these things tucked away for safekeeping in the hope that she will appreciate the maxim that anything is possible in America.

Ladies and gentlemen, pick a better country.

I am proof that America works. I am an American hero because I've stayed the course, and America has not let me down.

I am arrogantly proud to be a fully vested American, and I've got a big mouth about it.

God bless America.

Epilogue:
Aunt Merle and the
New York *Daily News*

"**I** know it was you by da hat."

In those weeks in early 1994 when my phone was ringing off the hook because of national publicity about me, I picked up my home phone one night to be greeted by those words of excitement from my aunt Merle in Brooklyn.

At first I had no idea what she was talking about. She rambled on in her delightful West Indian accent; I could hear paper rustling as she talked.

It turned out she was looking at that day's edition of the *Daily News*, which carried an article about me entitled "Black Rushin' Spoken Here?" A big picture of me in my fedora was in the center of the page, and a photo of Rush Limbaugh was in the lower right-hand corner. The article posed the question yet again about whether I was the "black Rush Limbaugh."

The article said that I had critics, but it also spelled out enough of my message to make sense to Aunt Merle.

I hung up the phone smiling at the irony of life.

Aunt Merle's dread—that my picture would turn up in the *Daily News*—had come to pass. But luckily for me, my head wasn't bowed to shield my face from the camera, and my picture hadn't run in the crime section. I was relieved that, despite all of my critics, she thought I was doing the right thing, upholding the honor of our American family.

If you want to read more of Ken Hamblin's common sense and plain talk about the issues that concern the millions of men and women who still believe in the American Dream, order his monthly newsletter, *KEN HAMBLIN Talks with America*, by calling 800-408-2427.

To get the latest information about the Ken Hamblin radio show, or to send e-mail to Ken, check out Ken's home page on the internet:

http://www.hamblin.com

To mail Ken a message: Ken Hamblin, P.O. Box 562, Castle Rock, CO 80104

About the Author

An avid motorcyclist, private pilot, photographer, filmmaker, skier, fly fisherman, scuba diver, entrepreneur, and media personality, Ken Hamblin is living proof that the American Dream is accessible to everyone. He worked as the first black photographer for the *Detroit Free Press* from 1969 to 1970. During the 1970s, he produced and hosted a variety of television programs for WTVS, Channel 56, in Detroit and ran an independent film production company. He began his first radio talk show in 1982 on Denver's KOA. Today he broadcasts a nationally syndicated weekday show from Denver, reaching 2½ million people. He also writes a weekly opinion column for the New York Times Syndicate and writes twice a week for the *Denver Post*. Hamblin lives with his wife, Sue, in Colorado.